D0108388

Gender and Thought

Mary Crawford   Margaret Gentry
Editors

Gender and Thought: Psychological Perspectives

Springer-Verlag
New York Berlin Heidelberg
London Paris Tokyo

Mary Crawford
Department of Psychology
West Chester University
West Chester, PA 19383
USA

Margaret Gentry
Department of Psychology
Hamilton College
Clinton, NY 13323
USA

Library of Congress Cataloging-in-Publication Data
Gender and thought: Psychological perspectives/edited by Mary
    Crawford and Margaret Gentry.
        p.   cm.
    Based on a conference held in April, 1987, at Hamilton College.
    Bibliography: p.
    ISBN 0-387-96891-1
    1. Sex differences (Psychology)—Congresses.   2. Women—
Psychology—Congresses.   3. Feminist psychology—Congresses.
I. Crawford, Mary.   II. Gentry, Margaret.
BF692.2.G467   1989
155.3′3—dc19   88-8482

Printed on acid-free paper.

Typeset by ASCO Trade Typesetting Ltd., North Point, Hong Kong.
Printed and bound by R.R. Donnelley and Sons, Harrisonburg, Virginia.
Printed in the United States of America.

9 8 7 6 5 4 3 2 1

ISBN 0-387-96891-1 Springer-Verlag New York Berlin Heidelberg
ISBN 3-540-96891-1 Springer-Verlag Berlin Heidelberg New York

This book is dedicated
with love to the spirit of
Nancy Datan

Preface

The juxtaposition of "gender" and "thought" in the title of this book is deliberately (and, I hope, intriguingly) open-ended. "Gender and thought" refers to how the social circumstances of being female or male lead to the development of sex-differentiated cognitive schemata and abilities—the agents, processes, and outcomes of gender role socialization as applied to cognition. It also refers to the maintenance of gender differentiation. Femininity and masculinity can be regarded as social codes or conventions that function to prevent people from making some observations and connections, while making others seem natural and normal. Questioning the practice of differentiation is difficult because gender has functioned as a largely nonconscious ideology. What is taken for granted, what is "obvious" about human nature, is the most difficult to analyze.

The phrase "gender and thought" also subsumes issues about the production of scientific knowledge on gender. For example, feminist psychologists are actively debating whether some research methods or epistemological approaches are particularly suited for feminist inquiry. Others are analyzing how attempts to reconceptualize the study of women and gender become integrated into "mainstream" psychology and change (or fail to change) prevailing paradigms.

Happily, the reader of this book will not need to choose from among this trio of possible meanings for the juxtaposition of gender and thought. Questions of gender socialization, gender maintenance, and the production of knowledge about gender are all addressed in its pages. The authors draw on a rich variety of methods including field study, laboratory experiment, and large-scale survey. Their work reflects the diversity of topic, method, and level of analysis that characterizes contemporary feminist psychology.

Although most chapters are relevant to more than one of the three areas I have outlined, each can stand as a particularly good example of one of these areas of inquiry. The processes involved in becoming gendered and some consequences of those processes are directly addressed by Jacquelynne Eccles and by Hazel Markus and Daphna Oyserman. Eccles describes the social influences shaping gender differences in mathematics performance, and Markus and Oyserman examine how that most fundamental cognitive structure, the self-schema, develops differently for boys and girls.

The maintenance of gender relations and gender distinctions in social interaction is scrutinized by Nancy Henley, Faye Crosby and her colleagues, and Nancy Datan. Reviewing research on sex bias in language, Henley shows a variety of cognitive effects and provocatively compares biased language to propaganda. Crosby and her colleagues show the limits of individuals' ability to perceive discrimination. Datan dissects the messages conveyed to women who have breast cancer—messages that reinforce a constricting ideal of femininity, while at the same time portraying it as forever unattainable for the female cancer patient.

Epistemological and methodological questions in understanding gender are the focus of chapters by Rhoda Unger, Mary Crawford, and Michelle Fine and Susan Gordon. Unger contrasts two paradigmatic approaches in psychology, "reality constructs the person" and "the person constructs reality," and examines their utility—and limitations—for the study of gender. My own chapter critiques a feminist research project on women's ways of knowing from two epistemological perspectives, raising questions somewhat parallel to Unger's about the strengths and shortcomings of different feminist approaches to science. A radical vision of psychology transformed to a science that can truly encompass women's realities, along with a documentation of how little transformation has occurred thus far, is provided in the chapter by Fine and Gordon.

But to summarize each chapter in a sentence and to pigeon-hole each as addressing only one question cannot do justice to their complexity or the relationships among them. Margaret Gentry, in her Introduction, gives a more detailed overview of the chapters and draws from each in examining the meanings of gender.

This project was conceived shortly after I accepted what would be a two-year visiting appointment (1986–88) as holder of the Jane Watson Irwin Chair in the Humanities at Hamilton College.

As a researcher and teacher in psychology and women's studies, I wanted to share insights from current theory and research on gender with the Hamilton community. The idea of organizing a conference on gender and thought originated in a conversation with Doug Herrmann, chair of Hamilton's Psychology Department. Margaret Gentry was soon recruited as co-planner and the conference took place at Hamilton in April 1987.

One of our goals as conference coordinators was to create an environment in which students and scholars could interact comfortably and explore issues together. Each presentation was followed by both two discussants and a general open floor for comments and criticism.[1] The essays added later had their genesis in that interaction. In preparing this volume, we have tried to echo the conversational dialogue of a good conference. We let our authors know that readable, lively prose would be welcomed, and that they should feel free to expand on the implications of their research.

Mary Crawford

---

[1] Faye Crosby, Nancy Datan, Jacquelynne Eccles, Nancy M. Henley, and Rhoda K. Unger presented papers at the conference. Serving as discussants were Roger Chaffin, Amy H. Gervasio, Louise Kidder, Suzanne Lovett, Margo MacLeod, Jeanne Marecek, Margaret Matlin, Elizabeth Potter, Dean Rodeheaver, and Hy Van Luong.

Acknowledgments

The conference that provided the genesis for this book took place at Hamilton College in April 1987. Mary Crawford held the Jane Watson Irwin Chair in the Humanities at Hamilton for 1986–1988 and Margaret Gentry was awarded a Margaret Scott Bundy Fellowship for Spring 1987, providing opportunities for the editors to work together. Funding for the conference was provided by the Jane Watson Irwin Fund, the Kirkland Endowment, Faculty for Women's Concerns, and the Psychology Department of Hamilton College. We gratefully acknowledge those who supported our project by helping to fund it.

We would also like to acknowledge the numerous individuals who have worked behind the scenes in making both the conference and the book possible—our families, friends, colleagues, students, and secretaries. Without their support and assistance, none of this would have been possible.

Contents

Contributors

Mary Crawford
Department of Psychology
West Chester University
West Chester, Pennsylvania 19383

Faye J. Crosby
Department of Psychology
Smith College
Northampton, Massachusetts 01063

Nancy Datan
Human Development
College of Human Biology
University of Wisconsin
  at Green Bay
Green Bay, Wisconsin 54311-7001

Jacquelynne S. Eccles
Research Center for Group
  Dynamics
Institute for Social Research
University of Michigan
Ann Arbor, Michigan 48106-1248

Michelle Fine
University of Pennsylvania
Graduate School of Education
Philadelphia, Pennsylvania 19104

Margaret Gentry
Department of Psychology
Hamilton College
Clinton, New York 13323

Susan Merle Gordon
University of Pennsylvania
Graduate School of Education
Philadelphia, Pennsylvania 19104

Nancy M. Henley
Department of Psychology
University of California
Los Angeles, California 90032

Hazel Markus
Research Center for Group
  Dynamics
Institute for Social Research
University of Michigan
Ann Arbor, Michigan 48106-1248

Marion O'Connell
Smith College
Northampton, Massachusetts 01063

Daphna Oyserman
School of Social Work
Hebrew University of Jerusalem
Jerusalem, Israel

Ann Pufall
Department of Psychology
Smith College
Northampton, Massachusetts 01063

Rebecca Clair Snyder
Department of Rutgers
  University
New Brunswick, New Jersey 08903

Rhoda K. Unger
Department of Psychology
Montclair State College
Montclair, New Jersey 07043

Peg Whalen
Smith College
Northampton, Massachusetts 01063

Introduction
Feminist Perspectives on Gender and Thought: Paradox and Potential

Margaret Gentry

"Equality" has been the preeminent value in American culture since our
first self-evident truth declared that "all men are created equal." Although
equality and difference are not necessarily antithetical, equality within our
culture has been taken to depend on sameness: that is, historically equality
has evolved in favor of standardized rules that demand the same qualifications, afford the same opportunities, and offer the same rewards to all.
Generally, standardization of criteria dominates diversity, which is considered irrelevant when equality is applied as a principle. This operationalization of equality as sameness cuts right to the heart of the paradoxical status
of gender in the United States. For although we base equality primarily on
sameness, our ideology of gender is based on the idea that men and women
are fundamentally different. Consequently, we expect women to be different from men (e.g., in traits, values, and skills), and yet to obtain equality
women must be the same as men.

Consider this paradox in light of the defeat of the Equal Rights Amendment. For the majority of U.S. citizens, including many opponents of the
ERA, there was little disagreement about the historical fact that women
have been subjected to overt discrimination or about the belief that women
should no longer be systematically excluded from our institutions of business, learning, and government. Instead, opposition to the ERA focused
primarily on two issues. First was the extent to which gender differences
are significant and fundamental in our ideology of gender. That is, to what
extent do we believe that gender differences reveal the "true" nature of
men and women? Opponents tended to view differences as fundamental,
and therefore we "interfere" with them at our peril. If, for example,
women are believed to be "naturally" better parents or characteristically
less aggressive or more emotional than most men, then surely women
should occupy different spheres in life than men or hold different niches in
the same sphere. To want to occupy sex-inappropriate realms is "unnatural."

The second issue of disagreement was the extent to which the remedy for
gender discrimination has already been achieved by, in our minds, editing

our first guiding principle to read "all men [and women] are created equal." If, as according to many ERA opponents is the case, the existing laws and standards that we live by are essentially nondiscriminatory, then a direct and specific amendment to address gender discrimination is super-fluous. Women are equal because, in this view, society has implicitly agreed to expand its rules to include women. Thus, opponents of the ERA argued paradoxically that women are fundamentally different from men in nature but, in a world where equality depends on standardization, already men's equals.

The defeat of the ERA represents our culture's collective unwillingness to engage in substantive discussion about our ideology of gender (i.e., un-examined fundamental assumptions about gender) and about the need to assess and adapt this view in order to meet and change social realities. Matters were "resolved" like many final exams I have read—by a clock that ran out, rather than by a decisively reached judgment on the issues in-volved. How telling that women gained "equality" not by amending the fundamental assumptions of our government but by simply assuming that "men" means women too. Although a restipulation of the term "all men" was found politically inadequate to redress racial and ethnic discrimina-tion, precisely this stipulation has been left to carry the burden of redress-ing gender discrimination.

The interim result is that women are allowed to adapt to patriarchal institutions, but institutions are under few compulsions to adapt their rules and customs to women. Women may individually overcome their gender disadvantage, but the fairness of policies that make traditionally female roles, traits, responsibilities, and values a disadvantage in the first place remains closed to discussion. Failing to challenge masculinist standards may permit women to become part of a generic category of "men" and achieve some level of equality, but it is an equality *to* men, based on similarity to men. Furthermore, it is a nonreciprocal equality. That is, while women are adapting to a dominant male standard in many institutions, men are not rushing to participate in areas of life traditionally dominated by females such as homemaking and childrearing. As research documents, these tasks continue to be done primarily by women (e.g., Atkinson & Huston, 1984; Pleck & Rustad, 1980). Thus, women must accommodate their husbands' careers, their own careers, and domestic demands even as they pursue their "equal" opportunity to careers.

No clear consensus has yet evolved on the questions of how to change or replace patriarchal rules, institutions, or governments. But whatever their views on particular remedies, feminists in general agree that society's ideology of gender cannot be changed by simply *adding* "women" to the standards and social domains previously created and occupied by men. They resist this prevailing view of equality on both the personal basis of their own life experiences and the intellectual basis of feminist scholarship that has been emerging recenty from academic fields. The personal and social consequences of our ideology of gender will not be changed through silence. A direct examination is required.

The political parable of the ERA parallels the feminist predicament in scholarship, where field after field has grudgingly opened the doors to women—and even "permitted" academics to place gender at the heart of their scholarship—but has precluded a direct debate and examination of the field's operative assumptions. Feminist scholars may enter the field of play provided they leave *ideological* challenges to the rules of the game back in the locker rooms. Gender can be addressed as long as it does not challenge fundamental beliefs or can be co-opted and removed from its political context.

Has psychology marginalized and co-opted feminist scholarship? Clearly some inroads into mainstream psychology have been made. Feminist work appears somewhat more frequently in mainstream journals than in the past; individuals who are feminists have gained recognition in the field; certain findings from feminist scholarship are routinely cited in introductory texts; and most studies using humans now at the least mention the gender of the participants. Perhaps, however, the questions that feminists should be asking are not so much what has been accomplished but what has been left out in the adjustments in the field and how seriously have feminist challenges to psychological theory, methodology, and ideology been taken.

Michelle Fine and Susan Merle Gordon (Chapter 7) argue that psychology has marginalized feminist work by resisting its integration into mainstream psychology and by being slow to engage in debate about the nature of gender at the level of the field's own ideology and conduct. Although the nature of gender has been and continues to be a topic of great interest to psychology, it is discussed at the level of fact and objectivity and not at the ideological level—a level that would present challenges to traditional theory, method, and belief. By declaring gender a dichotomous variable that can be studied with traditional methods (e.g., by generating gender differences) and by adapting its methods and theory superficially (e.g., adding comparison groups of females or including gender in hypotheses), psychology has de-politicized the study of gender and has declared itself a gender-neutral discipline in a value-free pursuit of the "true facts" about gender.

Part of the field's reluctance to enter into debate about gender's theoretical and methodological challenges to the discipline may also be attributed to feminist psychologists' reluctance to ask the challenging questions. Faced with masculinist norms regulating training, promotion, job security, and publication, such reluctance is understandable. After examining the integration of feminist work into mainstream psychology journals and feminist journals of psychology, Fine and Gordon note that:

Feminist psychology published within *our* representative divisional journal does reform the samples, methods, and questions of psychology as well as broaden the scope of interpretation. But we also reproduce the individualism and conservatism of the larger discipline. Most feminist psychologists have yet to declare questions of power primary; to establish white, heterosexual, patriarchal control as central to relations and representations of gender; and to take seriously the spaces that women create as retreats, as celebrations, as moments of resistance, and as the closets for our social transformations. Even among ourselves, feminist psychologists, by necessity or desire, appear to be playing to a male psychological audience. In our attempts to bring feminism to psychology we have perhaps undermined the politics and scholarship of feminism, refused questions of power asymmetry and defaulted to the benign study of gender differences. (p. 151)

This book, like the debate over the ERA or the debate over the inclusion of feminist scholarship in psychology, addresses the issues of sameness and difference. Rather than explicitly asking or answering the question, "Are men and women the same, different, or both the same and different?," our authors address issues of how to conceptualize and reconcile sameness and difference and how to synthesize diversity. It is apparent that the authors in this book approach the study of gender in different ways. They do not address the same topics or use the same methods to study gender, nor do they analyze gender-related issues at the same level. Yet within this diversity are common threads that tie the authors' chapters together so that the different methods used and the specific topics addressed inform each other. Although the chapters differ from one another, each engages our assumptions about gender directly, attempting to make this ideology's terms explicit and to trace its pragmatic consequences for women's lives.

One image frequently used to describe the coherence of traditional science is that of the jigsaw puzzle. As individual researchers work on one piece of a puzzle, they see themselves fitting it together with others to form ultimately a whole picture. Depending on the field, one's pieces may be small, or obscurely related, but the individual's efforts are compensated by the big picture believed to be accruing. As the puzzle becomes more complete, the difficulties and the process of the work disappear. The puzzle becomes coherent to the extent it is "solved" and the big picture becomes clear. "Progress" is achieved as the gradual bits of information lock into a fixed pattern of evidence. Researchers work in relative isolation to come up with discrete answers, but they expect their work to enter the picture seamlessly in the end.

This image for unifying separate research into a coherent whole may work particularly well for the natural sciences, in which findings are perceived as historically absorbing and cancelling previous gaps in knowledge. But do the social sciences work in this way? And is the puzzle an appropriate image for feminist research on gender? As a sociocultural phenomenon, gender is less of a picture waiting to be discovered than it is part of our changing and changeable social fabric. For this reason, expecting feminist views on gender to provide a fixed solution, a single picture, waiting to be pieced together miscasts this work as incoherent. The potential of feminist approaches to research on gender can perhaps be better grasped if we consider an alternative image of coherence: a quilt.

Quilting has traditionally been a social process, the coming together of different individuals to work cooperatively in creating a new and unique quilt. Although the pattern of some quilts may be predetermined and old patches are sometimes recycled in new quilts, each quilt differs in the fabric, color combination, and stitching used to create it. Individuals may contribute separate patches to the quilt, but they cannot work for long in isolation from one another if the quilt is to have a harmony in the overall pattern. Therefore, the talk around the quilting frame—in the margin of the ongoing work—is essential in constructing the quilt. Individual differences in stitching the separate squares are respected, for the goal is not to erase each hand's work but to stitch the squares together with interconnecting threads. Once the top layer of a quilt is pieced together it is quilted through several layers to give it warmth and substance. The outcome of the quilting process is both a work of art and a functional product you can put next to your body or over your child to provide warmth.

Feminists work from the fabrics of their own lives. Even when studying an issue in an area such as the natural sciences where the answer may be found in uncovering an existing pattern, they bring to their work new ways of creating and applying knowledge, based on the personal experiences and intellectual perspectives of feminism. The threads of feminism can connect different quilt squares together *across* both disciplines and subfields within disciplines, and *through* both different levels of analysis and different levels of application. As feminists, we ideally want our work to be both scholarly contributions (i.e., art) and works that function within everyday life. We cannot rely on the notion that our scholarly ideas will trickle down from the academy to affect and benefit the world around us. To create a harmonious integration of art and utility there has to be dialogue among the quilters.

Feminist psychology and feminism in general seem to be at the point of trying to piece together the individual parts of a quilt. The overall pattern of the quilt that we want to create is still emerging. No one knows what a feminist psychology will look like any more than we know what equality in a post-patriarchal world will look like. We are beginning to piece the separate parts together—to explore the kinds of stitching to use in connecting the pieces and how to place the separate pieces into the pattern. But we have not stopped questioning the process of quilting itself. Sometimes, it appears that we are working on different levels (e.g., theoretical–methodological, personal–interpersonal–societal–cross-cultural, academic–activist) rather than stitching the levels together. To many academics trained in the traditional notion of science, such a state of affairs may appear contradictory or lacking in cohesion; for some, no matter how intricately made or how joint the effort of the many different hands, the end-product of such a process is an inferior product, unworthy of being called art. As feminists continue to construct a feminist version of psychology, they must not lose heart that their quilt may be considered by some to be a "marginal" art or that they may themselves be located at the margins of their discipline. Their quilt is already functional and the conversations around the margins are vibrant and empowering.

This book can be read, of course, the way edited volumes often are. Each chapter presents topical intersections of gender and thought, which can be taken separately as discrete papers with their own specialized interests. Reading the volume in this manner is perhaps more like the jigsaw approach, where one focuses on only those topics that are of interest and fits those chapters into existing perspectives. Reading the book in this way, you may miss the common threads that were apparent in the conversations with the conference participants when many of these papers were presented as talks. As colleagues, friends, and co-workers, the authors shared with those who attended the conference a dialogue that continually drew multiple relationships among their work. The transition from conference to book leaves behind those conversations in which their papers, the "patches," fit like parts of a single quilt into complex patterns of shared experience and sensibility. The richest way to read their work is by actively addressing their diversities. Rather than random pieces of an enormous puzzle, their differences function as a division of labor and insight in a rigorous tacit collaboration.

The chapter in this book that provides definition to the patterns underlying the other chapters is Rhoda K. Unger's "Sex, Gender, and Epistemology." Her chapter is a meditation on how researchers' most basic premises about reality affect the questions they ask and limit what they may learn. Unger steps back from her own extensive empirical work on gender issues to examine the various epistemological frameworks from which gender has been and can be viewed. As a pragmatic researcher, she identifies particular problems for methodological refinement and invention. As a scholarly thinker, she presents the larger philosophical context in which our efforts to understand gender rely on the particular framework through which we view it.

Unger describes the shifts in psychology between two alternative paradigms used to investigate gender—one that reality constructs the individual, the other that the individual constructs reality. Most of the past psychological research on gender and thought, like most of psychology, has used a logical positivist approach to the study of gender, presupposing that there is a "reality," either biological or social, that structures a person's cognitions and behavior. It assumes that this reality can be discovered and that there are general laws that can be used to predict behavior. Intrinsic in almost all conceptualizations of gender based in logical positivism are two important beliefs. First, gender is an organismic variable, a quality that is essential and inherent. Second, this quality of the individual is believed to distinguish between males and females in most areas of thought and behavior. In comparison, social constructionism questions the existence of a "reality" that influences the individual, focusing instead on how individuals construct, interpret, and perceive their subjective and social worlds. In this approach, gender is more akin to a belief system (Deaux & Kite, 1987), a system of social classification used to interpret and construct social interaction, or a lens or framework for analysis rather than an inherent characteristic of individuals.

As Unger points out, although the social constructionist framework is more agreeable to many feminists than a logical positivist one, it is not necessarily feminist. Nor does it necessarily reject many of the fundamental beliefs underlying logical positivism. Current interpretations of social constructionism in psychology are primarily empiricist in nature and in search of generic predictors of behavior. It does, however, introduce the possibility of transforming the questions we ask and the methods we use. One place to look for the new questions and methods may be in the inconsistencies, contradictions, and paradoxes of gender. The use of these phenomena to study gender is particularly appropriate to the social reality of women whose lives are spent in reconciling their experiences as women in a world that has been shaped and dominated by men.

The value of paradox, according to Unger, is that it promotes the examination of the belief systems that produce the paradox and it can lead to a fuller understanding of the questions that must be asked.

Philosophers value the study of paradox because it prompts questions about the nature of a given belief system that can produce such conceptual "traps." A more familiar analogy for psychology is the study of optical illusions, which are "perceptual paradoxes" in the sense that identical physical stimuli produce several different sensory responses. When we find an optical illusion, we do not question the nature of physical reality. Instead, we analyze neural and perceptual mechanisms to see how the multiple reality is created. Similarly, the study of social paradoxes can lead to a richer conceptualization of what must be known. (p. 32)

One way of creating a richer conceptualization of gender is to view gender from several epistemological frameworks in turn. The frameworks should display their distinct patches of knowledge in a field where consistency and diversity remain in view. Just as a quilt of identical squares would be useful but stark, a view of gender restricted to a single method or paradigm is a less powerful, undynamic, and incomplete way of gathering our questions.

Thus, the paradox, apparent in this book and in Unger's chapter, of feminist psychologists striving toward new and feminist conceptualizations of gender while still grounded in empiricism presents different ways of restructuring questions and methods. Feminists can challenge empiricism, an empiricism that is weak in its capacity for eliciting social reality as women perceive and function within it by redefining method and problem. They can also step back to challenge the fundamental philosophical assumptions of how we define and study gender. That is, feminists may be able to hold open and debate the operative assumptions of doing science while continuing to practice their craft. One danger for feminists in this approach is in focusing on the challenges to empirical methods without addressing the challenges to epistemology. The result of such an approach is that challenges to systems of belief are reduced to controversies over method and "facts."

Nancy Henley's chapter, "Molehill or Mountain? What We Know and Don't Know About Sex Bias in Language," on masculine generic language illustrates how a nonconscious ideology of gender can promote a sexist practice in the face of a large body of empirical evidence arguing against its use. Henley comprehensively reviews the empirical work on masculine generic language, or the practice of using "he" to mean "he or she," and she concludes that such language does not function generically. Men and women both tend to visualize or assume "men" to be the referent of "he" even when the context is open to "he or she." Women interpret the generic as including females more frequently than do males, probably an adaptive cognitive difference given the power differential of men and women. Furthermore, Henley presents evidence that the use of generic language may negatively affect how women are perceived and how they process information.

Faced with empirical evidence arguing against the use of masculine generic language, how can there still be a controversy? In this particular case the data contradict traditional language usage by challenging the assumption of men as the prototypical human—that is, the facts rebut our ideology. When confronted with the empirical evidence, proponents of masculine generic language claim that the studies make too much of a social practice that is part of the noble tradition of language, and, after all, we should not tamper with tradition. They argue that the facts are incomplete or open to alternative explanations and that decisions about language usage should not be made on the basis of such evidence. However, when proponents are confronted with philosophical arguments against the use of masculine generic language they fail to recognize the sexist ideology from which such a practice springs. They claim the practice is not worth debating, that everyone knows "he includes she," and they demand scientific proof that the use of masculine generic language is harmful. One must then engage in renewed debate over empirical evidence. However, as Henley puts it, "We do not need to prove that language of itself influences behavior to find sex bias in language offensive, just as we find racist language is inexcusable and intolerable apart from any empirical findings of actual harm" (p. 59).

The debate on the masculine generic echoes the debate on the ERA. The question, "Does he include she?", is equivalent to the question,

"Does all men include women?". By asserting that "he includes she," proponents of generic language manage to defy both fact and logic. By trivializing the importance of keeping women legally and linguistically in a paradoxical position of difference-blind equality, the champions of this tradition put the issue of equality beneath our consideration. Feminists who study the fallacy are making a mountain out of a molehill, and activists who advocate change are attacking the pillars of tradition. Thus, despite the availability of an array of remedies—from the so-called cumbersome "he or she" to the colloquial pluralism of "they" to an as of yet uninvented true generic—the masculine generic persists, reducing the assumptions of difference between women and men that we all hold in practice to the status of sameness in principle.

Mainstream research on gender in psychology also reflects the societal debate of the sameness/difference paradox. For the most part, difference between female and male has been the prevailing assumption about gender. Exceptions to this belief have, of course, occurred. Until recently, however, they have occurred primarily when trying, often as an afterthought, to fit women into a model based, in principle, on men.

Although feminist psychologists who study gender are challenging the notion of gender as difference (Deaux, 1984; Hare-Mustin & Marecek, 1988; Unger, 1979), gender as a key discriminator between people persists not only in psychological research but also in social life and personal ideology. Why is the concept of gender as difference so prevalent and so resistant to change? Like most nonconscious ideologies or assumptions, the belief of gender as difference functions subtly, making it difficult to step outside this "reality" to criticize this conceptualization of gender or to develop alternative accounts of gender. For many reasons, it is critical for feminists to be able to step outside—not necessarily reject—the notion of gender as difference between males and females. Perhaps most importantly, a construction of gender as difference obscures differences among women, differences among men, and similarities between women and men of the same race and class. Thus, gender difference comes to possess an importance that overshadows or eliminates other comparisons. The existence of these differences in a world where the basic criterion for equality does not recognize difference makes it extremely difficult to reconcile the existence of women's divergent life circumstances with society's conceptualization and operationalization of equality.

Although many feminists have downplayed observed gender differences, some feminist psychologists are now reinterpreting the concept of gender difference. Researchers such as Carol Gilligan (1982) and Mary Belenky, Blythe Clinchy, Nancy Goldberger, and Jill Tarule (1986) accept the assumption that women differ from men, but they cast the contrast in a positive light, so that difference reaffirms the uniqueness and special qualities of women. Faced with the prevailing view of gender as difference in both academic and everyday life, it is not surprising that difference has resurfaced; and the temptation to offer a perhaps overly positive view of difference is understandable given that women have historically been viewed in a more negative light. As Mary Crawford points out in her chapter, "Agreeing to Differ: Feminist Epistemologies and Women's Ways of Knowing," there are, however, problems in this approach which she illustrates with an analysis of *Women's Ways of Knowing* by Belenky, Clinchy, Goldberger, and Tarule.

Clearly, the work of Belenky et al. is feminist in its values and goals, attempting to illuminate the previously ignored experiences of how women acquire knowledge and know reality. One problem that Crawford points out is in how the researchers give voice to the experiences of women. Although the work originates in feminist theory, the methods used appear to be intended to comply with prevailing empirical standards. In and of itself, this would be less of a problem if the methodological design and execution of the research were not flawed according to such standards. It was proposed earlier that perhaps feminists could work within an empirical framework as they challenged the underpinnings of that framework. The trap that Belenky et al. have fallen into is in challenging the underpinnings of masculinist research on empiricism's terms and failing to execute those terms adequately. Consequently, empiricists who are so inclined can discount the ideological challenges raised by this work by calling it "bad science" and ignoring the underlying issues. And feminists who are so inclined can discount the methodological limitations and focus on the similarity of the experiences reported in this research to their subjective experiences and to those of women they know. Neither group must face or resolve the contradictions of feminism and empiricism.

Crawford also points out that extolling one's virtues can have unforeseen political consequences. Although researchers are not necessarily responsible for the political purposes to which their work is used, there is a danger for feminists when a theory, even one shaped by feminist norms, ends up being in synchrony with masculinist beliefs. Feminist scholarship that reaffirms gender difference, especially difference that reinforces stereotypical views of gender such as "men think rationally and women think intuitively," is easily fitted in with existing beliefs about women and men. The popular press can present such scholarship as "facts" in ways that dichotomize the sexes, make the differences appear universal, and attribute a biological etiology to them. In a world where equality is based on sameness and where more social power is accorded to males, reaffirming that women differ from a male standard is almost always interpreted as deficiency. Attempts may be made to bring women's ways of thinking into line with men's ways of thinking to achieve sameness, or the differences may be called on to justify women's exclusion from educational or career opportunities.

Theoretical speculation about the nature of difference does not have to be divorced from empiricism or popularized as universal facts. In fact, such speculation may push psychology toward alternative explanations for gender differences and toward hypotheses that invite further empirical testing. Especially when difference is viewed as a consequence of social interaction, new theoretical models can expose implications for psychology and societal beliefs. The chapter, "Gender and Thought: The Role of the Self-Concept" by Hazel Markus and Daphna Oyserman invites such reflection. Their chapter questions not the existence or nature of gender differences in cognition, but the source from which differences arise. According to their framework, different types of self-concepts result from different types of social interactions, with women having a more collectivist or connected sense of self and men a more individualistic or egocentric sense of self. After presenting their model, they examine male–female differences in perceptual and cognitive processes from that perspective, concluding that a self-schema approach presents a plausible alternative to the more traditional biologically oriented explanation for these differences.

Rather than trying to recast the notion of difference, Markus and Oyserman use it to offer alternative ways of conceptualizing the cause of difference. If gender differences in cognition are a function of the varying types of social interaction available to males and females, then they are social constructions and as such may appear more amenable to being changed or reconstructed than the alternative biological bases for difference. The popular interpretation of any biologically based difference between males and females is such that difference is seen as inevitable or immutable. Such a belief is no more accurate than the belief that social constructions are always easily changed (Angoff, 1988). Moreover, it can have serious political implications. Markus and Oyserman suggest hypotheses that could provide feminists with an opportunity to investigate the divergent social experiences of women and men and the effects of these on cognition in an empirical fashion. What Markus and Osyerman have done is to create new and feminist theoretical hypotheses without tearing their work from the field of psychology. They set their ideas out expecting to have their patch of the quilt tested against established fact and theory.

Regardless of the way feminist psychologists approach the study of gender, they are constantly confronted with the sameness/difference paradox which permeates the study of gender. Perhaps the area in which the debate over difference has been the loudest, both in psychology and the popular press, has been gender differences in cognitive abilities such as mathematics. Gender differences in scores on tests such as mathematical achievement tests and SATs have reinforced the underlying masculinist belief that girls are less gifted mathematically than boys. These "facts" of differing test scores are frequently interpreted within a biological framework that implies the inevitability of difference. Jacquelynne Eccles has addressed these issues in her investigation of mathematical performance. She and her colleagues have pursued the question of why scores differ in a series of carefully crafted and sophisticated empirical studies.

In her chapter, "Bringing Young Women to Math and Science," Eccles presents a social constructionist model to explain why girls choose to enroll in fewer math courses than boys. This model assumes that girls' choices and performance in math courses are not based on fixed differences in ability or in past success or failure in math, as most interpreters of test scores assume. When Eccles looked beyond the scores and figures of enrollment in math courses, she found that girls typically do not differ significantly from boys in math-related attitudes or confidence and often outperform boys early in their careers. It is only later that they lag behind in performance and opt out of advanced courses in mathematics. In other words, by viewing their math history over time, we find that girls do not exhibit a consistent "deficit." This fact alone is telling and typical of gender controversies. The later divergence in scores is cited and posed as a "finding," while the earlier lack of difference, which does not fit in with stereotypes of gender or with the commonly held belief that innate ability explains gender difference in mathematics, is frequently ignored. Eccles' work rebuts the idea that there are large and essential differences in the mathematical abilities of boys and girls and suggests instead that girls are constructing a different view of their abilities from their social interactions than are boys.

Eccles' work confirms the value of and need for empirical work, and shows that such research must be attuned to the nuances of the socially constructed reality of the subjects. Psychology has habitually studied gender, a variable dependent by definition on social construction, in ways that strip it of its social context. Although this may be most evident in research emanating from a logical positivist perspective, it is also apparent in social constructionism. As Unger (Chapter 1) states:

Perhaps the greatest danger of a cognitive perspective is that psychologists will come to believe that all the questions about sex and gender can be answered within the paradigm, and we will forget that there are real societal forces that impact on the individual's ability to influence his or her own reality. (p. 24)

While Eccles recognizes and suggests ways of changing some of these social forces as they affect most young girls, Faye J. Crosby's research examines how individuals' cognitive processes at work in institutions and the workplace impact on adult women's construction of reality. Like Eccles, Crosby's empirical work programmatically probes the nuances behind discrimination and begins to suggest a necessarily detail-oriented route to change. Also like Eccles, she justifies the close attention paid to environmental cues and details by observing a compelling factual contradiction: despite a changed corporate and cultural code from overt discrimination against women to equal treatment of women, all indicators of working women's *actual treatment* in terms of hiring, promotion, pay, and firing continue to find a consistent pattern of de facto discrimination. Equality by fiat simply has not arrived. Yet the discrimination that persists is conducted in millions of job decisions whose makers are confident they do *not* discriminate. How can we account for this apparent paradox?

The chapter, "The Denial of Personal Disadvantage Among You, Me, and All the Other Ostriches," by Crosby, Pufall, Snyder, O'Connell, and Whalen builds on Crosby's work on the "firefly phenomenon," presented at the 1987 conference and documented elsewhere (Crosby, Clayton, Alksnis, & Hemker, 1986; Twiss, Tabb, & Crosby, 1989). The firefly phenomenon is a cognitive process by which individuals recognize certain patterns such as sex discrimination when presented with aggregate information but cannot recognize the phenomenon in the individual case— just as it is easy to see a group of fireflies but much more difficult to catch a single firefly. The everyday result of this cognitive phenomenon is that individuals who make policy at institutional levels cannot recognize discrimination in the individual case, although they are able to recognize it in the context of aggregrate information (i.e., information about the institutional history of cases).

In everyday behavior we rarely stop to examine decisions in the context of aggregate information; thus, we may act with the intentions of not discriminating in any one case only to find ourselves creating a pattern of discrimination. An institution must thoroughly and rigorously examine its practices before it can have the background information with which to recognize discrimination and redress it. The difficulty is in convincing individuals, both male and female, who believe that they are operating fairly case by case, that they must look at the overall pattern. Crosby's research makes the point that viewing discrimination on a case by case basis does not provide the necessary information needed to detect patterns of discrimination.

Crosby and her colleagues extend this work in this volume to suggest that not only is it hard to recognize discrimination against others when taken case by case but individuals may also have difficulty recognizing that they themselves are victims of discrimination. Sampling a group of lesbians and a group of working class students, these contributors examine the extent to which individuals who are likely to be on the receiving end of discriminatory behavior recognize that they have experienced discrimination. One of the most important lessons that we can learn from this line of research is that the need to reform and change the workplace cannot be judged only by how upset individual workers are. Individuals who have been discriminated against may not recognize this discrimination and therefore may not press for change. Pairing this perspective of the worker with administrators' inability to recognize discrimination on a case by case basis (an inability common to individuals irrespective of gender and gender beliefs) suggests a need for more rigorous examination of the ways decisions are made in the workplace.

Unspoken assumptions about gender keep us from recognizing how our ideology affects us; similarly, our assumptions about the field of psychology keep us from recognizing or imagining what the field could be. Michelle Fine and Susan Merle Gordon in their chapter, "Feminist Transformations of/Despite Psychology," open a window through which we can begin to imagine the possibility of feminist change in psychology.

While feminist psychology exists as a *potentially* expansive field of intellectual and political inquiry, it remains bound by a discipline designed to flatten, depoliticize, and individualize. These unacknowledged contradictions fill that which is called feminist psychology. They pervert our scholarship, as they erode the politics of our work. Perhaps more than in other disciplines, feminists inside psychology, however, have choices. While broadening our audience beyond the discipline may be costly to those who remain in the academy, it is also compelling to imagine psychology deployed in ways that demystify ideology, that disrupt the seeming neutrality of relationships and structures, and that open ideological and material choices for all women. (p. 158)

The chapter by Fine and Gordon presents the reader with a project of imagining a political, feminist psychology that could be used to transform psychology and, more importantly in their opinion, a psychology that can transform everyday life. They describe new ways of learning that are constructed from and embedded in the social context of women's lives and suggest how interrogating these arenas is a political act that challenges and intentionally confuses social theory, method, and politics. They argue that to understand women's lives we must study the traditional work of women—relationships and keeping secrets—and what they call the subversive work of women—imagining what could be by untying political contradictions and studying that about gender which has been ignored.

Nancy Datan embodied the feminist possibilities Fine and Gordon imagine. She came to the 1987 conference four months after a mastectomy and several days after her last chemotherapy treatment. A scarf, instead of a wig, decorated her baldness; a sweater, instead of loose clothing, represented her rejection of a prosthesis. Standing at a podium and taking deep breaths when the waves of nausea hit, instead of sitting in a chair, she demonstrated her strength and stamina. Nancy Datan rejected the cancer victim's costume and bearing and spoke freely of the secrets of a mastectomy—its disguises, its effects on relationships, its political and personal meanings.

In Datan's chapter, "Illness and Imagery: Feminist Cognition, Socialization, and Gender Identity," she simultaneously examines society's prescriptions of what it is to be female from the viewpoint of herself as a feminist, a social scientist, and a woman, all of which were essential components of her life. Drawing on the work of Audre Lord she identifies the socially constructed image of a woman with breast cancer—that of a mutilated victim who is "deficient" by traditional standards of attractiveness—and reconstructs the image to one of a warrior campaigning against an enemy. Using her personal experience as a starting point, Datan takes us with her as she conducts an ethnographic study of the medical profession's images of women with breast cancer.

It is a central tenet of feminism that women's invisible, private wounds often reflect social and political injustices. It is a commitment central to feminism to share burdens. And it is an axiom of feminism that the personal is political. It is in that spirit that I ask you to come with me in imagination where I hope nobody will ever go in fact, to a hospital bed on the morning after a mastectomy (p. 175). . . . A mastectomy, it seems, ushers in a lifetime of round-the-clock disguise: so I discovered after I found that I underestimated the power of a nonconscious ideology. Breast cancer is not a cosmetic disease, but it is embedded in a larger social and political phenomenon. Thus, if one rejects the a priori assumption that a missing breast demands an all-out coverup, one finds oneself at war with the very material [Reach to Recovery materials] that is meant to promote healing. (p. 178)

Datan sees her experiences as representative of a common lot, but she remains aware of the distinctions and diversity of women as a group. She does not expect that everyone who has had a mastectomy should live on her terms. "Breast cancer is a trauma; if a women feels she is entitled to four silicone breasts after a mastectomy, I applaud her originality" (p. 181). Instead she takes issue with the lack of tolerance for individual choice in coping with illness and with rigid definitions of femininity. The medical profession treats a woman with breast cancer as a fractured whole to be pieced together into a fixed picture of what a woman should be, and there is a preferred step-by-step way of reconstructing the whole so that she fits conventional standards of attractiveness. In this way the woman's condition can be erased from view. Datan urges us not to hide the differences, but to let the stitches and the scars and the wounds exist socially.

Cancer may go into remission, but breasts do not grow back; to accept the message of Reach to Recovery is to accept mutilation as a core feature of one's postsurgical identity, and thus to accept the status of victim. And for victims the most appropriate response is grief. Survivors, by contrast, command our respect. (p. 186)

What is remarkable about Nancy Datan's chapter and her life is that she was able to do what few of us can—she was able to live the academic and personal roles with equal fervor and commitment. At a time when most of us would be dealing at a personal level with breast cancer and the loss of a breast, Nancy took the tools of her trade and worked with them to integrate the personal and professional levels of her life. She challenges her colleagues to bring their personal experiences as women and men to bear on the creation of knowledge. She is the quilter who pieces together individual squares of a quilt sewing through multiple levels of epistemology, empiricism, feminism, and personal life. Her company in our efforts to examine the nonconscious ideology of gender makes us strong. Her quilt keeps us warm. We dedicate this book to her.

Acknowledgments. I am grateful to Amy Gervasio, Nancy Rabinowitz, and Peter Quinn for their comments on earlier drafts of this chapter. I am especially grateful to Michael Gervasio for the gentle guidance, nurturance, and encouragement he has provided in the writing of this chapter and the editing of this volume. I owe him a tremendous intellectual debt.

REFERENCES

Angoff, W.H. (1988). The nature-nurture debate, aptitudes, and group differences. *American Psychologist, 43*, 713–720.

Atkinson, J., & Huston, T.L. (1984). Sex role orientation and division of labor early in marriage. *Journal of Personality and Social Psychology, 46*, 330–345.

Belenky, M.F., Clinchy, B.M., Goldberger, N.R., & Tarule, J.M. (1986). *Women's ways of knowing: The development of self, voice, and mind.* New York: Basic Books.

Crosby, F., Clayton, S., Alksnis, O., & Hemker, K. (1986). Cognitive biases in the perception of discrimination: The importance of format. *Sex Roles, 14*, 637–646.

Deaux, K. (1984). From individual differences to social categories: Analysis of a decade's research on gender. *American Psychologist, 39*, 105–116.

Deaux, K., & Kite, M.E. (1987). Thinking about gender. In B.B. Hess & M.M. Ferree (Eds.), *Women and society: Social science research perspectives.* Beverly Hills, CA: Sage.

Gilligan, C. (1982). *In a different voice: Psychological theory and women's development.* Cambridge, MA: Harvard University Press.

Hare-Mustin, R., & Marecek, J. (1988). The meaning of difference: Gender theory, postmodernism, and psychology. *American Psychologist, 43*, 455–464.

Pleck, J.H., & Rustad, M. (1980). *Husbands' and wives' time in family work and paid work in the 1975–1976 study of time use* (Working paper No. 63). Wellesley, MA: Wellesley College, Center for Research on Women.

Twiss, C., Tabb, S., & Crosby, F. (1989). Affirmative action and aggregate data: The importance of patterns in the perception of discrimination. In F. Blanchard & F. Crosby (Eds.), *Affirmative action: Social psychological perspectives.* New York: Springer-Verlag.

Unger, R. (1979). Toward a redefinition of sex and gender. *American Psychologist, 34*, 1085–1094.

1
Sex, Gender, and Epistemology

Rhoda K. Unger

It has been argued by Buss (1975) and others that psychology as a discipline tends to alternate between two basic paradigms explaining the relationship between humans and their environment. These two basic conceptual paradigms are: (1) reality constructs the person, and (2) the person constructs reality. Paradigm (1) postulates a model of a reality that is stable, irreversible, and deterministic. It further postulates that this reality is discoverable through the proper application of scientific methodology and that individual differences are a result of the impingement of that reality on the developing organism. This deep structure underlies such diverse schools of thought as behaviorism, psychoanalysis, and sociobiology. These theoretical frameworks do not question that reality exists. They differ merely on the aspects of reality they stress as having the most impact on individual behavior.

Recently, psychology appears to have undergone a "cognitive revolution" (Gardner, 1985; Neisser, 1967). The former paradigm has been replaced by a keen interest in the active role of the individual in constructing his or her own reality. This model postulates that reality is largely a matter of historical and cultural definition (Gergen, 1985). It emphasizes the power of ongoing social negotiation in the creation of individual behavior and is more willing to take a less deterministic view of causality in general. Those who espouse a strong social constructionist viewpoint appear to be more likely to attribute individual differences to chance (nonpredictable or noncontrollable events) and, in the most extreme views, despair of the possibility of any generalizable laws of human behavior at all.

Although the social constructionist viewpoint is much more congenial for feminists in psychology (Unger, 1984–1985), I shall argue that sex and gender pose problems for both paradigms. I shall review briefly some of the major strengths and weaknesses of each in terms of sex and gender research, discuss what I see as some important conceptual and methodological trends in the area, and, lastly, discuss some of my own research and theorizing that bears on attempts to integrate apparently dichotomous views.

Reality Constructs the Person

Behaviorism, sociobiology, and psychoanalysis share a commitment to a fixed past as a major determinant of the individual's current behavior. They differ in the phenomena or processes they stress as the most important creators of that past. However, the explanatory power of schedules of reinforcement, genes, or familial psychodynamic processes is based on sometimes unstated assumptions about their connection with basic psychobiological mechanisms.

In these theoretical frameworks, sex is a biological given or an organismic variable. This assumption, of course, is stated explicitly by sociobiologists who assume that current differences between men and women are evolutionarily adaptive and interfered with by society at our peril. This view is most clearly spelled out in the title of the book *The Tangled Wing: Biological Constraints on the Human Spirit* (Konner, 1981).

Classic psychoanalytic theory and even some of its more feminist derivatives, however, also assume psychobiological mechanisms. Biology is introduced by the universal fact of motherhood and the inevitable conflicts produced by the relationship between the custodial parent (almost always the mother) and the developing child. Feminist psychodynamic theories appear to differ from classical Freudian ones by stressing power rather than sexual-erotic mechanisms, and by their belief that the psychodynamic consequences of the basic human family structure are not primarily due to the gender of the chief custodian. They tend to argue that the role of primary childrearer (linked to females, to be sure, by the biological necessity of childbearing) is the major determinant of gender-related differences between the sexes.

Behaviorism seemed to avoid biological assumptions. In its classic form, it tries to avoid the need to utilize variables from any other level of disciplinary discourse. Its essence is to restrict psychology to a few simple, easily observable and categorizable behaviors in order to facilitate the examination of the relationship between behavioral output and its outcomes (so-called reinforcers). In so doing, however, it has limited itself to behaviors that are devoid of much meaning for the human subject—of either sex—and has had to examine these subjects in a controlled environment—a situational context that eliminates any opportunity for the organism to select alternative behaviors. As a "science" that seeks to establish universal "laws of behavior" from an examination of the behavioral similarities between pigeons, rats, and humans, it has had little to say about the similarities or differences between various groups of human beings. In theory, behaviorism has ignored sex as a variable. In practice, even the rats were male.

What, if anything, have we learned about sex and gender from schools of thought emanating from reality constructs the person assumptions? Sociobiologists have compiled a long list of supposed sex differences based on the adaptive value of sex-specific behaviors for the survival of males and females of various species. They have little to say about the rich variability of sex-related behaviors in human cultures of the past and present. And they offer us little in the way of specific mechanisms to explain sex differences (other than their primary notion of relative reproductive economy for mammalian males—who may scatter their plentiful sperm widely—and mammalian females—who produce relatively few eggs and must cherish their scarce offspring).

Unfortunately, the area of psychology that has had the most to say about sex differences—the subfield of individual differences—is also the area that is most intellectually and historically akin to sociobiology. It has been noted that Galton, the founder of this field, was a strong believer in social Darwinism. He viewed women and colored people as inferior to men and the British (Buss, 1976). The area of individual differences has produced little in the way of a theoretical rationale for its data on differences between various groups and, in fact, has given us little explanation as to why some "causal" variables (such as sex, race, and class) should be studied, whereas others (such as height, physical appearance, or hair color) can be ignored.

The area of individual differences has remained a virtual catalog of behavioral phenomena with the mechanisms left unspecified. Since no systematic theory exists, it has been left to the user of this data base to determine when and why a specific sex difference may be cited. The consequences are obvious when one looks at various introductory textbooks in psychology written by authors with various theoretical perspectives. "Sex differences" in an almost infinite variety of behaviors are cited. There is, however, little consistency in whether or not a particular behavior is cited in different texts, and there is no agreement about what comprises a usable sex difference—in terms of statistical size, generality of occurrence, or cross-situational consistency.

Unfortunately, many early feminists in psychology took this data base seriously (Rosenberg, 1982; Shields, 1975). Early researchers worked to demonstrate that many so-called sex differences could not be verified empirically. Since the list of potential sex differences is potentially infinite, however, they may have spent their lives on issues that later psychologists regard as of no particular importance. The number of possible sex differences is not an important issue in the current feminist agenda. Much more pressing is the issue of how sex difference as a conceptual tool is deployed and manipulated.

Since behaviorism excludes questions about sex and gender entirely, the only other area utilizing this paradigm within which we may look for information is psychodynamic theory. It is noteworthy that this is the area from which feminist scholars outside psychology derive most of their inspiration. It has been largely ignored, however, by the majority of researchers within psychology, who primarily derive from a social psychological framework.

An extensive critique of psychodynamic theories about sex and gender would be tangential to the main thrust of this chapter. I shall therefore limit my discussion to a few remarks about what I see as the major problems of the psychodynamic view of women and men, as well as some benefits feminist social psychologists can derive from the theory. The major problem of the psychodynamic perspective for social psychology is the unexamined psychobiological connections discussed above. It is not clear what causal mechanisms best explain gender differences in the developing child. It is also not clear what role cultural prescriptions about gender-appropriate characteristics for boys and girls, and fathers and mothers, play in the development of such gender-related behaviors as intimacy, relatedness, individualism, or aggression.

Psychodynamic theory roots the individual in a historical time and place. I believe it is this aspect of the theory that makes it attractive to feminist scholars in other academic disciplines. They tend to find the logical positivist underpinning of traditional experimental psychology sterile because they are unwilling to conceptualize human beings devoid of their situational context (Unger, 1983). They also question the morality of the subject-as-object relationship specified by traditional psychology and deny the possibility that researchers can divorce themselves from their subject matter in order to measure human phenomena in an objective manner. They may also resent the arrogance of psychologists in defining themselves as the "measurers" of human beings. While these are all valid criticisms, some of the lack of communication between feminist scholarship and feminist psychology may be attributed to lack of awareness of the former about paradigm shifts within psychology as a discipline. In particular, there appears to be little knowledge about those aspects of the psychology of sex and gender that utilize the "person constructs reality" paradigm.

The Person Constructs Reality

As in the case of the "reality constructs the person" paradigm, there are a number of ways researchers can deal with phenomena having to do with sex and gender using "person constructs reality" assumptions. All these perspectives involve a formulation of human beings as consciously aware individuals who actively select and influence their environment, as well as being influenced by it. This positing of human subjects as agents of their own reality underlies the various perspectives influenced by the "cognitive revolution" within psychology.

In the new psychology of sex and gender, maleness and femaleness are seen as social stimuli that provide valuable information for organizing reality to both actors and observers (Deaux & Major, 1987). Observers use information about sex to determine whether the individual is behaving in a role-consistent manner. Identical male and female behaviors are rarely evaluated similarly, because sex and role are highly confounded in our society. In the absence of disconfirming information, individuals are evaluated in terms of the gender consistency of their behavior. Deviation from normative gender/role prescriptions has a major impact on how the individual is perceived by others. It is difficult to tell, in fact, how often, and to what extent, negative judgments of women's behavior in certain social contexts are due to their role deviance, rather than their gender deviance.

The observer's beliefs about sex as a social reality are confirmed by gender-characteristic styles of self-presentation and by the differential distribution of females and males into roles with divergent degrees of status and power. Individuals may maintain gender-characteristic behaviors because of both intrapsychic needs for self-consistency and pressure from others to behave in a socially desirable manner. Ultimately, the individual may lose sight of distinctions between herself and her role. She may become the person society prescribes.

What evidence supports this theoretical framework for sex as a cognitive variable? The analytic methodology of social psychology is very useful here. For example, it can be demonstrated that sex is a salient social category even under the most impersonal of circumstances and even when it may be useless or counterproductive as a source of information about the person (Grady, 1977). Very few individuals appear to question what makes sex such an apparently useful source of information.

There is evidence, moreover, that people use sex-related information differently, depending on whether they are making judgments about themselves or others (Spence & Sawin, 1985). Males and females also use different categories in evaluating their own gender identity: males use *attributes*, such as strength or size, and females use *roles*, such as mother or wife. Neither group, however, appears to regard either sex or gender as anything other than a simple, unitary, "fact of life."

One of the most difficult questions in understanding sex as a cognitive variable is determining when it is salient for the individual and when it is not. Sex-related effects do not appear in every possible social context. They have a "now you see them, now you don't" quality, which makes analysis difficult (Unger, 1981). Some important work has been devoted to developing typologies of contexts in which sex-related effects appear. A number of intriguing findings have emerged.

First, sex appears to be an important cue for behavior when the individual is a member of a statistically rare category for the social context in which he or she appears. This condition applies to sex both as a self-label (McGuire, McGuire, & Winton, 1979) and as a label used by others (Taylor, Fiske, Close, Anderson, & Ruderman, 1977, cited in Taylor & Fiske, 1978). It is possible that statistical deviance heightens the expectation of role deviance.

Second, sex-related differences in social behaviors appear to be maximized when such behaviors are subject to public scrutiny, as compared to situations in which individuals believe that their behaviors are private and anonymous (Eagly, Wood, & Fishbaugh, 1981; Kidder, Belletirie, & Cohn, 1977). Public behavior appears to conform to sex-stereotypic assumptions much more than does private behavior. What is particularly important about these findings is that they derive from one of the very few methodologies that permit social scientists to manipulate societal norms within a laboratory context. The difference between public and private represents a difference in assumptions about the probability with which others will evaluate one's behavior. For example, males are found to be more concerned with equity and justice in public than in private (Kidder et al., 1977). It is difficult to argue that long-standing personality traits underlie sex-characteristic behaviors that are so easily influenced by social comparisons.

Third, sex-characteristic patterns of behavior can be made to conform to the expectations of others. Laboratory models of the "self-fulfilling prophecy" have demonstrated that gender-linked "personality traits" (such as "sociability") of the target person may be altered by changing the expectations of the individual with whom they are interacting. Effects are produced by manipulating the beliefs of the observer about other gender-relevant characteristics of the target individual, such as her physical attractiveness (Snyder, Tanke, & Berscheid, 1977).

Physical attractiveness is associated with assumptions of further gender-appropriate characteristics for both males and females. Handsome males are seen as particularly likely to possess masculine characteristics, and beautiful females are seen as possessing feminine attributes (Lemay & Unger, 1982). In contrast, lack of attractiveness is associated with perceptions of social deviance in a variety of situational domains. For example, less attractive males and females are seen to be more likely to be campus radicals than are their more attractive counterparts (Unger, Hilderbrand, & Madar, 1982).

Fourth, developmentally and culturally consistent patterns of behaviors directed toward males and females can be identified that may be related to sex-related differences in personality. For example, the most persistent contexts in which females are helped more than males are those involving travel outside the home (Piliavin & Unger, 1985). Young girls are helped more than boys when they request assistance from their teachers or adult mentors (Serbin, Connor, & Citron, 1978). Interestingly, girls also request more help when they are placed in the kind of structured activities that preschool girls appear to prefer (Carpenter, Huston, & Holt, 1986). Together, these data suggest that social and environmental constraints induce helpless or dependent behaviors in females that are frequently attributed to personality traits or even biological determinants.

Although this kind of constructionist paradigm has produced some very interesting information about sex and gender, there are dangers as well as strengths in the cognitive paradigm. Problems will probably emerge more clearly as the territory is further explored, but a few "traps" are already evident. One major problem is how to distinguish compliance with a gender-prescriptive reality from the actual self as actor. A useful tool in this regard is the methodological distinction between public and private behavior discussed above. One may assume that private behavior is less constrained by social desirability and therefore more closely represents the self as actor.

A more serious problem for cognitive theories about sex and gender involves the search for general laws that regulate behavior. Research has already shown that people use different information about sex and gender to organize their own behavior as contrasted to the behavior of others. Males and females may also use different sources of information to answer identical questions about their gender-relevant attributes (Spence & Sawin, 1985). The "same" information about sex and gender may be used differently by children of different ages (Katz, 1986). We therefore have every reason to believe that such information will also be used differently by individuals of different cultures, social classes, or ethnicities. We must be as wary of overgeneralizing a "female" consciousness as we have been of overgeneralizing from males to females or from the American middle class to everyone else. The search for truly general laws must be conducted with acute attention paid to the influence of transitory contextual variables.

On the other hand, the analysis of reality as individually constructed and highly subjective also carries traps with it. If everyone constructs their own reality, what criteria do we use to test the validity of their constructs? Some personal realities appear to be more functional than others, but utility may come at the cost of the individual's excessive compliance with societal norms. Functional analyses of both intrapsychic and behavioral coping may be greatly influenced by the values of the evaluator (Fine, 1983–1984). Middle-class investigators may too easily blame the victim and ignore the constraints of environments unfamiliar to them.

A focus on events that take place "inside one's head" may also make it easier to ignore external realities that are not under the person's control. For example, current analyses of stereotyping consider stereotypic perception as a normal variant of information seeking and cognitive processing. In a sense, stereotypes offer a kind of cognitive economy for the individual who needs to evaluate information about a wide assortment of different people. Stereotypes provide an easy way to select and remember information about others (Deaux, 1985; Hansen, 1980; Snyder & Uranowitz, 1978). These analyses, however, tend to ignore the fact that this kind of cognitive economy is not helpful to those individuals who are grouped as members of target populations. Nor do social analyses based on information processing explain individual differences in the extent and kind of stereotypes produced. Lastly, our fascination with the more powerful segments of society has produced little work on the consciousness of the victims of prejudice. Faye Crosby's (1982) and Kenneth Dion's (Dion, 1975; Dion & Earn, 1975) excellent work in this area are notable exceptions.

In sum, the "person constructs reality" paradigm as currently applied to sex and gender has both pluses and minuses. It takes a big step forward by providing psychologists with a theoretical rationale for measuring perceptions and cognitions about females and males. It also places explanations for sex-related differences within the framework of social reality rather than physical or biological reality. However, cognitive psychology does not explain how social reality is translated into individual reality. We need to explain when and why people are different as well as when and why they are similar. Some questions that need to be resolved include: Why do perceptions and cognitions about males and females appear to be consistent across a wide variety of times and places? Why do females concur with a social reality that is harmful to themselves as individuals? How do we explain those individuals who appear to be "invulnerable" to sex-characteristic attributions about themselves or others?

There is also a difference between a cognitive and a feminist perspective on sex and gender. Perhaps the greatest danger of a cognitive perspective is that psychologists will come to believe that all the questions about sex and gender can be answered within that paradigm, and we will forget that there are real societal forces that impact on the individual's ability to influence his or her own reality. The major social fact that has been ignored is the differential nature of social power (Unger, 1986). People of some social groups have more ability to impose their definitions of reality than do others. Their definitions influence the extent to which members of oppressed groups make use of resources theoretically available to all (Sherif, 1982). We need to understand how individuals incorporate an inegalitarian reality into their personal identities. But we also need to recognize that society is inegalitarian and that systems as well as individuals must change.

Theoretical and Empirical Work in an Alternative Epistemology

It is important for feminist psychologists to develop theories and to conduct empirical work that takes into account the alternative paradigms discussed earlier and transcends them. In the last few years I have been conducting work in two areas: one on the impact of values on thought and the other—more theoretical—on the nature of the interactive relationship between the person and the social environment. In working empirically and theoretically through these two areas, I have found neither paradigm adequate, and their condition as an "either/or" choice for a feminist conceptual framework is problematic.

This work is by no means complete (if it ever will be), but I want to share some of it here in terms of where I see the work fitting into the psychology of sex and gender, some of the results and problems of trying to work between paradigms, and some of the ironies involved in putting theory into practice. Because I am concerned with the epistemological relationship of this work to the epistemology of psychology, my discussion is less historical than is usually the case. In other words, I present the research questions and ideas in which I am interested in terms of their conceptual meaning for me, rather than in terms of how they represent the "inevitable" progression of the field. Indeed, I argue that psychology's lack of awareness of its own epistemology and its lack of attention to the reflexive connection between researchers and their research account for its inability to achieve a dialectical synthesis between the person and reality.

The Impact of Values on Thought

There is a body of evidence showing that individual researchers within the social sciences espouse different beliefs about the relationship between the person and reality that is similar to the more generic epistemologies discussed above. Not only has psychology shifted back and forth between two alternative epistemologies, but individual psychologists appear to agree predominantly with one or the other of these world views. Various researchers have conferred different terms for these positions, such as nature–nurture (Pastore, 1949), objectivist–subjectivist (Coan, 1979), or, most recently (by analogy to C.P. Snow) psychology's two cultures (Kimble, 1984). These varying epistemological viewpoints appear to be deeply embedded and not consciously attended to by most individuals.

Since feminism has been a major force in the critique of methodology and conceptualization in psychology (Gergen, 1985; Unger, 1983; Wallston, 1981; Wallston & Grady, 1985), it would not be surprising if feminist scholars share an epistemology that differs from others in the field. It is also likely that our epistemology will be consistent with a "person constructs reality" (i.e., social constructionist) framework. On the basis of these hypotheses, I constructed an instrument—the Attitudes about Reality Scale (AAR)—designed to measure epistemological position on a continuum ranging from a strong belief in a logical positivist framework to a strong belief in a social constructionist world view. Beliefs about how the world works were evaluated across a variety of conceptual domains involving such issues as: whether power is personal or social in nature; whether group differences may be best explained by biological or environmental factors; the value and efficacy of individual efforts to change society; and the nature of science and its impact on society (Unger, Draper, & Pendergrass, 1986).

Both feminist scholars (Unger, 1984–1985) and students enrolled in courses on women (Unger et al., 1986) hold more socially constructionist views than comparable others. In sum, they tended to agree with statements indicating that power is conferred by society; that differences between groups can be explained better by environmental than by biological factors; and that science is influenced by cultural values and is not an altogether positive force in the solution of human problems. Feminists also believe that success is not always the result of merit. Although they appear to be aware that individual behavior is constrained by social and cultural forces, feminists paradoxically also strongly agree with statements suggesting that individuals can have an impact on society. In some ways, they seemed to be espousing an inconsistent epistemology—believing that humans are a product of their social reality, while at the same time asserting the ability of the individual to change that reality.

Research in cognitive processes involving sex and gender suggests that neither sex nor gender is used holistically. What is particularly striking is the ability of the individual to process identical information about the self and others differently. For example, we have found enormous differences in agreement with a statement acknowledging sex, race, or class discrimination depending on whether the statement is worded in the first or third person singular (Unger & Sussman, 1986). Women seem to be able to notice the existence of sex discrimination for others, while they deny the relevance of this information to themselves (Crosby, 1982).

Feminists and other social activists appear to be aware that society is unfair and yet believe that they can have an impact on it. This distinction between the self and others probably helps to explain why scores on the AAR do not correlate significantly with traditional measures of internal–external locus of control, which word statements about the relationship between behavior and its outcome in terms of the self. Beliefs about the social construction of reality for others, however, do correlate significantly with a lower belief in the just world (Rubin & Peplau, 1973) and a belief in the social, political, and economic equality of the sexes (Spence & Helmreich, 1978). In contrast, those who believe in more logically positivist explanations about how the world works also show more traditional patterns on these measures; for example, they believe that the world is a fair place, that people get what they deserve, and that traditional gender roles are appropriate and correct.

Not all women are feminists, nor are all feminists female. One of the surprising findings in our studies using the AAR Scale is that when environmental context is held constant (i.e., male and female subjects are selected from the same classes), subject sex differences are far less important than are course differences. In other words, epistemological position is predicted better by the individual's self-selection of what to learn about than by his or her biological or social category.

These data lead to several other interesting questions. How do people develop a social constructionist epistemology? And what is the relationship between social constructionism and the belief in feminism (defined broadly as commitment to the social, economic, and political equality of the sexes)? We have found that social constructionism is significantly correlated to a number of biographical and demographic markers that are consistent with a problematic relationship with American society as a whole. Thus, social constructionists are more likely to be members of a minority religion or espouse no religion at all; they are more likely to be politically liberal; and they are very likely to be found among students who attend college at an untraditionally older age (Unger et al., 1986).

Those who label themselves as feminists appear to have the most socially constructionist views of any group yet tested. These results are consistent with a study of feminist psychologists by Mary Ricketts (1986) using Coan's Theoretical Orientation Scale. She found that feminists were more subjectivist in their views than other women attending conferences on the psychology of women, and that lesbian feminists were the most subjectivist of all. Commitment to various subdisciplines within psychology was less important in predicting epistemological position than were self-assessed ideological and sexual labels.

These findings are difficult to explain except in terms of identification with marginal groups within society. As a pioneering paper by Helen Hacker (1951) asserts, membership in an oppressed group is not the same as membership in a minority group. The awareness that discrimination is due to one's group membership rather than to one's personal failures crucially changes one's perceptions. Social activists appear to be able to maintain a contradictory cognitive schema that acknowledges both social injustice and the efficacy of individual efforts to change society (Forward & Williams, 1970; Sanger & Alker, 1972). Such contradictory belief patterns may be supported by identification with a socially stigmatized group.

Different life experiences appear to be related even to the epistemologies that scholarly researchers develop (Coan, 1979; Sherwood & Nataupsky, 1968). We still know little, however, about the relationship between particular life circumstances and epistemological position. Crosby and Herek (1986) have found, for example, no connection between men's knowledge about the experiences of the women in their lives and their perception of sex inequality. It is possible that different epistemologies lead people to perceive identical circumstances in a different way. The AAR Scale was constructed, in part, as a kind of verbal Rorschach test to get at this question of differing interpretations. Whether one views a "fact" as an enduring truth or a probabilistic statement will probably make a difference in how one responds to an item such as "The facts of science change over time." We are presently conducting research to find out whether people with different epistemologies interpret similar words differently.

These data suggest there is a relationship between personal epistemology and the epistemological frameworks developed by psychologists. Moreover, personal circumstances appear to influence world views in the same way for both scholars and "ordinary people." Since people use the same information to construct conflicting explanatory structures, they may be unaware of the extent to which their subjective realities diverge.

THE RELATIONSHIP BETWEEN THE INDIVIDUAL AND HER SOCIAL ENVIRONMENT

Research on personal epistemology as well as on the whole field of sex and gender prompts a difficult and crucial question: How does the individual acquiesce in the construction of a reality that is harmful to that individual? It was easier when we could dichotomize society into *us* and *them*, but it is clear that both sexes are part of the reality with which we deal. The question of the extent to which people incorporate the social categories known as norms and roles versus the extent to which people maintain their individuality is one of the basic questions that a true social psychology of people will have to resolve. Circumstances change, but people can also perceive them differently and thus change these circumstances. The processes by which we reconstruct our social categories are fundamental if we are to understand the way individuals produce social change.

In several recent papers, I have discussed the nature of the "invisible" social frameworks that direct behaviors into what we consider to be masculine or feminine traits (Unger, 1985, 1988). A major feature of this theoretical framework is its use of the interpersonal transaction as a unit of analysis rather than the individual alone. In brief, I have argued that stereotypes are a fundamental part of consensual reality, that there are many more cognitively contradictory perceptions of females than males, and that these contradictory perceptions are an important force in shaping gender-characteristic behaviors in our society. I have focused most on the construction of double binds for women, particularly when they step into the world outside the role prescriptions for domesticity. Double binds put the individual at risk regardless of the behavior she manifests. However, since the preferred unit of analysis in our society (as well as within psychology) is the individual, women attribute the inevitable negative consequences of their behavior to themselves rather than to situational constraints. Even our vocabulary for analyzing this kind of social process is miserly compared to our rich vocabulary for documenting every nuance of intrapsychic traits and characteristics.

This theoretical framework is tied to the empirical data on personal epistemology discussed earlier in several ways. First, it places the primary explanation for phenomena related to sex and gender within a social constructionist framework. The terms social and constructionist are both critical here. Individual behavior is defined as meaningless outside a social context, in which both females and males come to share the dominant ideology of a society. This framework posits the dominant ideology, however, as manifested through ongoing relationships, rather than as simply incorporated as a stable aspect of personality within the individual's psyche.

Cognitive mechanisms mediate interpersonal interactions. These mechanisms include: biased perceptions about the sexes, such as the belief that males are more logical than females (Broverman, Vogel, Broverman, Clarkson, & Rosenkrantz, 1972); the ability to screen and remember evidence differentially depending on its consistency with one's cognitive schema (Skrypnek & Snyder, 1982); as well as attributional processes that "explain" sex-related outcomes that are inconsistent with perceptual paradigms in ways that maintain preferred reality. Thus, when women are portrayed as more successful than men, this unexpected outcome is explained by their greater luck, effort, or other unstable cause (Hansen & O'Leary, 1985). Individuals may choose explanations that are harmful to themselves rather than question the social reality of which they are a part. Women's tendency to deny the impact of sex discrimination on themselves while recognizing its impact on other women (Crosby, 1982) illustrates this pattern of thinking.

Second, this theoretical framework acknowledges the difference between the social and "real" self. Individuals, especially those from socially marginal groups, are likely to be isolated within those social contexts in which biased definitions play a large part. They have no opportunity to validate outcomes in terms of the reality of others like themselves and thus have no alternative but to share dominant reality with its value-laden definitions of others in their social category. Distinguishing oneself from others in a devalued category is probably an effective mechanism for defending oneself against depression. This mechanism, however, also ensures that those in a position to change the dominant ideology about members of their group will also be less likely to identify with it.

Development of group consciousness appears to play a crucial role in the formation of a cognitive framework that avoids blaming the victim for her failure to surmount her circumstances (Rosenthal, 1984). This form of consciousness may be facilitated by childhood circumstances that indicate a lack of accord with the dominant values of American society. A social constructionist framework, however, may also lead one to seek information that is consistent with a less meritocratic belief structure. Such information is most likely to be found in situations where people who identify with socially marginal groups are also likely to be found. Hence, biographical background, present information base, and reference group all contribute to our belief structures (Unger et al., 1986).

The Problem of Inconsistency

What are we to make of all this complexity? Clearly, we cannot view sex and gender as holistic concepts, despite the fact that individuals in our society rarely examine their underlying assumptions for either others or themselves (Spence & Sawin, 1985). Assumptions about the sexes are also clearly tied to a complex network of assumptions about how the world works and which strategies are most useful for dealing with that world.

Since we pay little attention to our underlying belief structures, we have little opportunity to examine them for inconsistencies or to alter them in the face of conflicting evidence.

Personal epistemology appears to be relatively consistent over a large variety of conceptual domains and fairly stable over time (Unger et al., 1986). People appear to establish systematic belief structures similar to those found among established scholars before being trained in a particular discipline's epistemological assumptions (King, 1980). Social constructionist epistemology appears to be associated with social marginality in such areas as religion and sexual orientation, as well as gender ideology.

Although we have not yet done analyses for other groups, active feminists appear to be able to incorporate an ideology that insists on the possibility of both societal and personal control (Unger, 1984–1985). I would argue that such a paradoxical epistemological position is particularly adaptive to a contradictory reality. Feminists recognize the power of consensually defined social reality, while at the same time recognizing that individuals have the power to evade sex-biased definitions of their behavior. It is possible, for example, that female supervisors may exchange structural criticisms of established corporate policy when among females of equal company rank but frame the same issues in more guarded, individualistic terms when among subordinates or males of any rank. Judith Laws (1975) suggested such a dual consciousness in her early and important work on academic tokenism, but I know of no clear empirical test of this hypothesis. Proof of such contradictory patterns may necessitate the selection of social contexts in which alternative verbal and nonverbal definitional processes apply.

In the examination of the evasion of sex bias, however, the irony of trying to avoid the pitfalls of either logical positivist or constructionist models becomes evident. Social constructionists cannot ignore the fact that the power to define reality is more in the hands of some social groups than others. The governing groups tend to enforce and apply their own epistemological position. Thus the evidence we generate to support the social construction of gender-based reality will be evaluated in terms of both professional and personal epistemology. I have provided data to suggest that feminist epistemology is quite distinct as a constructionist way of looking at the world. Nevertheless, the methods that I have used to demonstrate this point are clearly logical positivist. How am I to deal with this inconsistency?

Scholars in a number of disciplines have attempted to avoid the assumptions of logical positivism by using various deconstructionist techniques. Such methodologies involve letting each person construct her own reality. Personal reality is seen as having no meaning apart from its historical and cultural context or the personal circumstances of the individual's life. Evidence about shared reality is provided through a comparison of shared stories.

This kind of methodology, however, is inconsistent with the desire of most psychologists to find generic predictors of human actions. Feminist social psychologists therefore must live with even more inconsistency than other feminist scholars. Any self-assessment method, as contrasted to psychodynamic or phenomenological approaches, appears to strip behavior from its historical and cultural context. What is the relationship between the response to items on a paper-and-pencil scale and the response to similar issues of effectiveness and merit in the context of personal evaluation? I can measure generic consistency in social constructionist beliefs only by using a measure that may strip these beliefs of their social meaning.

Some of these same kinds of inconsistencies emerge in attempts to analyze the ongoing perceptual dynamics in the relationships between individuals. Double binds are constructed by means of unexamined and contradictory definitions of normative female behavior (Unger, 1988; Wood & Conrad, 1983). They are effective largely because they are invisible to the participants in a social transaction. Not only do we lack a vocabulary to describe these social constraints, but attempts to bring them into awareness will probably cause them to disappear. Ironically, the "Heisenberg principle" is a concept shared with physics that psychologists have been less willing to acknowledge than operationalism or experimental methodology. Physicists recognize that they cannot predict the behavior of single electrons, but psychologists are less willing and less able to abandon the individual. Our apparent inability to deal with the subjective without losing the objective and vice versa is exemplified by psychology's endless cycling between the two basic paradigms with which I introduced this chapter. It has split psychologists into "two cultures" (Kimble, 1984) and threatens to tear apart the field as a unitary discipline.

The Uses of Paradox

It is easy for psychologists to get caught in dualisms (c.f. Coan. 1979, for a list of some of the dualisms uncovered by his Theoretical Orientation Scale). Contradiction, however, may be used to avoid some apparent dichotomies. The person versus situation controversy may be resolved, for example, by noting that persons bring symbolic constraints to situations (in terms of the way they perceive and define the world). These cognitive frameworks influence how they perceive and explain the mechanisms of interpersonal control found within most relationships between the sexes outside the home. We need to integrate findings on contradictory perceptions about men and women and about self versus others in identical circumstances. Unexamined contradictions in such perceptions help explain how people acquiesce to social schemata that are potentially harmful to them.

Similarly, dualisms involving internal versus external causality can be transcended by looking for methods that vary the extent of social coercion in apparently identical behavioral contexts. Private versus public behavior is one method by which societal prescriptions may be varied. Other methods may involve alteration of the "rules" for socially desirable behavior or the imposition of salient stimulus persons who embody particular gender-prescriptive norms. For example, work by Mark Zanna and his associates (von Baeyer, Sherk, & Zanna, 1981) has demonstrated differences in self-presentation style based on women's assumptions about an interview with a sexist or nonsexist employer.

A final duality involves the person versus society. Research on feminist epistemology indicates that a belief in the efficacy of the person may be linked to identification with a reference group whose consensual validation of reality resembles one's own. Some kinds of research questions can be formulated only if we accept the validity of a number of definitions of personal reality and are able to measure the discordance between various constructs. Thus, our American belief in individualism and the meritocracy may be possible only if those who construct this reality benefit from it and are able to discount the realities of others who do not. More communal analyses of social welfare may be easier for those who define human society more inclusively and who find the status quo less personally beneficial or rewarding.

Philosophers value the study of paradox because it prompts questions about the nature of a given belief system that can produce such conceptual "traps." A more familiar analogy for psychology is the study of optical illusions, which are "perceptual paradoxes" in the sense that identical physical stimuli produce several different sensory responses. When we find an optical illusion, we do not question the nature of physical reality. Instead, we analyze neural and perceptual mechanisms to see how the multiple reality is created. Similarly, the study of social paradoxes can lead to a richer conceptualization of what must be known.

Social contradictions exist because people either accept several conflicting definitions about the same person or differ as to when particular definitions should be applied. Psychology lacks the criteria to determine whose definitions are more valid, or even if "validity" has any meaning in consensually defined reality. Our yardsticks cannot be merely methodological—they must be conceptual and moral as well. We need a different, transcendant model for human beings. Perhaps the kind of person who functions best in a socially constructed world is one who can live in each reality as though it were the only one, but who knows that it is possible to stand outside them all.

REFERENCES

Broverman, I.K., Vogel, S.R., Broverman, D.M., Clarkson, F.E., & Rosenk-rantz, P.S. (1972). Sex-role stereotypes: A current appraisal. *Journal of Social Issues*, *28*, 59–78.

Buss, A.R. (1975). The emerging field of the sociology of psychological knowledge. *American Psychologist*, *30*, 988–1002.

Buss, A.R. (1976). Galton and sex differences: An historical note. *Journal of the History of the Behavioral Sciences*, *12*, 283–285.

Carpenter, C.J., Huston, A.C., & Holt, W. (1986). Modification of preschool sex-typed behaviors by participation in adult-structured activities. *Sex Roles*, *14*, 603–615.

Coan, R.W. (1979). *Psychologists: Personal and theoretical pathways*. New York: Irvington.

Crosby, F.J. (1982). *Relative deprivation and working women*. New York: Oxford University Press.

Crosby, F.J., & Herek, G.M. (1986). Male sympathy and the situation of women: Does personal experience make a difference? *Journal of Social Issues*, *42*, 55–66.

Deaux, K. (1985). Sex and gender. *Annual Review of Psychology*, *36*, 49–81.

Deaux, K., & Major, B. (1987). Putting gender into context: An interactive model of gender-related behavior. *Psychological Review*, *94*, 369–389.

Dion, K.L. (1975). Women's reaction to discrimination from members of the same or opposite sex. *Journal of Research in Personality*, *9*, 294–306.

Dion, K.L., & Earn, B.M. (1975). The phenomenology of being a target of prejudice. *Journal of Personality and Social Psychology*, *32*, 944–950.

Eagly, A.H., Wood, W., & Fishbaugh, L. (1981). Sex differences in conformity: Surveillance by the group as a determinant of male nonconformity. *Journal of Personality and Social Psychology*, *40*, 384–394.

Fine, M. (1983–1984). Coping with rape: Critical perspective on consciousness. *Imagination, Cognition, and Personality*, *3*, 249–267.

Forward, J.R., & Williams, J.R. (1970). Internal–external control and black militancy. *Journal of Social Issues*, *26*, 75–92.

Gardner, H. (1985). *The mind's new science*. New York: Basic Books.

Gergen, K.J. (1985). The social constructionist movement in modern psychology. *American Psychologist*, *40*, 266–275.

Grady, K.E. (1977). *The belief in sex differences*. Paper presented at the meeting of the Eastern Psychological Association, Boston.

Hacker, H.M. (1951). Women as a minority group. *Social Forces*, *30*, 60–69.

Hansen, R.D. (1980). Commonsense attribution. *Journal of Personality and Social Psychology*, *39*, 996–1009.

Hansen, R.D., & O'Leary, V.E. (1985). Sex-determined attributions. In V.E. O'Leary, R.K. Unger, & B.S. Wallston (Eds.), *Women, gender, and social psychology* (pp. 67–99). Hillsdale, NJ: Erlbaum.

Katz, P.A. (1986). Modification of children's gender-stereotyped behavior: General issues and research considerations. *Sex Roles*, *14*, 591–602.

Kidder, L.H., Belletirie, G., & Cohn, E.S. (1977). Secret ambitions and public performance: The effect of anonymity on reward allocations made by men and women. *Journal of Experimental Social Psychology*, *13*, 70–80.

Kimbe, G.A. (1984). Psychology's two cultures. *American Psychologist*, *39*, 833–839.

King, D.J. (1980). Values of undergraduate students and faculty members on theoretical orientations in psychology. *Teaching of Psychology*, *7*, 236–237.

Konner, M. (1981). *The tangled wing: Biological constraints on the human spirit*. New York: Harper & Row.

Laws, J.L. (1975). The psychology of tokenism: An analysis. *Sex Roles*, *1*, 51–67.

Lemay, M.F., & Unger, R.K. (1982). *The perception of females and males: The relationship between physical attractiveness and gender*. Paper presented at the meeting of the Eastern Psychological Association, Baltimore.

McGuire, W.J., McGuire, C.V., & Winton, W. (1979). Effects of household sex composition on the salience of one's gender in the spontaneous self-concept. *Journal of Experimental Social Psychology*, *15*, 77–90.

Neisser, U. (1967). *Cognitive psychology*. New York: Appleton-Century-Croft.

Pastore, N. (1949). *The nature–nurture controversy*. New York: King's Cross Press.

Piliavin, J.A., & Unger, R.K. (1985). The helpful but helpless female: Myth or reality. In V.E. O'Leary, R.K. Unger, & B.S. Wallston (Eds.), *Women, gender, and social psychology* (pp. 149–189). Hillsdale, NJ: Erlbaum.

Ricketts, M. (1986). *Theoretical orientations and values of feminist psychologists*. Unpublished Ph.D. dissertation, University of Windsor.

Rosenberg, R. (1982). *Beyond separate spheres: Intellectual roots of modern feminism*. New Haven: Yale University Press.

Rosenthal, N.B. (1984). Consciousness raising: From revolution to reevaluation. *Psychology of Women Quarterly*, *8*, 309–326.

Rublin, Z., & Peplau, A. (1973). Belief in a just world and reactions to another's lot: A study of participants in the national draft lottery. *Journal of Social Issues*, *29*, 73–93.

Sanger, B.P., & Alker, H.A. (1972). Dimensions of internal–external locus of control and the women's liberation movement. *Journal of Social Issues*, *29*, 115–129.

Serbin, L.A., Connor, J.M., & Citron, C.C. (1978). Environmental control of independent and dependent behaviors in preschool boys and girls: A model for early independence training. *Sex Roles*, *4*, 867–875.

Sherif, C.W. (1982). Needed concepts in the study of gender identity. *Psychology of Women Quarterly*, *6*, 375–398.

Sherwood, J.J., & Nataupsky, M. (1968). Predicting the conclusions of Negro–White intelligence research from biographical characteristics of the investigator. *Journal of Personality and Social Psychology*, *8*, 53–58.

Shields, S.A. (1975). Functionalism, Darwinism, and the psychology of women: A study in social myth. *American Psychologist*, *30*, 739–754.

Skrypnek, B.J., & Snyder, M. (1982). On the self-perpetuating nature of stereotypes about women and men. *Journal of Experimental Social Psychology*, *18*, 277–291.

Snyder, M., Tanke, E.D., & Berscheid, E. (1977). Social perception and interpersonal behavior: On the self-fulfilling nature of social stereotypes. *Journal of Personality and Social Psychology*, *35*, 656–666.

Snyder, M., & Uranowitz, S.W. (1978). Reconstructing the past: Some cognitive consequences of person perception. *Journal of Personality and Social Psychology*, *36*, 941–950.

Spence, J.T., & Helmreich, R. (1978). *Masculinity and femininity: Their psychological dimensions, correlates, and antecedents*. Austin: University of Texas Press.

Spence, J.T., & Sawin, L.L. (1985). Images of masculinity and femininity: A reconceptualization. In V.E. O'Leary, R.K. Unger, & B.S. Wallston (Eds.), *Women, gender, and social psychology* (pp. 35–66) Hillsdale, NJ: Erlbaum.

Taylor, S.E., & Fiske, S.T. (1978). Salience, attention, and attribution: Top of the head phenomena. In L. Berkowitz (Ed.), *Advances in experimental social psychology*, Vol. 11. New York: Academic Press.

Unger, R.K. (1981). Sex as a social reality: Field and laboratory research. *Psychology of Women Quarterly*, *5*, 645–653.

Unger, R.K. (1983). Through the looking glass: No Wonderland yet! (The reciprocal relationship between methodology and models of reality.) *Psychology of Women Quarterly*, *8*, 9–32.

Unger, R.K. (1984–1985). Explorations in feminist ideology: Surprising consistencies and unexamined conflicts. *Imagination, Cognition, and Personality*, *4*, 395–403.

Unger, R.K. (1985). Between the "no longer" and the "not yet": Reflections on personal and social change. First Carolyn Wood Sherif Memorial Lecture. Presented at the meeting of the American Psychological Association, Los Angeles.

Unger, R.K. (1986). Looking toward the future by looking at the past: Social activism and social history. *Journal of Social Issues*, *42*, 215–227.

Unger, R.K. (1988). Psychological, feminist, and personal epistemology: Transcending contradiction. In M. Gergen (Ed)., *Feminist thought and the structure of knowledge* (pp. 124–141). New York: New York University Press.

Unger, R.K., Draper, R.D., & Pendergrass, M.L. (1986). Personal epistemology and personal experience. *Journal of Social Issues*, *42*, 67–79.

Unger, R.K., Hilderbrand, M., & Madar, T. (1982). Physical attractiveness and assumptions about social deviance: Some sex by sex comparisons. *Personality and Social Psychology Bulletin*, *8*, 293–301.

Unger, R.K., & Sussman, L.E. (1986). "I and thou": Another barrier to societal change? *Sex Roles*, *14*, 629–636.

von Baeyer, C.L., Sherk, D.L., & Zanna, M.P. (1981). Impression management in the job interview: When the female applicant meets the male (chauvinist) interviewer. *Personality and Social Psychology Bulletin*, *7*, 45–51.

Wallston, B.S. (1981). What are the questions in psychology of women? A feminist approach to research. *Psychology of Women Quarterly*, *5*, 597–617.

Wallston, B.S., & Grady, K.E. (1985). Integrating the feminist critique and the crisis in social psychology: Another look at research methods. In V.E. O'Leary, R.K. Unger, & B.S. Wallston (Eds.), *Women, gender, and social psychology* (pp. 7–33). Hillsdale, NJ: Erlbaum.

Wood, J.T., & Conrad, C. (1983). Paradox in the experience of professional women. *Western Journal of Speech Communication*, *47*, 305–322.

2
Bringing Young Women to Math and Science

Jacquelynne S. Eccles

A growing concern has been expressed by educators and policymakers alike over the small number of women pursuing careers in the scientific, mathematical, and technical fields (e.g., Sells, 1980). Despite efforts to ameliorate this through affirmative action and scholarship programs, employment statistics indicate that men and women are still entering these career fields in disproportionate numbers (Bureau of Labor Statistics, 1980). Women are less likely than men to enter professions that are math related. For example, in 1983, women received only 13.2% of all undergraduate degrees in engineering and only 27% of all undergraduate degrees in the physical sciences. In contrast, females received 68% of the undergraduate degrees in psychology and sociology and 75% of the undergraduate degrees in education (Vetter and Babco, 1986).

These differences are even more dramatic at the graduate and professional levels. In 1984, for example, less than 10% of the master's degrees and less than 6% of the doctorates in engineering went to women. In this same year, women received 50–51% of the doctorates in education, the humanities, and psychology, and they received 58% of the doctorates in health-related sciences (Vetter and Babco, 1986).

Many researchers have expressed an interest in this problem. Although females receive less encouragement to continue their mathematical and physical science studies and to pursue mathematical or technical careers, findings from a wide variety of sources indicate that the sex differences in career plans are not solely the result of systematic discrimination (see Eccles, 1987a, b). On the contrary, all too often females choose to limit, or to end, their math training while still in high school or soon after entering college. College-bound high school females take about one-half year less mathematics and about one year less physical science than their male peers—despite the fact that females, in general, get better grades in math and science than males (*Women and Minorities in Science and Engineering*, 1986). For these females, this choice effectively eliminates many career options related to math and physical science before they enter college. In fact, only 20–22% of female high school graduates have enough high school mathematics to qualify them for a quantitative major in college. The comparable figure for male high school graduates is 28%. And only 4.5% of female high school graduates express any interest in a quantitative college major (Vetter & Babco, 1986).

Why do females limit their options in this way? The search for an understanding of the motivation/attitudinal determinants of achievement-related behaviors is not new to psychology. Much of the relevant work in the 1950s and 1960s was stimulated by the expectancy-value theory of Atkinson and his colleagues (e.g., Atkinson, 1964). This theory focused attention on individual differences in the motive to achieve and on the effects of subjective expectation on both this motive and the incentive value of success. Some investigators, using new techniques to measure achievement motives, have continued to explore the implications of motivational mediators for achievement behaviors (e.g., see Spence and Helmreich, 1978). Much of the work of the last decade, however, has shifted attention away from motivational constructs to cognitive constructs such as causal attributions, subjective expectations, self-concept of ability, perceptions of task difficulty, and subjective task value. The theoretical and empirical work presented in this chapter fits into this tradition.

Building on the works of motivational and attribution theorists such as Jack Atkinson (1964), Virginia Crandall (1969), Kurt Lewin (1938), and Bernard Weiner (1974), my colleagues and I have elaborated a model of academic choice. Drawing upon the theoretical and empirical work associated with decision making, achievement, and attribution theory, the model links academic choices to expectancies for success and to the importance of the task's incentive value. It also specifies the relation of these constructs to cultural norms, experience, aptitude, and a set of personal beliefs and attitudes associated with achievement activities (see Eccles-Parsons et al., 1983); achievement activities in this model are any activities that involve evaluating one's performance or products against a standard of excellence. We believe that this model is particularly useful for analyzing sex differences in students' course selection and career choice and in guiding future research efforts in this domain.

A general summary of the mediators and their relation to expectations, values, and achievement behaviors such as persistence, performance, and choice is depicted in Figure 2.1. This model is built on the assumption that an individual's interpretation of reality has a more direct influence on one's expectancies, values, and achievement behavior than one's actual past successes or failures. If actual performance directly predicted and accounted for subsequent academic choices, we would expect more females than males to enter math and science fields. By placing the influence of experience on achievement beliefs, outcomes, and future goals in a more complex cognitive framework, the model allows us to address several mediating factors, which may offer more sound explanations and remedies. These mediating factors include causal attributional patterns

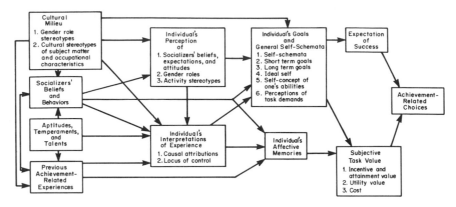

FIGURE 2.1. Developmental model of educational and occupational choices. (Adapted from Eccles, 1985a.) This model outlines the longitudinal relationships between the constructs listed in each box. The arrows indicate the hypothesized relationships and the presumed causal direction of the relationships at any one point in time. For example, it is assumed that the constructs in the boxes in the far left column are causally prior in their influence on all boxes to the right of this column. Similarly, it is assumed that the impact of the experiences implicit in the boxes in the far left column on expectations for success and subjective task value are mediated by the constructs listed in the boxes in the middle two columns (i.e., the individual's perceptions and interpretations of experience, the individual's emerging goal hierarchy and self-schemata, and the individual's affective memories of their experiences). Finally, it is assumed that the influence of all constructs in columns to the left of the fifth column on achievement-related choices (such as course enrollment decisions and occupational preferences) are mediated through their impact on the individual's expectations of success in the various options considered and the subjective value of the various options considered to the individual. Full elaboration of the model can be found in Eccles-Parsons et al. (1983); detailed discussion of the model's implications for an understanding of the impact of gender roles on achievement choices can be found in Eccles (1984, 1987a, b).

for success and failure, the input of socializers (primarily parents and teachers), gender-role stereotypes, and one's perceptions of various possible tasks. The model assumes that each of these factors contributes to both the expectations one holds for future success and the subjective value one attaches to any particular achievement task. Expectations and subjective value, in turn, directly influence achievement-related behaviors, including decisions to engage in particular achievement activities, the intensity of effort expended, and actual performance.

Eccles-Parsons et al. (1983) review extensively the literature supporting the importance of these cognitive mediators for career choice. Readers interested in a full discussion of these factors will find that article germane. The general trend in the literature, however, based on studies ranging from such diverse fields as mathematical modeling of decision making to career counseling and guidance, supports the importance of these mediating constructs in achievement task and/or career choice (see Betz & Hackett, 1981, and Eccles, 1987a, b for additional reviews).

In this chapter, I summarize the findings from work conducted with my colleagues on the importance of expectancies (defined in terms of confidence in one's abilities and performance) and values (defined in terms of interest in the subject matter, and the perceived importance and utility of the subject area) on math course enrollment decisions. Throughout, I discuss in particular the role teachers and parents play in socializing males and females to hold different expectancies and values toward math. The findings discussed come from two large-scale longitudinal studies my colleagues and I have conducted at the University of Michigan over the last ten years. These studies differ only in the samples included. The measures used are either quite comparable or exactly identical across these studies. Separate studies were run to test the generalizability of our findings across populations and to extend our study to the parents and teachers of our student samples. The findings reported in this chapter replicate across the studies. For ease of presentation, most of the specific data outlined in this chapter come from a single two year longitudinal study of approximately 500 predominantly white, middle-class fifth to twelfth graders in southeastern Michigan and their parents and math teachers. Details of the method of this study can be found in Eccles (1985a), Eccles, Adler, and Meece (1984), Eccles-Parsons (1984), Eccles-Parsons, Adler, and Kaczala (1982), and Eccles-Parsons, Kaczala, and Meece (1982). We refer to this sample in this chapter as our primary sample.

Confidence and Values

Given both the empirical and theoretical importance of confidence and value in mediating course choice and occupational decisions, we assessed the role these beliefs have in explaining sex differences in the choice of mathematics. But before we could do this, we needed to translate these theoretical constructs and the relationships implied in our model into the concrete beliefs and specific relationships that operate in the complex environment in which students actually make course enrollment and occupational choices. As a first step in this process, we investigated secondary school students' decisions about enrolling in optional high school courses. In analyzing this specific context, it became clear immediately that we needed to study more than just mathematics and science. Too often researchers think about math and science enrollment decisions as if these are the only subjects that students are choosing to take. This is clearly not the case. Students at the senior high school level have to make some very complex decisions about what they want to spend their time doing. The decision to drop mathematics is rarely made in isolation from the students' decisions regarding other subjects. Math courses must compete with an array of subjects, such as a second foreign language, band, art, and home economics. With very few slots available for electives, students make scheduling trade-offs among those subjects they expect either to enjoy the most or to benefit their long-range goals. The decision not to take an advanced math or a physical science course often reflects a preference for other goals or subjects rather than a fear of math or physical science. Since, for college-bound females, these competing concerns are often related to language, our studies have examined attitudes toward both mathematics and English in order to gain a richer picture of this complex choice process.

Both our understanding of the factors leading females away from math and science and our ability to develop effective intervention strategies depend on our obtaining this richer and more ecologically valid picture of the decision making process underlying course choice. Obtaining such a picture requires our understanding of the courses taken as well as the courses not taken and of the reasons behind each type of choice. Studying secondary school students' confidence in their own abilities in math and English (defined in terms of how good they think they are in the subject area and how well they expect to do in the subject area) and secondary school students' perception of the value of math and English (defined as interest in the subject, and perceived importance and utility value of the subject area for long- and short-term goals) seemed a reasonable first step.

Empirical Findings

Males' and females' attitudes toward math and English, and toward themselves as learners of math and English, diverge consistently in all studies of people over the age of 12. In our samples, these differences begin to emerge at about the seventh grade and become stronger over the high school years. Figure 2.2 illustrates the relative confidence males and females from our primary sample reported in their math and English abilities (Eccles, 1985).

In this sample, there were no major sex differences in confidence for either subject prior to seventh grade. In fact, if anything, the elementary school females reported slightly more confidence than the males in their English ability. Sex differences, however, began to emerge in junior high school, at which point the females had lower estimates of their math ability than did the males. The size of this sex difference grew as the students moved into high school. This general developmental pattern characterizes the results for our second sample as well. In the second sample, however, the sex difference favoring English for females was stronger.

Even more striking than the sex differences within subject area is the subject matter difference among the females. As these females moved into junior high school, a growing discrepancy between their view of their math skills and their view of their English skills emerged. Apparently even

ABILITY

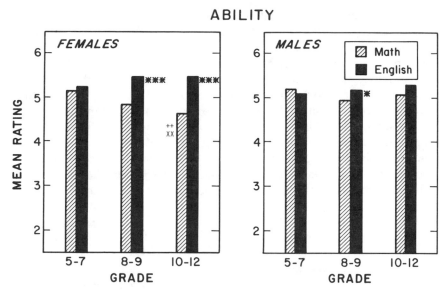

FIGURE 2.2. Grade level, sex, and subject matter differences in self-concept of ability. (Adapted from Eccles, 1985a.) This figure illustrates the mean ratings of males and females from different grade levels on a measure of their self-concepts for their math and English abilities. The measure has a score range from 1.0 to 7.0 and is based on the mean of several items that consistently factor together across our various samples. These data are taken from a cross-sectional study of 668 students from a predominantly white middle- to upper-class, Midwestern community designated as our primary sample in the text of this chapter. Significance levels are indicated with three symbols: asterisks (*) indicate the subject domain comparisons within sex and age group; pluses (+) indicate sex comparisons within age group and subject domain; crosses (×) indicate age comparisons within sex and subject domain. In each case, one symbol indicates a significance level of at least .05; two symbols indicate a significance level of at least .01; and three symbols indicate a significance level of at least .001.

among females who are doing very well in mathematics, who are on a college track, and who are enrolled in advanced level high school math courses, females express greater confidence in their English abilities than their math abilities. The males in this sample did not show this difference. Unlike the females, these males on the average did not seem to favor one subject area over the other. It is possible that there may be more individual variation among males with some favoring English and others favoring math. If so, then as a group, males' preferences would average out and result in nearly equal group levels of confidence. In support of this suggestion, the variability in these males' scores was significantly greater than the variability in these females' scores. In contrast, among the females we found a consistent average population effect. In general, these data suggest that most females underestimate their math abilities as they get older and feel increasingly more confident about their English abilities than about their math abilities.

This pattern of results is mirrored in students' attitudes toward the value of math and English. We asked males and females how useful math and English were for their future goals. We also asked them how much they liked math and English, and how important they thought being competent in each subject was for their own self-concept. Figure 2.3 illustrates the findings in our primary sample (Eccles, 1985a). As was true with confidence in their abilities, the females showed a linear decrease over age in their assessment of the value of mathematics. This pattern was not evident in the male population as the males moved through these secondary school

SUBJECTIVE TASK VALUE

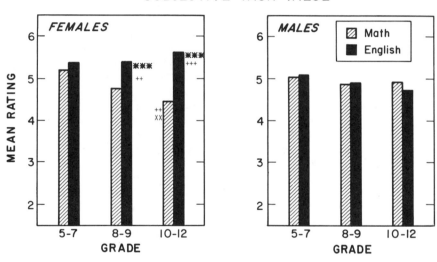

FIGURE 2.3. Grade level, sex, and subject matter differences in subjective task value. (Adapted from Eccles, 1985a.) This figure illustrates the mean ratings of males and females from different grade levels on a measure of their self-concepts for their math and English abilities. The measure has a score range from 1.0 to 7.0 and is based on the mean of several items that consistently factor together across our various samples. These data are taken from a cross-sectional study of 668 students from a predominantly white middle- to upper-class, Midwestern community designated as our primary sample in the text of this chapter. Significance levels are indicated with three symbols: asterisks (*) indicate the subject domain comparisons within sex and age group; pluses (+) indicate sex comparisons within age group and subject domain; crosses (×) indicate age comparisons within sex and subject domain. In each case, one symbol indicates a significance level of at least .05; two symbols indicate a significance level of at least .01; and three symbols indicate a significance level of at least .001.

years. The confidence pattern was further paralleled by a growing discrepancy between the value that the females attached to mathematics and English. Again, in contrast, the males' responses were about equal for the two subjects. As the females moved through high school, they reported valuing English increasingly more than they valued mathematics.

Given these results, is it any wonder that these females elect to drop mathematics in the twelfth grade when they must choose between taking an advanced math course and another subject in which they are more interested? In general, these females were more likely to elect advanced level courses in English, foreign languages, or social science than advanced level courses in either mathematics or physical science. As a consequence, they were less likely than the males to enroll in an advanced math or physics course (Eccles et al., 1984). We would predict exactly this result *unless* someone intervened and gave the females new information that would lead them to reevaluate either their assessments of the importance of mathematics or their estimates of their mathematical aptitude, or both.

Origins of Sex Differences in Confidence and Subjective Task Value

From where do these attitudinal differences come? Several mechanisms are suggested in Figure 2.1. Beginning at the far left of Figure 2.1, we hypothesized that these differences are due to general cultural factors such as the gender-role stereotypes both of different subject areas and of the sex differences in the distribution of specific talents in the population. These stereotypes are hypothesized to have a direct effect on the individual's self-perceptions and subjective task values. I discuss the evidence for this link first. In addition, these stereotypes are hypothesized to have an indirect influence on the individual through their influence on socializers' beliefs and behaviors. That is, culturally held gender-role stereotypes are presumed to affect the attitudes and behaviors of socializers (in this case parents and teachers), which in turn affect the self-perceptions and task values that males and females develop as they grow up. I discuss the evidence for these links second, focusing first on parents and then on teachers. Finally, in the model in Figure 2.1, we hypothesized that previous achievement-related experiences influence the development of females' and males' attitudes toward mathematics both directly through their impact on the individual's affective memories and indirectly through their impact on the individual's interpretative framework. I discuss evidence for these links last, focusing on classroom experiences. The fourth and final set of influences listed in the far left column is aptitudes, temperaments, and talents. Although much debate has occurred regarding the possible role these factors may play in shaping sex differences in math and science, no definitive conclusions have been reached by the scientific community (see Eccles, 1987b; Eccles-Parsons, 1984; Halpern, 1986; Steinkamp & Maehr, 1984, for discussion). In contrast, it is quite clear that social forces do affect females' interest in math and science, as is documented in the next sections. Consequently, given the focus in this book on gender role as a belief system and given my commitment to studying intervenable causes of females' under representation in math and science, I do not discuss the possible influence of sex differences in aptitudes, temperaments, and talents further. In summary, in this chapter I discuss three of the possible mechanisms outlined in Figure 2.1: gender-role congruence, parent influences, and teacher influences.

GENDER-ROLE CONGRUENCE

Gender roles can affect both confidence and value. One critical feature of the female gender role in this culture is a belief in the relative incompetence of females in mathematical and technological fields—a belief that females are unlikely to have math talent or to be very skilled in technical areas. To the extent that a female incorporates this cultural belief into her self-concept, she is likely to have less confidence in her math abilities than in her English abilities.

To test this prediction among the secondary school students in our primary sample, we compared the females' ratings of themselves on the Personality Attributes Questionnaire (PAQ) to their ratings of their own math ability and of the difficulty of math as a subject area. The PAQ is a scale designed to assess self-perceptions of one's femininity, masculinity, and androgyny (Spence & Helmreich, 1978). As predicted, the masculine and the androgynous females had more confidence in their math ability, higher expectations for their own performance in math, and rated math as easier than did the feminine females (Kaczala, 1981).

It is also probable that the extent to which parents have incorporated this belief system into their view of the world will influence their judgments of their daughter's math abilities. To test this hypothesis, we compared the strength of parents' ratings of mathematics as a stereotypically male talent with their ratings of their own sons' or daughters' math talent controlling for the actual performance level of the children. As predicted, parents who endorsed the gender-role stereotype that males have more math talent than females either underestimated their daughters' math talent or overestimated their sons' math talent depending on the sex of their child (Jacobs, 1987).

Gender-role beliefs should also affect parents' attributional explanations for their children's performance in mathematics. Given that parents in general believe that males have more math talent than females, they should be less likely to attribute a female's successes in math and physical sciences to high ability than to her hard work, diligence, and effort. And in fact, we found exactly this attributional pattern. Parents in our follow-up studies were more likely to attribute their sons' math successes to talent and their daughters' math successes to effort and, as a consequence, to rate their sons as more talented in math (Yee & Eccles, in press). These attributional biases, in turn, were linked to a decline in their daughters' confidence in their own math abilities, even though the young women continued to get just as high grades in their math and science courses as their male peers (Eccles et al., 1987; Eccles-Parsons, Adler, & Kaczala, 1982). Thus gender roles do appear to undermine females' interest in mathematics by diminishing both females' own confidence in their mathematical abilities and parents' view of their daughters' math talent.

Gender roles can also influence enrollment and occupational choices through their direct impact on interests and values. In particular, gender roles can undermine females' interest in mathematics and physical sciences by their impact on females' personal values and perceptions of the importance of mathematics and technological professions. Through their impact on both the view one has of oneself and the view one has of the world, gender roles can affect the value individuals come to attach to various school subjects, college majors, and future occupations. As we mature, we develop a view of who we are and who we would like to be. Obviously, this view includes many characteristics. The professional and academic goals we set will depend not only on our intellectual confidence and values but also on our personal values and self-definition. Just as students do not schedule elective math courses in a vacuum, females do not define their adult career choices as if severed from their other interests and images of themselves as females. Two major differences in the male and female gender role may generate different views of "appropriate" professions. Females show a greater interest in other people, as opposed to things; and they show a greater interest in helping and nurturing, as opposed to trying to take things apart and manipulate mechanical objects (Eccles, 1987b; Gilligan, 1982; Huston, 1983). We would expect this distinction to be reflected in a divergence in the occupational goals that males and females adopt.

During our childhood, we also develop images of different occupational fields, for example, engineers, physicists, or scientists. Sally Boswell (1979) asked elementary and senior high school students what they thought scientists did. Not surprisingly, the children, both males and females, conjured up an image of a person wearing a white coat and working in front of an array of test tubes. *He* was isolated in a laboratory, worked long hours, and had no time for *his* family or *his* friends. When the children were asked to imagine an engineer, they conjured up an image of a man in a hardhat looking for oil in the Arabian desert. Most females, who are developing images of themselves as helpful and nurturing toward other people, would not find the image of scientist or engineer very attractive or very compatible with their self-image. Thus, we would expect them to have difficulty imagining themselves doing such work for the rest of their lives. As a consequence, these occupations should have—and in fact do have—less positive value for females (see Eccles, 1987b).

As mathematics and physical science courses are often prerequisites for entry into these professions, we would accordingly expect these subject areas to have less value to females, especially those who have incorporated the female gender role into their own identity. To test this suggestion, we compared the females' PAQ classification score with their ratings of the value of mathematics. Consistent with the findings for confidence in one's math ability, androgynous females rated math as more interesting, more important, and more useful than did feminine females (Kaczala, 1981).

If, as I have argued, these stereotypical gender-role beliefs undermine the value females might otherwise attach to technological occupations, then they can obviously undermine the value females attach to the mathematics courses that are prerequisites to entry into such fields. When we asked our primary sample why they were taking mathematics, only a few claimed they were taking math for the love of the subject. Most reported taking mathematics because it was required for their occupational goals, or because it was required to get into a good college (Eccles-Parsons et al., 1983). If one is not going into a field that requires math, why (they argue) should one bother taking nonrequired math? Unfortunately, few educators and parents give the students a positive answer to this question. In addition, these adults often give students erroneous information about the level of mathematics required in various fields (see Eccles, 1985b; Fox, Brody, & Tobin, 1980; Steinkamp & Maehr, 1984). Thus females are likely to have had insufficient math training for even those scientific fields that they are likely to enter, such as psychology.

This pattern of misinformation and lack of encouragement is compounded by the lack of role models available to children in either the media or their own experience. Females rarely observe examples or images of women performing in math-related technical professions. As a result we have a situation in which there are few incentives for most females either to take advanced courses in math and physical science or to consider seriously math-related occupations, and strong, and fairly consistent, gender-role prescriptions against consideration of nontraditional educational and occupational choices. Is it any wonder then that females are less likely to make such nontraditional choices when it comes time for them to make these decisions?

SOCIAL FORCES: PARENT INFLUENCES AND TEACHER INFLUENCES

Neither sex-differentiated beliefs and self-perceptions nor gender-role beliefs develop in a vacuum. Ample evidence documents the fact that peers, friends, siblings, parents, TV, and school personnel all contribute to the shaping of these beliefs over time (see Huston, 1983; Eccles, 1985b; Eccles

& Hoffman, 1984; Eccles-Parsons, 1984). The model depicted in Figure 2.1 focuses attention on the role parents and teachers play in shaping children's self-perceptions and task values. And, not surprisingly, the studies we have done based on this model reflect this orientation. Our data document the role of parents and teachers in shaping and perpetuating sex-differentiated self-perceptions, and both educational and occupational preferences. In the next sections, I summarize these findings separately for parents and teachers. But first I summarize briefly our general findings on the relative influences of parents and teachers.

In our studies, parents appear to play the more central role in the creation of sex-differentiated values and self-perceptions. As I argue below, these effects are not necessarily intentional; in fact, the parents are often unaware of the things they do that discourage their daughters from studying math and science. Consequently, their gender-role stereotyped behaviors and expectations are often immune to modification based on their children's actual talents and performance. In contrast, the teachers' role is more one of reinforcing children's gender-role stereotyped beliefs than one of creating them. Because of the demands inherent in teaching and supervising a large number of children at one time, teachers are usually more reactive than proactive in their interactions with students. Consequently, teachers often unintentionally reinforce the gender-role–related beliefs the children bring with them to the classroom. In our numerous hours of classroom observation, we rarely saw a teacher attempt either to modify their students' beliefs or to expose the children to experiences that would challenge their preconceived beliefs, self-perceptions, and aspirations. Consequently, although teachers could be a powerful force for change, they typically are too reactive and too overwhelmed with the day-to-day realities of their classrooms to have much of an impact on most children's gender-role stereotyped self-perceptions and values. These points are elaborated below.

Parents

Our data quite consistently show that parents, to a greater extent than teachers, have gender-role stereotyped beliefs about their children's academic competencies (Eccles & Jacobs, 1986; Eccles et al., 1987; Eccles-Parsons, Adler, & Kaczala, 1982). Let me give some examples from the parents of our primary sample. As noted earlier, these males and females had always done equally well in mathematics. In addition, their teachers reported that they had worked equally hard in mathematics. Yet, when we asked their parents how much effort they thought their daughter or son needed to exert in order to do well in math, both mothers and fathers of daughters reported that their child had to work harder than did the mothers and fathers of sons. When we asked them how hard math was for their child, both parents agreed that math was more difficult for daughters than for sons. When we asked them how important it was to take math, both parents rated math, especially advanced high school math, and both physics and chemistry, as more important for sons than for daughters. Similarly, parents of sons were more likely to report that math is relatively more important than other subjects than parents of daughters. In contrast, parents rated English and American history as more important for daughters to take than for sons. Finally, both mothers and fathers agreed that they would be more likely to encourage their sons to take advanced math.

These results did not reflect a general lack of confidence in their daughter's academic abilities. In general, these females got better grades in school than their male peers. And when we asked the parents to indicate their perception of their child's general school performance, both fathers and mothers reported that the females were doing better in school than the males were (Eccles-Parsons, Adler, & Kaczala, 1982).

Similar sex-of-child effects characterized the parents' causal attributions for their children's success in mathematics. We asked parents in a second sample to recall a time when their child had done especially well in mathematics and to rate how important they felt natural talent, skill, and effort were in accounting for this performance. Parents of sons rated natural talent a more important reason for their child's performance than parents of daughters. In contrast, parents of daughters rated hard work (effort) as a more important reason for their child's performance than parents of sons (Yee & Eccles, in press).

These causal attributions, in turn, have the expected impact on parents' views of their children's mathematical talent (Yee & Eccles, in press). Parents who attributed their child's math success more to natural talent than to effort (the male pattern) developed more confidence in their child's math ability than parents who attributed their child's math success relatively more to hard work than to natural talent (the female pattern)—even though both groups of children had earned equivalent grades in mathematics.

Furthermore, longitudinal analyses indicate that parents' confidence in their child's math abilities has a direct impact on their children's self-perceptions and values as predicted by the model illustrated in Figure 2.1 (Eccles-Parsons, Adler, & Kaczala, 1982). Parents', especially mothers', confidence in their children's math abilities and parents' estimates of how hard their child is having to work in math seemed to mediate the impact of the children's grades on the children's confidence in their math abilities. Apparently, parents provide their children with an interpretative framework for understanding what grades mean about one's abilities. And since parents think math is harder for daughters than for sons, females develop less confidence in their math abilities than males.

In addition, perhaps because parents think math is harder for daughters than for sons, and English is easier for daughters than for sons, they rate advanced math and the physical sciences as less important than other subjects for daughters but not for sons. Consequently, parents are less likely to encourage females to take advanced math courses. Since parental advice is noted by students as one of the most important influences on high school course decisionmaking (Eccles-Parsons et al., 1983), these parental beliefs about the relative importance of mathematics appear to play a major role in determining sex differences in math course enrollment decisions.

Teachers

A great deal of research has focused on the role teachers may play in either creating or perpetuating sex-differentiated self-perceptions and educational choices. Social scientists have taken two approaches to this topic.

The first and most classic approach has been to look for differential treatment in the classroom by using carefully designed observational systems. This approach investigates whether teachers treat males and females differently, and whether these differences convey the subtle message that females are not expected to go on or to excel in math and physical science. There has been a long tradition of research on these issues involving many studies looking at teacher–student interaction. Three findings emerge with some consistency. First, there has been a major historical change. The differences reported by researchers in the 1960s are more difficult to document today. Either teachers have become more sensitive to the differences on which observers focus and therefore act more equalitarian when the observers are there, or teacher training has been effective at producing teachers who are more equalitarian in their treatment of males and females in their math classrooms.

Despite this historical change, however, two differences still characterize many classrooms: (1) males are yelled at and criticized publicly more than females, and (2) males are more likely than females to monopolize teacher–student interaction time (see Eccles & Blumenfeld, 1985). The second characteristic emerges only in some classrooms and seems to reflect the fact that a few males are allowed to dominate the class time in these classrooms. The teachers are not interacting more in general with the males in these classrooms: rather, a few males are receiving much more interaction than all the other students. We have now observed in over 150 math classrooms in southeastern Michigan; in 40 of them, we coded every interaction the teacher had with each student over a ten-day period. Over half the students *never* talked to the teacher during the ten days. Others had 14 or more interactions with the teacher *every hour*. Most of these latter students were males.

The second approach to the study of teacher influences has used a very different strategy. Researchers in this tradition identify a set of characteristics that makes some classrooms special and then observe and compare these classrooms to more typical ones. For example, both Pat Casserly (1975) and Jane Kahle (1984) have identified "superb" teachers and then compared their classroom techniques with those used by more "mediocre or average" teachers. Casserly and Kahle used criteria such as average student achievement level to define these "superb" and "average" teachers. Following a similar strategy, we have identified classrooms in which there were few sex differences in the students' attitudes toward math and compared them to classrooms in which the males had more positive attitudes toward math and more confidence in their math ability than the females.

Even though researchers have used a variety of criteria to define their classroom types, there has been reasonable consistency across studies regarding the distinguishing characteristics of good and/or "nonsexist" classrooms. In our study, for example, we compared classrooms in which the males and females had similar confidence in their mathematical ability to classrooms in which the males had substantially higher confidence in their math ability than the females (Eccles, MacIver, & Lange, 1986; Eccles-Parsons, Kaczala, & Meece, 1982). Important procedural differences emerged. Classrooms in which there were no sex differences were more orderly, had less of both extreme praise and criticism, and were more businesslike. The teacher also maintained tighter control over student–teacher interactions, ensuring equal student participation by calling on everyone, rather than focusing on the small subset of students who regularly raised their hands. In contrast, classrooms marked by sex differences in the students' attitudes were characterized by student–teacher interactions dominated by a few students. Essentially, these teachers were more reactive, focusing their attention primarily on those students who raised their hand or insisted on attention in other ways. Consequently, a running dialogue emerged between the teacher and two or three students, who usually sat in the front of the room and regularly raised their hands. More often than not these "stars" were white males. Other students rarely volunteered and were never called upon to participate. They sat out of the teacher's view, and as long as they did not cause a disturbance or start trouble, they were allowed to be nonparticipants. The latter group of students included both the males for whom the teacher had low expectations and most of the females.

A further difference emerged with some consistency. The classrooms in which males and females had similar views of their abilities were less public and more private. Essentially, these classrooms were characterized by more dyadic interactions between the teacher and the student and less public drills involving the whole class. Consequently, the students spent less time waiting to be called on and competing for public attention, and more time working on problems and consulting individually with the teacher when help was needed. This teaching style appears to have a beneficial effect on females, perhaps because it induces a less competitive classroom environment. It is an environment that allows students to work individually and receive feedback without the entire class focusing publicly on the interaction.

The importance of general classroom climate, especially competitiveness, has emerged in a study we just completed that looks intensively at math instruction in sixth and seventh grades (Eccles, MacIver, & Lange, 1986). In this study we gathered information on general classroom climate from the students, observer, and the teachers in 110 mathematics classrooms. We used the students' reports of their confidence in their math abilities and the value they attached to mathematics to classify each classroom into one of the following three categories: (1) girl-friendly classrooms—the classrooms in which the females had more favorable attitudes toward mathematics than the males, (2) boy-friendly classrooms—the classrooms in which the males had more favorable attitudes than the females, and (3) neutral classrooms—the classrooms with no consistent pattern of sex differences in the students' self-perceptions and perceived math values. We then compared the classroom climate measures for the girl- and boy-friendly classrooms. The girl-friendly classrooms, relative to the boy-friendly classrooms, were characterized by less social comparison and competition among the students, by more teacher stress on the importance and value of mathematics, and by a warmer, fairer teacher as perceived by the students themselves. These results suggest that females develop more favorable attitudes toward math and more confidence in their math abilities in classrooms characterized by relatively low levels of competition, relatively high levels of personal contact with the teacher, and relatively low levels of public drill and practice.

Casserly (1980), using a different criterion for excellence, found a very similar pattern of results. She identified the 20 school districts in the United States that had the most favorable record of females going on to take Advanced Placement courses in math and science.[1] She then observed and interviewed these districts' teachers in an effort to identify their particular teaching skills and strategies. Five characteristics emerged with great regularity: (1) These teachers were more likely to use either cooperative learning strategies or individualized learning strategies than public drill. (2) They were less likely to use competitive motivational strategies; that is, they did not try to pit the students against each other in order to motivate their performance. (3) They used more hands-on learning and more problems with practical implications and opportunities for creative solutions. (4) Rather than drilling their math and science students on a canon of "correct" textbook information, these teachers designed more active, open-ended learning situations. They would pose a problem (e.g., "build a

---

[1]These districts also had the best record with males. Apparently, the techniques that worked for females also worked with males.

bridge that can bear a maximum amount of weight") and then divide students into teams. These teams could solve the problem in a variety of ways. (5) These teachers also engaged in a great deal of active career guidance in the classroom, stressing the importance and usefulness of math and science for the students' other courses and for their future career choices.

Kahle (1984) has done a similar study in science classrooms. She found that a very similar cluster of techniques were characteristic of science teachers who have been labeled as "outstanding." These teachers tended to use multiple texts, to carefully supplement their texts with information and pictures indicating the involvement of all nationalities, races, and both genders in math and science, and to avoid the use of sexist or racist material. Like the teachers in Casserly's study, they provided active career guidance during class time.

The "outstanding" teachers Kahle studied also relied heavily on hands-on experiences in which all students were required to participate actively. Use of computers in the classroom provides an excellent example of the importance of this type of teacher control. Too often, when computers are introduced into classrooms (especially at the elementary level), the pattern of a single male dominating their use emerges. This pattern is most evident in classrooms where the students are allowed to control access to the computers. A similar pattern often emerges with other types of scientific or laboratory equipment (Wilkinson & Marrett, 1985). In Kahle's optimal classrooms, opportunities were more evenly distributed and enforced: everyone participated, the "boss" in laboratory groups rotated, everyone took a turn with the equipment, and students had equal time on the computer. Enforcing this pattern is not easy. Teachers must be extremely organized and committed to equal distribution of opportunities for working with the equipment. Instead, all too often, a few students, usually white males, take over and other students, usually females, watch or play a more passive role (Wilkinson & Marrett, 1985). The monopolizing of computer time occurs particularly when the teacher is uncomfortable with this new technology. Such teachers often find a confidant in the classroom, usually a student familiar with computers and to whom the teacher delegates authority. This person then monitors who gets access to the computer, and how long they may use it. More often than not, this person is a white male since this is the group of children who, by a large margin, are most likely to have had the privilege of someone buying them a computer to use at home and providing them with the opportunity to learn about computers in either computer camps or out-of-school computer classes (Kiesler, Sproul, & Eccles, 1985b).

These studies, and several others like them, suggest that teachers may be providing a subset of males with more opportunities to learn and to practice leadership skills in science and math classrooms than they provide for the vast majority of females. In some cases, this may be due to conscious sexist attitudes and beliefs. For example, some teachers may believe that males are more talented in math and science and therefore focus their mentoring efforts on the males. But more often this appears to be due to the teachers' unconscious passive reactions to individual differences in behaviors and skills which the children bring to the classroom. Gender-role socialization outside the school leads males and females to have different skills and interests. Consequently, in the classroom, males and females display different behaviors—with males demanding more attention and more leadership opportunities by being more assertive and by having more out-of-school experience with math and science equipment such as computer and laboratory equipment. Since females typically do not protest the differential treatment that results, even well-intentioned teachers may fail to see the sex inequity of their classroom protocols for equipment use and participation. And unless truly committed to sex equity, even these teachers will do little to ensure equal participation and to try to counteract and modify males' and females' gender-role stereotyped self-perceptions and values.

In conclusion, it appears that there are certain kinds of learning environments that are not particularly conducive to most females' motivation to study math and science. These characteristics include competition, social comparison, high use of public drill, and domination of student–teacher interaction by a few students. In contrast, there are certain kinds of learning environments that appear to be more beneficial to females. These include controlled hands-on experience, use of nonsexist and nonracist materials, cooperative or individualized learning formats that ensure full participation by *all* children in the class, and active career counseling. Kahle has labeled this latter type of classroom a "girl-friendly" classroom. What is interesting about this set of characteristics is that they facilitate the motivation and performance of minority students and low achieving males as well (Malcolm, 1984). Apparently, only a few students benefit from competitive environments in which a select group of students tend to monopolize the teacher–student interaction. The rest of the class suffers either in terms of their motivation or in terms of their actual learning. Looked at in this light, the call for structuring classes and materials "more effectively" for females is *not* a call for special or remedial attention. Rather, it is a call for more conscientious distribution of the teacher's efforts as a resource for all students and for the use of instructional techniques that foster interest in mathematics and science even among students who are not intrinsically interested in the subject matter.

Conclusions

I began this chapter by presenting a model for understanding individual differences in achievement choices and then used this model to analyze why females are underrepresented in fields related to mathematics and the physical sciences. Consistent with the expectancy-value theoretical framework on which the model is based, I argued that the underrepresentation of females in mathematics and science resulted most directly from sex differences in students' confidence in their math and English abilities and the relative value they attach to activities and careers involving mathematics and physical science compared to the value they attach to other subject matter areas and occupational fields. Evidence was presented to support this hypothesis.

Again consistent with the model, I argued that these sex differences in beliefs result from the impact of our culturally based gender-role system on the beliefs and behaviors of those individuals responsible for the rearing and education of our children. Adults in this culture both act out and believe in traditional gender-role prescriptions regarding appropriate activities for males and females. They also believe that the sexes differ in their "natural" talents and interests, and these beliefs influence their perceptions of their own children's talents and interests despite evidence that the distribution of particular talents is very similar for males and females during the preadolescent years. As a consequence of these nonconscious beliefs, parents and teachers treat males and females differently, form different expectations and aspirations for females and males, and provide males and females with different interpretations of reality and different advice regarding their future options. As a result of these experiences, and in the absence of accurate information on which to base their stereotypes of adult occupations, young women, compared to young men, develop less confidence in their math abilities, less interest in studying math and physical science, and less interest in pursuing careers in math and science-related fields.

How can we change this cycle? Although parents seem to have the most powerful direct influence on the origins of these differences, teachers are well situated to intervene in this system. As I argued earlier, much of the problem stems from gender-role stereotyped values and self-perceptions. One of the ways that "superb" teachers produce positive outcomes is by active career counseling, equalitarian creative hands-on teaching practices, and active attempts to change their students' gender-role stereotyped beliefs, self-concepts and values. They change the females' views of who they are and who they can become. In so doing they change the value females attach to mathematics. By providing students with a reason for studying math and/or science, and by telling them how these subjects relate to the occupational world, these teachers give students a reason for wanting to learn math. In essence they provide an answer to the question "Why should I study more mathematics?" for those students who do not find math especially interesting or enjoyable. By providing all students the opportunity to participate fully in the class, they facilitate the acquisition of confidence in one's abilities and interest in the subject. Although teachers do not generally have a lot of influence, these exemplary teachers suggest that teachers make a difference if they decide to. But to do this requires an active commitment to nonsexist, nonracist instruction and guidance.

Even more importantly, it involves a commitment to go out of one's way to encourage young women to consider the fields of math and science. Teachers are in a unique position to identify talented, motivated students and to communicate their confidence in these students to both the students and their parents. This feedback is especially important for females and minority children, who appear less likely than males in general to label themselves as talented in math or science. By providing good female students and their parents direct explicit feedback regarding their talents and potential, teachers can counter the tendency of females and their parents to attribute young women's academic successes to hard work rather than talent. Providing this feedback also enlists the parents as allies in the resocialization process. Most parents want the best for their children, but because they themselves were raised in a gender-role stereotyped culture and have had little exposure to nontraditional models or information, they often overlook nontraditional career possibilities for their children and misinterpret their children's school performances. If a teacher, as a recognized expert, takes time to discuss their child's math or scientific talent and the vocational options it opens to her, parents of daughters may become as willing to encourage their children to think about careers in fields related to math or science as parents of sons are.

All these recommendations require very active involvement on the part of the teachers. Such involvement has been made easier by the development of good curricular materials for women students. These materials provide teachers with films and posters that will expose the students to minority and female role models in fields associated with math and science. Such materials can suggest new job options to students which they might otherwise not have known or not have considered. Students may also glean more realistic images of the familiar professions they had viewed in simpler, more stereotypic terms. By pointing out these options to females, teachers can motivate them to imagine themselves in these fields and thus to open themselves to the possibility of pursuing such occupations.

In closing, it seems evident to me that at this historical point in our culture, "equal treatment" in schools is not enough to increase the probability that young women will seriously consider nontraditional educational or vocational options. It certainly is the minimum to which we must aspire. But since children are exposed to a heavy dose of gender-role socialization outside school, they come into the classroom with well-formed, gender-role stereotypic beliefs about what is appropriate for them to think about in terms of their long-range vocational goals and their view of their own competencies. And their typical experiences in school and at home do nothing to counteract these beliefs. Consequently, when they reach the age where affirmative action programs are in place, they have already lost access to many possible options as a result of earlier educational and occupational decisions. If we are to get women involved in math and science, and if we are to change the impact of gender-role beliefs on females' self-perceptions, then we must use the classroom to counteract the years of socialization messages the children have received from billboards, parents, TV, and the culture at large. Equal *access* to classes and even equal performance in lower level classes are not adequate for overcoming what parents and teachers may consider (or fail to see) as "trivial" daily inequities in classroom structure and home environments. "Equal opportunity" must be viewed more hour-by-hour, rather than solely by policy decree, and it must begin very early for the effects of unequal treatment and gender-role stereotypes are already evident when children enter elementary school. Only active interventions will get students to reconsider their view of themselves, of math and science, and of the options that they should consider open to them in adulthood.

Acknowledgments. Work for this chapter was supported in part by grants to the author from the National Institute of Mental Health (MH31724) and the National Institute of Child Health and Human Development (HD17296).

References

Atkinson, J.W. (1964). *An introduction to motivation.* New York: Van Nostrand.

Betz, N.E., & Hackett, G. (1981). The relationship of career-related self-efficacy expectations to perceived career options in college women and men. *Journal of Counseling Psychology, 28,* 399–410.

Boswell, S. (1979). *Nice girls don't study mathematics. The perspective from elementary school.* Symposium paper presented at the meeting of the American Educational Research Association, San Francisco.

Bureau of Labor Statistics (1980). *Employment and earnings.* Washington. DC: U.S. Department of Labor.

Casserly, P. (1975). *An assessment of factors affecting female participation in advanced placement programs in mathematics, chemistry, and physics.* Report to the National Science Foundation, Washington, DC.

Casserly, P. (1980). An assessment of factors affecting female participation in advanced placement programs in mathematics, chemistry, and physics. In L.H. Fox, L. Brody, & D. Tobin (Eds.), *Women and the mathematical mystique* (pp. 138–163). Baltimore: Johns Hopkins University Press.

Crandall, V.C. (1969). Sex differences in expectancy of intellectual and academic reinforcement. In C.P. Smith (Ed.), *Achievement-related behaviors in children.* New York: Russell Sage Foundation.

Eccles, J.S. (1985a). Sex differences in achievement patterns. In T. Sonderegger (Ed.), *Nebraska Symposium of Motivation, Vol. 32.* Lincoln, NE: University of Nebraska Press.

Eccles, J.S. (1985b). Why doesn't Jane run? Sex differences in educational and occupational patterns. In F.D. Horowitz & M. O'Brien (Eds.), *The gifted and talented: A developmental perspective.* Washington, DC: APA Press.

Eccles, J.S. (1987a). Gender-roles and achievement. In J. Reinisch, L.A. Rosenblum, & S.A. Sanders (Eds.), *Masculinity and femininity, Vol. 1*. New York: Oxford University Press.

Eccles, J.S. (1987b). Gender roles and women's achievement-related decisions. *Psychology of Women Quarterly, 11*, 135–172.

Eccles, J.S., Adler, T.F., & Meece, J.L. (1984). Sex differences in achievement: A test of alternate theories. *Journal of Personality and Social Psychology, 46*, 26–43.

Eccles, J., & Blumenfeld, P. (1985). Classroom experiences and student gender: Are there differences and do they matter? In L.C. Wilkinson & C. Marrett (Eds.), *Gender influences in classroom interaction*. Hillsdale, NJ: Erlbaum.

Eccles, J., Flanagan, C., Goldsmith, R., Jacobs, J., Jayaratne, T., Wigfield, A., & Yee, D. (April 1987). *Parents as socializers of achievement attitudes*. Symposium paper presented at the biennial meeting of the Society for Research in Child Development, Baltimore.

Eccles, J.S., & Hoffman, L.W. (1984). Socialization and the maintenance of a sex-segregated labor market. In H.W. Stevenson and A.E. Siegel (Eds.), *Research in child development and social policy, Vol. I*. Chicago: University of Chicago Press.

Eccles, J.S., & Jacobs, J. (1986). Social forces shape math participation. *Signs, 11*, 367–380.

Eccles, J., MacIver, D., & Lange, L. (April 1986). *Classroom practices and motivation to study math*. Symposium paper, AERA, San Francisco.

Eccles-Parsons, J. (1984). Sex differences in math participation. In M.L. Maehr and M.W. Steinkamp (Eds.), *Women in science*. Greenwich, CT: JAI Press.

Eccles-Parsons, J., Adler, T.F., Futterman, R., Goff, S.B., Kaczala, C.M., Meece, J.L., & Midgley, C. (1983). Expectations, values and academic behaviors. In J.T. Spence (Ed.), *Achievement and achievement motivation*. New York: Freeman.

Eccles-Parsons, J., Adler, T.F., & Kaczala, C.M. (1982). Socialization of achievement attitudes and beliefs: Parental influences. *Child Development, 53*, 310–321.

Eccles-Parsons, J., Kaczala, C.M., & Meece, J.L. (1982). Socialization of achievement attitudes and beliefs: Classroom influences. *Child Development, 53*, 322–339.

Fox, L.H., Brody, L., & Tobin, D. (Eds.) (1980). *Women and the mathematical mystique*. Baltimore: Johns Hopkins University Press.

Gilligan, C. (1982). *In a different voice*. Cambridge, MA: Harvard University Press.

Halpern, D.F. (1986). *Sex differences in cognitive abilities*. Hillsdale, NJ: Erlbaum.

Huston, A.C. (1983). Sex-typing. In P. Mussen and E.M. Hetherington (Eds.), *Handbook of child psychology, Vol. IV*. New York: Wiley.

Jacobs, J.E. (April 1987) *The relation between parents' and adolescents' gender role stereotypes and ability beliefs*. Symposium paper presented at the biennial meeting of the Society for Research in Child Development, Baltimore.

Kaczala, C.M. (April 1981). *Sex-role identity, stereotypes and their relationship to achievement attitudes*. Symposium paper presented at the biennial meeting of the Society for Research in Child Development, Boston.

Kahle, J. (1984). *Girl-friendly science*. Paper presented at the meeting of the American Association for the Advancement of the Sciences, New York.

Kiesler, S., Sproull, L., & Eccles, J.S. (1985). Pool halls, chips, and war games: Women in the culture of computing. *Psychology of Women Quarterly*, *9*, 451–462.

Lewin, K. (1938). *The conceptual representation and the measurement of psychological forces*. Durham, NC: Duke University Press.

Malcolm, S. (1984). *Equity and excellence: Compatible goals*. Washington, DC: AAAS Publications.

Sells, L.W. (1980). Mathematical filter and the education of women and minorities. In L.H. Fox, L. Brody, & D. Tobin (Eds.), *Women and the mathematical mystique*. Baltimore: Johns Hopkins University Press.

Spence, J.T., & Helmreich, R.L. (1978). *Masculinity and femininity: Their psychological dimensions, correlates, and antecedents*. Austin: University of Texas Press.

Steinkamp, M.W., & Maehr, M.L. (Eds.) (1984). *Women in science, Vol. 2*; *Advances in motivation and achievement*. Greenwich, CT: JAI Press.

Vetter, B., & Babco, E. (Eds.) (February 1986). *Professional women and minorities*. Washington, DC: Commission on Professionals in Science and Technology.

Weiner, B. (1974). *Achievement motivation and attribution theory*. Morristown, NJ: General Learning Press.

Wilkinson, L.C., & Marrett, C. (Eds.) (1985). *Gender influences in classroom interaction*. Hillsdale, NJ: Erlbaum.

Women and minorities in science and engineering (January 1986). (NSF 86–301). Washington, DC: National Science Foundation.

Yee, D., & Eccles, J. (in press). Parents' causal attributions for their children's mathematical performance. *Sex Roles*.

3
Molehill or Mountain? What We Know and Don't Know About Sex Bias in Language

Nancy M. Henley

Language is at the core of human interaction, and it is at the core of our beings, our sense of self. An attack on our language is in a very real sense an attack on ourselves; as we know, wars large and small have been fought over language. Small wonder then that people are upset about the issue of sex bias in language. We are upset as speakers of the language because we identify with it: an attack on our language as unfair says that we are ourselves unfair. And we are upset as referents of the language (particularly women and girls) because in referring to us the language often seems to be attacking us. Why do I say the language, and not its speakers, are attacking us? Because well-meaning, nonsexist speakers may, simply by conventional usage, unwittingly use the language as conscious misogynists do: to trivialize, ignore, and demean females. Thus the problem is located in the common language, not solely or necessarily in the intents of its speakers.

In this chapter, I examine what we know and must learn about sex bias in American English. Many readers are already familiar with arguments against sexist language and perhaps tired of protests whose empirical base they have not seen. But much empirical evidence has accumulated. *My intent here is to examine and evaluate the evidence*, not just to repeat arguments. A burgeoning of research on language and gender in recent years has produced new evidence that is not yet widely known. This body of work raises theoretical and practical issues that go beyond those usually addressed.

Two things should be made clear at the outset. First, this chapter is not about sex *differences* in language usage, but about sex *bias* in language itself (though sex differences, where they exist, are also implicated in sex bias). Second, I do not intend the following evidence to test the question of whether we should or should not use sex-biased language. We do not need to prove that language of itself influences behavior to find sex bias in language offensive, just as we find racist language inexcusable and intolerable apart from any empirical findings of actual harm. The evidence is presented here to address a series of questions that arise in the investigation of sex-biased language, to give us a fuller understanding of such language and of the theoretical issues it involves, and to indicate areas for further investigation. However, although it is not required for our rejection of sexist language, the evidence certainly adds specific grounds for concern about the use of sex-biased forms.

Does Our Language Treat the Sexes Unequally?

The answer is clearly yes. There are at least three ways we can point to sexual imbalance in language:

1. *Language deprecates women.* A few examples will suffice. Nilsen (1977b) reported a dictionary study of 517 words visibly marked for + Masculine or + Feminine. There were 385 masculine terms and 132 feminine ones, but negative feminine words outnumbered masculine ones. Of those marked for + Prestige, masculine outnumbered feminine words six to one. Similarly, Stanley (1977) found 220 terms for a sexually promiscuous woman and only 22 for a promiscuous man. Farmer and (W.E.) Henley (1890–1904/1965) cite over 500 English terms for *prostitute*, but only 65 for *whoremonger*. Schulz (1975) reports on a tendency among English words for women to acquire debased or obscene reference (e.g., *lady*, *dame*, *madam*, *mistress*), while their equivalent masculine terms escape such pejoration (e.g., *lord*, *baronet*, *sir*, *master*).

2. *Language ignores women.* The most pervasive example comes with the use of the masculine as a generic form, as in *chairman*, *spokesman*, *the man for the job*, *the man in the street*, *the working man*, *the black man*, *men of good will*, "the brotherhood of man and the fatherhood of God" (BOMFOG, as Merriam [1974] has termed it); or, and I quote, "the development of the uterus in man" (cited in Miller & Swift, 1976). *He* is of course also frequently used to refer to an unknown or unspecified human being, as in "anybody who has not passed in a paper should raise his hand," or "whoever opened the door left his keys in it." This imbalance when we speak about human beings makes the masculine form *unmarked* (as linguists call it), while the feminine is *marked*; that is, to denote the female an additional marker must be used.

3. *Language stereotypes women and sometimes men.* Our traditional titles of address do not differentiate males by marital status (*Mr.*) but do differentiate females (*Miss*, *Mrs.*), indicating a difference in our perception of the importance of that status in the two sexes. Usage can of course also stereotype: the generic use of the masculine falls down in referring to stereotypical female classes such as nurses and secretaries, when the feminine form *she* is often used generically. Similarly, we indicate our sexual stereotypes by marking gender in many terms, especially

occupational ones, such as in "woman doctor" or "male nurse." An analysis of 5 million words in children's schoolbooks found that women more often than men were referred to in terms of their relation to others. For example, *wife* occurred three times as often as *husband*, and *mother* occurred more frequently than *father* (Graham, 1975). These various imbalances in linguistic forms and in usage reflect cultural norms and stereotypes of women and men.

This small selection of examples merely documents what most of us already know. Far from treating the sexes equally, our language is biased in at least three ways: it affords many more positive terms for male than for female, tends to designate human beings as male, and reflects gender stereotyping in usage. The largest body of research in this field addresses the second type of bias, the masculine generic form[1], a usage that does not acknowledge the existence of the female. I limit myself in this chapter to consideration of that usage.

Does Language Only Reflect Thought, or Does It Affect It?

The foregoing facts are so well known that they often (perhaps reasonably) evoke the response "So what?" That is, the culture is sex biased, and the language reflects that fact. Without saying "so what," Susan Sontag (1973) took this position 13 years ago in an article in *Partisan Review*. She first expresses most eloquently the meanness of sexist cultural forms:

The forms of work, sexual customs, the idea of family life have to be altered; language itself, which crudely enshrines the ancient bias against women, cannot remain unaffected. For, however advanced our ideas, every time we speak we continue to affirm the superiority (activity) of men and the inferiority (passivity) of women. It is "grammatically correct" to assume that agents, active persons are men. Grammar, the ultimate arena of sexist brainwashing, conceals the very existence of women—except in special situations. (p. 186)

But she denies any effect of language on our thinking:

Language is not, of course, the source of the prejudice that identifies "men" as the human race, and associates most human activities with men only. Language merely expresses the sexist order that has prevailed throughout history. (p. 186)

---

[1] I prefer to use the term "masculine generic" rather than "generic masculine" because in the latter, *generic* used as an adjective implies that the masculine form does work generically, which is subject to empirical test. *Generic* is used as a noun to denote a word meant to reference a class of things, in this case human beings. There may be masculine, feminine, or unbiased generics. [My usage differs from that of Dubois and Crouch (1979), who use "masculine generic" and "generic masculine" interchangeably, to denote words referencing the class masculine.]

The well-known exchange, reported in *Newsweek* in 1971, between Harvard Divinity students who protested sexist language in the classroom and Harvard linguists who accused them of "pronoun-envy" shows the similar position many linguists have taken. These linguists wrote:

The fact that the masculine is the unmarked gender in English . . . is simply a feature of grammar. It is unlikely to be an impediment to change in the patterns of the sexual division of labor towards which our society may wish to evolve. (Martyna, 1983, p. 26)

It is true that any examples you can give of sexist language do not show that language is itself a culprit, that it *invokes* rather than simply *reflects* misogyny and stereotyping. In further support of the position that language merely reflects the culture, the argument can be made that everyone knows the masculine generic includes the feminine in it (or, as is often said, "the male embraces the female"). It is further argued that readers and hearers can distinguish when the masculine is used generically and when it is used specifically, that is, to refer to males. The argument continues that it is less awkward and more efficient and time-saving simply to use the masculine when referring to human beings. (Although sociologist Pauline Bart, on hearing this argument, remarked: "What do you do with the time you save?")

Others might argue that this battle has been fought and already won. Their evidence might include guidelines for nonsexist language within psychology (American Psychological Association, 1983) and other fields, newly published books scrubbed clean of sexism, and increasing personal effort at remembering to include females when speaking. While this trend is observable, unfortunately change is not as widespread as we would like to think. Some even feel that in the recent American political climate, exemplified by reversals of affirmative action practices and principles, attempts to change sexist language have been backsliding or forgotten. In addition, previous reports have observed several ways change may be thwarted: (1) despite the best intentions, authors who say they are adopting nonsexist language practices, such as alternating masculine and feminine generic pronouns, do not necessarily follow through (Blaubergs, 1978); (2) usage of new "nonsexist" forms, such as *chairperson* or *spokesperson*, in at least one university turned out to be sex-biased rather than generic; that is, the new forms were more often used to reference women —and lesser-power women at that—than to reference men (Veach, 1979); and (3) at one institution studied, change toward nonsexist forms did not necessarily occur simply because of promulgated policy but rather tended to occur only when there was monitoring and enforcement (Markowitz, 1984).

The battle then is not won. Sexist language persists, and the question of its influence remains. To answer this broader question of whether language is only *reflecting* sex bias we look first at several more specific questions.

We begin with the question of whether the masculine generic is interpreted generically.

Does *Man* Embrace "Woman"?

At least 16 articles or papers to date, encompassing about 20 studies, have examined the question of whether masculine generic language forms actually invoke a generic understanding. That is, these studies ask how effectively *he* and *man* perform their generic role and are interpreted as referring to female as well as male (DeStefano, Kuhner, & Pepinsky, 1978; Eberhart, 1976; Hamilton, 1985; Hamilton & Henley, 1987; Harrison, 1975; Harrison & Passero, 1975; Hyde, 1984; Kidd, 1971; MacKay, 1980c; MacKay & Fulkerson, 1979; Martyna, 1978; Moulton, Robinson, & Elias, 1978; Schneider & Hacker, 1973; Shimanoff, 1977; Sniezek & Jazwinski, 1986; Wilson, 1978; other studies relating to inclusivity are addressed under later headings). This line of work began in 1971 and was pursued by scholars in English, sociology, communication studies, and other fields. Psychology belatedly came to the issue with Wendy Martyna's ground-breaking dissertation studies in 1978.

Martyna (1978) in two of her studies (3 and 4) presented generic-topic sentences using *he*, *they*, or *he or she* to subjects by tachistoscope.[2] Subjects were then shown a picture of a female or male and required to make a fast "yes/no" decision on whether the picture was applicable to the sentence. This technique elicits people's first reactions, uncensored by their desire to be socially "correct," and closer to their likely responses in daily life. When *he* was used, subjects said "no" to the female picture, that is, the masculine generic sentence was not interpreted as referring to a female, in 11–25% of the judgments (experiments 3 and 4 respectively).[3] If *he* were acting generically, the subjects' responses should have approached 0% "no," since "yes" is the correct answer. In two other experiments (5 and 6), Martyna asked subjects to generate names, or choose names from a list, for subjects of sex-indefinite sentences using the same set of pronouns. For example, one item required names for "someone who always turns in his homework late," or "their homework," or "his or her homework." With the masculine pronoun, 88% of the names given were masculine names, while the unbiased forms elicited only 62–67% masculine names. When selecting names from an array (which put reminders of feminine as well as masculine names before the subjects), 61% still chose masculine

---

[2] A tachistoscope presents visual material (in this case text and pictures) very briefly, in specified fractions of a second.

[3] MacKay and Fulkerson (1979), in a similar experiment with aural questions, got 91% "no" with the masculine, and only 43% "no" with a neutral form. (Martyna does not report rejection rates for her pronouns other than masculine.)

names with the masculine pronoun, while the unbiased forms led to fairly equal choice of masculine and feminine names (51–52% masculine).

Two more of Martyna's experiments asked subjects to generate pronouns required to complete sentence fragments. When sentences were male-related, 96% of the completions employed *he*, and 90% of the mental images experienced—by both female and male subjects—were of males. When the sentence fragments were female-related, 87% of the sentences were completed with *she*, and 92% of the imagery, as expected, was of females. When the sentence fragments were neutral, 65% were still completed with *he*, but a sex difference emerged in imagery: 70% of the males reported having any imagery at all, but only 57% of the females did. In fact, among college students responding to neutral sentences, *all the imagery was male*; and while 51% of the male subjects reported having imagery, only 10% of the females did.

We return to this provocative difference in reported imagery later. On the question of genericness of the masculine, this study's findings do *not* explain whether the pronouns *we* generate influence our own imagery. Where greater male imagery is reported with greater generation of male pronouns, the relationship could be due to (1) the content of the sentence, when male-related, influencing both imagery and pronoun; (2) an underlying sexist attitude influencing both imagery and pronoun (when content is neutral); (3) the imagery causing the pronoun use; and (4) the pronoun use causing the imagery.

To get around these problems of confounding and of unknown direction of causality, Mykol Hamilton (in press) devised an ingenious design to assign subjects randomly to conditions of producing masculine or sex-neutral forms. She instructed them to complete sentence fragments using what she called either "traditional, formal" forms (including *he* as a generic pronoun) or "modern, informal" forms (including unbiased alternative pronouns such as singular *they*, *he or she*, etc.). Subjects were then asked to assign names to the persons their sentences were written about and to report any imagery they experienced. Subjects using the masculine ("formal") pronouns gave significantly more masculine names, and reported significantly more male imagery, than subjects using the unbiased ("informal") forms. This difference was independent of *both* individual propensity of any subjects to think of males more and of any signal that "modern, informal" usage might convey toward greater inclusivity. To separate these variables, Hamilton elicited sentence completions with the same two sets of instructions but changed conditions by inserting plural subjects in the sentences. Thus pronouns produced by subjects had to be *they* in every case. Sex of names assigned and imagery experienced did not differ significantly in the "formal" versus "informal" conditions. Therefore, the previous differences found with the *singular* conditions could be due only to the *pronoun* difference, not to concepts of formality/informality.

The research designs of Martyna and Hamilton exemplify some of the techniques used in the studies on this question. In summary, the 20 studies cited have presented subjects of ages varying from six years to adult with a variety of paradigms, in which they were given written or spoken phrases, sentences, paragraphs, or stories. The paradigms varied generic nouns or pronouns in masculine, feminine, and sex-unbiased forms. Subjects were asked to respond in equally various ways: by depicting the person or persons referred to (e.g., drawing a picture, bringing a picture to class, or selecting a picture from a given set); by describing, naming, or writing a story about the person; by choosing a "yes/no" or other multiple-choice response to answer whether a sex-specific word (female/male) or picture applies; or by reporting any imagery they experienced while reading or hearing the verbal material. In all these studies, when the masculine was used as generic, the pictures selected or drawn, the names used for the referents, the subjects of stories, the answers to questions of sex referred to, or the imagery seen were predominantly—and usually overwhelmingly—male. This uniformity of results bears repeating: *in no referential studies known to me has the masculine been found to reference females as readily as males.*[4]

So, does *man* embrace "woman"? According to these findings, *man* most readily embraces "man." The findings of this body of research lead to another question.

Do Males and Females Differ in Their Understanding of the Masculine Generic?

In at least eight studies cited above in which difference by subject sex was reported, females interpreted generics more generically—gave more female-related responses—than did males on at least one, and usually on all, measures (DeStefano et al., 1978; Hamilton, 1985; Hamilton & Henley, 1987; Harrison, 1975; Hyde, 1984; MacKay & Fulkerson, 1979; Martyna, 1978; Wilson, 1978). However, even the females generally gave

---

[4]There is a reported failure to find language effects in the research of Cole, Hill, and Dayley (1983), who conducted a series of experiments purportedly investigating the inclusiveness of masculine and unbiased pronouns. However, their criterion measure for whether females were included was in each case a semantic differential scale with adjectives associated with masculinity or femininity. This is a measure, then, not of inclusiveness of gender reference but of sex-stereotypic impression formation. Added together with the authors' admittedly erroneous assumption (without pretesting) that some occupations they used were sexually neutral, and with their intentional use of other clearly sex-stereotypic occupations, the main effect this research demonstrates is the tendency for overlearned occupational stereotypes to override any effects of pronoun differences in influencing sex-stereotypic impressions. It is not surprising, and it may be interesting, but it is certainly not evidence on the tendency to think of male referents.

more male- than female-related responses. Two additional studies found
no sex difference (Eberhart, 1976; MacKay, 1980c). But in none were
males found to be more inclusive in their interpretation than females.[5]
Why might this be?

Nilsen (1977c) argues that, for males, use of the masculine generic falls
under a rule of grammar which the linguist Labov (1969) has labeled
"Type I." Type I rules are learned naturally and early in life, and they
govern "automatic, deepseated, patterns of behavior which are not consciously recognized and are never violated" (p. 29). For females, she
claims, the masculine generic falls under a "Type II" rule, which is learned
formally, in school or through other instruction, and which may be violated
and corrected. This difference in relating to the masculine generic, Nilsen
believes, ensues from earliest language patterns, when children tend to use
the pronoun of their own gender to reference the subject of a generic sex-
neutral sentence. Later instruction imposes divergent adaptive tasks:

When boys grow up, they continue to use pronouns in approximately the same ratio
they used as children, but it is just the opposite for girls. Their adult speech is
expected to be an inverse picture of their naturally developed childhood speech.
(p. 178)

In other words, boys and men may not understand the generic meaning of
the masculine generic because they have never formally had to learn to
understand. Males may "naturally" use *he* to refer to any person, as they
did as children. But, like children, they may still think of "any person" as
like themselves, therefore masculine. Girls and women, on the other hand,
have had to learn formally to use the masculine generic. Barred from
continuing to refer to "any person" with their own pronoun, they *must*
believe in its inclusiveness, if they are to think of themselves and their sex
as existing. Silveira (1980) has a discussion of this "people = self bias,"
extending it to adults as well. The kicker or "so what?" question in all this
is discussed next.

Is There Actually Any Harm Done by the Masculine Generic Usage?

Protesters against sexist language have been challenged not only to show
that the absence of the feminine pronoun leads to masculine interpretation, but further to show that actual harm is caused by this form. The
anthropologist Gregersen (1979), for one, uses examples from various
languages to demonstrate that there is no correlation between the status

---

[5] Silveira's (1978) male subjects had equal reaction times for their responses to male
and female pictures, but the *n* was too small to make this finding reliable or
significant.

of women in a society and the gender differentiation present in its language: thus, he argues that biased language does not detrimentally affect women. The philosopher Levin (1981) takes a different tack and claims that unconscious word choices are related to human reality. In this view, when language acknowledges power, status, or physiological reality, it simply puts forward facts. Thus "desexing" language, according to Levin, is pernicious. Newspaper columnists and other writers have been ridiculing criticisms of sex-biased language for their triviality for years (for good reviews of these writings, see Martyna, 1983, and Nilsen, 1977a) and continue to do so. The assumption is widespread that the masculine generic does no harm. But in fact detrimental effects have been demonstrated in various areas.

Several studies have addressed *perceived qualification for jobs*, demonstrating that job descriptions using the masculine generic cause females to be discouraged from applying for the jobs (Bem & Bem, 1973; Stericker, 1981) and cause individuals to devalue females' ability to perform the jobs (Hyde, 1984, experiment 2). Silveira (1978) found that *cognitive processing time* (reaction time to correct response) was longer for subjects applying the masculine generic to a female picture than for those applying it to a male picture; Martyna (1978) and MacKay and Fulkerson (1979) present similar findings. Hamilton and Henley (1987) found *comprehension* of a science-fiction story (aurally presented) to be better (based on correct responses to comprehension questions) when it contained unbiased forms than when it contained male-biased ones. In a *memory* study, Crawford and English (1984) found in both of two experiments that females' recall for essays 48 hours later was worse when they were written with masculine generics than when with unbiased ones, and that the effect was stronger for good learners than for poor ones.

Henley, Gruber, and Lerner (1988) report an interaction of pronoun and subject sex on *self-esteem* among sixth-grade pupils who had read story booklets with masculine, feminine, or unbiased generic pronouns the week before. The boys had more positive change in self-esteem in the masculine pronoun condition, and the girls had more positive self-esteem change in the neutral pronoun condition. Martyna's results (1978, experiments 1 and 2) have implications for *self-relevance* of written materials: she found that seven times as many males as females reported self-imagery when the masculine pronoun was used with a sex-neutral topic sentence. Similarly, MacKay (1980a, experiment 1) found that female subjects rated masculine generic paragraphs as less personally relevant than sex-neutral ones, and males rated them oppositely. *Ambiguous interpretation* can be harmful also: Stopes (1908) and Martyna (1983) give instances from U.S. and Canadian law in which the masculine has at times been interpreted as including, and at other times as excluding, women. (According to Stopes, inclusion has been the rule when behavior is to be punished, and exclusion the rule when it is to be rewarded.)

The results from studies of detriment have not always been consistent or straightforward, but many anomalous findings may be laid to extraneous factors. In one example, a study of the effects of masculine or unbiased generics on perceived qualification for an honorary position concluded that the effects of language were nonsignificant (Caldie, 1981). However, examination of the materials used (Henley, 1987) shows that in them candidates are described as persons of achievement, and the literature on achievement and evaluation has long shown that antifemale bias is reduced when females are shown as having high achievement (for a review of this literature, see Wallston & O'Leary, 1981). In another exception, MacKay (1980a, experiment 2) found female subjects to report more rather than less personal relevance with the masculine than the sex-neutral form. He believed this result was obtained because the subjects of the second experiment were less feminist, however. And in another exception, Henley et al. (1988) had different results for both self-esteem and attitudes[6] with their three different age levels, which may be attributable to the differences in ages (development and/or environment) or to the quite different materials used in their three studies.

Despite the "plausible deniability" of the above results, the findings on detrimental effects are mixed, being fairly strong on cognitive effects and perceived qualification for jobs, but weaker on personality-related effects (e.g., self-esteem and self-relevance). Taken together, the direction of evidence on deterimental effects of the masculine generic is clear: it appears from these laboratory studies that much damage *is* being done. However, questions remain, and further research is needed. Beyond laboratory studies, what can we say about real-life effects?

Are Lesbians Homosexual? An Example Study with Real-World Effects

A very recent study by Hamilton (1988) bears extended reporting, because of its intertwining of "real-world" and laboratory events, and because of its implications for the effect of ambiguous generic reference on our crucial understanding of risk factors for acquired immune deficiency syndrome (AIDS). The research is also interesting because of a new slant it gives us on generics.

Hamilton conducted a content analysis of a sample of AIDS coverage in *The New York Times*, the *Los Angeles Times*, *Newsweek*, and *Time*, 1983–

---

[6]The materials used in the high school study had only masculine or feminine generics, unlike those used in the other studies, which included unbiased alternatives; therefore this study was not reported separately as a positive finding of detriment from masculine when contrasted with unbiased pronouns.

1985. She found that 100% of the references in headlines or titles taken alone, and 75% of the text and headline references taken together, used the generic reference terms "homosexuals," "gays," or "bisexuals" without specifying males. She estimated that for most people, often reading only headlines and sometimes reading articles as well, the exposure to generic-only reference falls between 75 and 100%. Did this exposure lead them to interpret the terms generically, and thereby to assume female and male gays were equally at high risk for AIDS?

To answer this question, a second study surveyed perceived risk for AIDS. Hamilton had college students rank order various groups according to what they considered the groups' relative risk of contracting AIDS. While nearly all subjects accurately ranked homosexual men as the number one risk group, 66% of the subjects incorrectly ranked homosexual women as at higher risk than male and/or female heterosexuals, with 51% putting lesbians above *both* heterosexual women and men. In fact, 16% of the respondents ranked lesbians second only to homosexual men, ahead of intravenous drug abusers and recipients of blood transfusions, and 30% put lesbians in third or fourth position. The truth, of course, is that of those named, lesbians are the *lowest* risk group.

Suspecting that her subjects' misinformation might have come from the media's failure to specify that the gays at risk are males, Hamilton conducted an experiment to examine this link. In this study, subjects read an informational paragraph on AIDS describing the risk associated with such factors as intravenous drug use, blood transfusions, and "homosexuality." "Homosexuality" was described in increasing degrees of specificity in the three conditions for subjects: with the words "homosexual," "homosexual men," or "homosexual men (but *not* homosexual women)." After reading one of these paragraphs, subjects rated different groups for AIDS risk on a scale of 1 to 5, with 5 representing most risk. Looking at ratings for risk to homosexual women, whose risk was the most misunderstood of all groups in the earlier survey, Hamilton found that with the least informative description ("homosexual"), lesbians were given an average rating of 3.0; with the more informative description ("homosexual men"), the rating dropped to 2.2; and with the "homosexual men (but *not* homosexual women)" description, it dropped to 1.6. Thus a specific link is established between generic language practices similar to those of the media and the public's lack of understanding of risk factors for a serious disease.

Further evidence for such a link comes from subjects' reasons for their rankings. They often stated that "AIDS is spread by homosexual activity" (with the rest of the syllogism implied: lesbians are homosexual; therefore lesbians spread AIDS). Many subjects further volunteered that they received their information through the media. The real-world effects this study taps are manifold. Besides the false beliefs whose prevalence has been demonstrated, there have been several newspaper reports of the canceling of lesbian blood donation drives because of fears in the general public (suspected or real) that lesbians' blood was not "safe." Further anecdotal information reported by Hamilton and in the *Los Angeles Times* indicates that lesbians sometimes shared the belief that they were at high risk for AIDS; they have also told of being shunned by heterosexual friends afraid of catching AIDS.

The intent of Hamilton's research is not, of course, to cause people to "more correctly" shun homosexual males, but rather to show that accurate reporting could help understanding and in fact combat homophobia. People should understand that it is not homosexuality *per se* that puts one at risk for AIDS, but certain practices, sexual and nonsexual, that open pathways for the transmission of the AIDS virus. Furthermore, heterosexuals may be underestimating their own degree of risk by projecting it onto homosexuals and not learning which sexual practices may be unsafe.

But wait a minute. The problem here seems not to be that the words *homosexual* and *gay* are *not* interpreted generically, but rather that they *are* being interpreted generically; that is, they appear to include women. (1) What's wrong with that? And (2) why is it that in this case a generic noun gets interpreted generically instead of as referring mainly to males? The answer to (1) is that in this case the *usage* of a generic term is inappropriate, not the interpretation of it. This is the other side of the masculine generic coin: rather than using masculine words for a sex-neutral class, the media are using sex-neutral words for a masculine class. The consequences obviously go beyond grammar. This example points to strong, real-life effects of ambiguous generic usage.

In answer to (2), the first fact is that these are sex-neutral, not masculine, generic terms. However, these sex-neutral nouns probably *are* being interpreted as referring primarily to males, since gay males do lead the list of people's estimated risk categories. This is an example of what has been called the "people = male bias." The fact that the media feel correct in using the generic noun to refer to a male group suggests that their writers are interpreting the generic as masculine, and the writers are probably correct in inferring that their readers will show this same tendency. Of course, the public has access to other information about gender and AIDS risk (e.g., friends, video images, stories on specific persons with AIDS), which probably acts as a concurrent source of information in citing gay males as at high risk. By enforcing the association between neutral generic terms and what the public knows to be a masculine group, the media may also be further enforcing the general association between generic human and male.

This case of distorted public knowledge on issues crucial to health shows the detrimental effect that insufficient gender marking, coupled with two types of bias, masculine and heterosexual, reinforcing each other, can have. It also illustrates well the pervasiveness of the bias to think of humans as male. This bias gives us something more to think about: Might the findings of male bias from the masculine generic be simply an extended case of the people = male bias (Silveira, 1980)? This question returns us to the earlier query.

Does Language Not Just Reflect But Influence Thought?

Hyde (1984) discusses the question "whether sexist language is primary and produces sexist thought, or whether sexist thought is primary and produces sexist language" (p. 705). Her research, and others', found that even when the sex-neutral pronoun was used, the percentage of female responses is still substantially low. These findings suggest to her that sexism in thought is primary. But, she points out, the child subjects in her experiments

had already been exposed to sexist language for six or more years of their lives, including hearing "he" and "they" used interchangeably in sentences of the sort used in [the] experiment. Thus the sexist thought . . . may be the product of years of exposure to sexist language, as well as many other factors. (p. 705)

In most of the studies comparing responses to neutral and masculine language forms, the neutral forms failed to elicit unbiased responses. Unbiased responses would have been, in the "choose examples" studies, 50% examples of males and 50% of females, and in the "does the female apply?" studies, 100% "yes." Even without the masculine generic, these studies' responses were biased toward the male: With sex-neutral language, the majority of chosen examples were of males and with the "does the female apply?" question, responses to the sex-neutral stimulus were not near 100%. These findings illustrate the strong effect of male bias in our culture in general, which has led so many to advise that we not bother to try to change the language, since it merely reflects the immense cultural bias (e.g., Lakoff, 1973; Nilsen, 1973).

However, the many experiments that hold the culture constant but vary the linguistic stimulus (by contrasting responses to masculine generic and unbiased generic forms) show that (at least) both forms of bias are operating—the bias induced by the masculine generic usage and the people = male bias: The difference between the male-oriented responses to sex-unbiased forms (from people = male bias) and the additional male-oriented responses to masculine forms shows the independent added bias from the language alone.

Why Does Human = Male? (Why Does Bird = Robin?)

Silveira (1980) has written about the relationship between masculine generic words and thinking. She cites the general bias in our culture for thinking of people as male. This people = male bias does not necessarily come from masculine generic language but is related both to the general sexism of the culture and to another type of bias of thought, the generic = specific bias. This bias is examined in the studies of categorization and typicality by Rosch and others (Rosch & Mervis, 1975). When we think of a category for which there is a generic term, such as *bird*, some examples of the category are more typical, seem to represent it better, than others. *Robin*, for example, is a typical bird; *chicken* is less typical. In a reaction time experiment, how long people take to decide that *robin* or *chicken* is an example of the category *bird* is one measure of those birds' typicality. The generic *bird* tends to take on the meaning of the specific *robin*, hence the generic = specific bias.

The specific that the generic category *human* tends toward is *male*. By using this measure of reaction time when categorizing, Silveira's (1978) experiment showed that subjects took longer to assign a female picture to a generic human category expressed in the masculine form than they took when it was expressed in a sex-neutral form. When *man* was used, woman was not a typical member of the category. Thus the people = male bias was not only operative but was strengthened when the masculine generic was used. The best answer to the question of whether language simply reflects or influences thought is that, of course, it does both.

Aren't You Just Trying to Revive the Discredited Whorfian Hypothesis?

Many readers have undoubtedly been wondering how long I could go on without invoking the beliefs of Benjamin Lee Whorf or his teacher, Edward Sapir (Sapir, 1949; Whorf, 1956), that the structure of language shapes the structure of thought. Those before me who have taken offense at sex bias in language have been accused of rampant or misguided Whorfianism (e.g., Gregersen, 1979; Schneider & Foss, 1977), and I have no doubt I am or will be too. However, if we were to be guided by Whorf's ideas, we could have stopped after the first few pages, having called attention to the bias which exists in the language. As Roger Brown has noted (1986, p. 243), for Whorf the demonstration of sexist bias in the language would have been enough to conclude that sexist thought is brought about by it. My examination of empirical evidence for the effect of the language in creating or enhancing sex bias need call on no presuppositions, but stands in the tradition of psychological hypothesis testing.

However, let us think about Whorf's ideas. Many have considered the Whorfian hypothesis a dead issue since the work of Heider–Rosch and others (Rosch, 1974) cast doubt on previous findings that how a language divided up the world, especially its color terms, determined the memorability of physical objects like color patches. However, there are at least two things to be said of the relation of Whorf's ideas to questions of sex-biased language. First, as some have already argued (Martyna, 1983; Shimanoff, 1977; Silveira, 1980), those who have called for change in sexist language have taken a "weak" Whorfian position (i.e., that language affects, or strongly affects, thought), usually considered an acceptable one, rather than the "strong" deterministic Whorfian stance (that language fully constrains thought) their critics have imputed to them. Second, the relation between language and thought, call it Whorfianism if you will, still has many unanswered and interesting questions.

Hamilton (1985), in the most thorough study known to me of the research on the Whorfian hypothesis together with the research on sex bias in language, points out that the two fields have been examining different corners of the universe: linguistic relativity studies have tended to be correlational, sex bias studies to be experimental; linguistic relativity studies have been concerned with a subject's language use, sex bias studies with a subject's reaction to language; linguistic relativity research has been concerned with both the physical and cultural domain, while sex bias research has concentrated on the cultural; relativity research has tended toward forced choice methods, while sex bias research has tended toward free choice methods. Small wonder that the findings have been different. Even within either field of research, not all domains have been researched with all methods. As it is likely that there are areas to which Whorfian predictions apply better than to others, the gaps in our research represent gaps in knowledge.

Is There Harm Done? Revisited

MacKay (1980c) has pointed out that the masculine generic bears a close resemblance to "highly effective propaganda techniques":

As a device for shaping attitudes, prescriptive *he* has the following advantages: *frequency* (over 10^6 occurrences in the course of a lifetime for educated Americans; see MacKay [1980b]); *covertness* (questioning the use of prescriptive *he* is difficult, since it usually is not intended as an open attempt to maintain or alter attitudes); *early age of acquisition* (prescriptive *he* is learned long before the concept of propaganda itself); *association with high-prestige sources* (it is especially prevalent in some of society's most prestigious literature, such as university textbooks); and *indirectness* (prescriptive *he* presents its message indirectly, as if it were a matter of common and well-established knowledge). (pp. 448–449)

In one sense, of course, most language may be seen as propaganda, since it conveys a particular cultural view of the world in much the way MacKay has described. But as the Whorfian research shows, other language forms do not all have the impact on cognition that the masculine generic seems to have. In addition, imparting the assumption that males are the prototypical humans is rather more insidious than imparting the assumption that the spectrum is partitioned into six or eight major categories. Our culture's implicit messages about valuing other human beings are to be taken seriously. Is the masculine generic usage then propaganda? From the evidence presented here, it might as well be.

What Is Still Needed?

That there have been any significant findings at all is surprising, given that subjects are immersed in sex-biased language in their daily lives. To bring them into the laboratory and expose one group to nonbiased language and another to the sex-biased language they are used to is much different from the more common experimental situation, which exposes subjects to variations on conditions that do not make up a major part of their lives, such as the presence of either pro or con arguments on political issues. Those subjects in the unbiased condition cannot be wrenched out of the language in which they are immersed. The slowness to research this aspect of sex bias perhaps reflects this problem. What we need here is some breakthrough methodology, short of what Silveira has pointed out would be ideal but impractical and unethical: raising children without exposure to masculine-biased language, and then introducing it, to see what effect it might have.

We need replication studies, especially of the newer research on the consequences of using the masculine generic. The provocative findings on memory, and the tentative findings on self-esteem, are important to subject to retesting and clarification. We need to know more about the point in children's lives when they learn this masculine generic form, especially about any differential effect on girls and boys. At present we have only anecdotal accounts of unhappiness in girls (Miller & Swift, 1976, p. 29). But how long-lasting is it, and how do boys react? We need more production studies to determine the circumstances in which production of masculine forms is more and less likely.

Both Martyna (1978) and Silveira (1980) have discussed Martyna's findings which suggest that female subjects are suppressing the male imagery that arises when *he* is used with neutral antecedents. Silveira cites avoidance of the masculine generic, which is more prevalent in females, as another form of resistance or coping with the alienation caused by masculine forms. However, this means of coping brings some alienation from the language and from the intelligentsia, hence from women's own intellect. These speculations are very much worth pursuing. We have just begun to explore the effects of sex-biased language on the affective aspects of our lives.

And while we have a number of studies of change in sex-biased forms, which there is not room to describe here (Adamsky, 1981; Bate, 1978; Dubois & Crouch 1979; Henley & Dragun, 1983; MacKay, 1980c; Markowitz, 1984; Veach, 1979), we need more such studies. For example, a randomly assigned sample of subjects who have not changed their sex-biased language might be given instruction and practice in so doing and later be tested for change in attitudes and other measures, compared with a control group that had no instruction and did not change its language.[7]

Finally, we need to think beyond the limits of reviewing research findings and confront the policy issues involved. Sex bias is not an accidental by-product of language: the society impresses its cultural forms into the service of its ideology. MacKay's image of the masculine generic as propaganda seems quite apropos. It is made to seem "natural," existing from beyond history, and "immutable." It is, of course, none of these, and it only has the advantages we grant to it. Psychology has been very responsive, as a profession, to changing its own sex-biased language. But it must share its information with a broader population—institutional and media decisionmakers, for example—to hasten that day when half the population no longer lives in the verbal shadow of the other half.

Acknowledgments. This chapter is a revision of an address, "Sex Bias in Language: What We Know and Don't Know," previously presented at the Eastern Psychological Association, another revision of which was presented at the Conference on Psychological Perspectives on Gender and Thought under the current title. Some parts originally presented at the Conference on Psychological Perspectives on Gender and Thought do not appear here but will appear in another forthcoming paper (Henley, 1987). I wish to thank Jeffrey Z. Rubin and Candace West for their very helpful comments on earlier drafts, and to express my appreciation for University Research Grants from the UCLA Senate Research Committee which partly supported preparation of this work.

REFERENCES

Adamsky, C. (1981). Changes in pronominal usage in a classroom situation. *Psychology of Women Quarterly*, *5*, 773–779.

American Psychological Association (1983). *Publication manual*, 3rd ed. Washington, DC: American Psychological Association.

Bate, B. (1978). Nonsexist language use in transition. *Journal of Communication*, *28*, 139–149.

Bem, S.L., & Bem, D.J. (1973). Does sex-biased job advertising "aid and abet" sex discrimination? *Journal of Applied Social Psychology*, *3*, 6–18.

Blaubergs, M.S. (1978). Changing the sexist language: The theory behind the practice. *Psychology of Women Quarterly*, *2*, 244–261.

Brown, R. (1986). Linguistic relativity. In S.H. Hulse & B.F. Green, Jr. (Eds.).

---

[7] Adamsky (1981) approximates such a study but subjects were not pretested on feminism or prior language change, not randomly assigned to condition, and were not given instruction to change their language.

One hundred years of psychological research in America (pp. 241–276). Baltimore: Johns Hopkins University Press.

Caldie, R.W. (1981). *Dominance and language: A new perspective on sexism.* Lanham, MD: University Press of America.

Cole, C.M., Hill, F.A., & Dayley, L.J. (1983). Do masculine pronouns used generically lead to thoughts of men? *Sex Roles, 9,* 737–749.

Crawford, M., & English, L. (1984). Generic versus specific inclusion of women in language: Effects on recall. *Journal of Psycholinguistic Research, 13,* 373–381.

DeStefano, J., Kuhner, M., & Pepinsky, H. (1978). *An investigation of referents of selected sex-indefinite terms in English.* Paper presented at Ninth World Congress of Sociology, Uppsala, Sweden.

Dubois, B.L., & Crouch, I. (1979). Man and its compounds in recent prefeminist American English. *Papers in Linguistics, 12,* 261–269.

Eberhart, O.M.Y. (1976). Elementary students' understanding of certain masculine and neutral generic nouns. *Dissertation Abstracts International, 37,* 4113A–4114A.

Farmer, J.S., & Henley, W.E. (1890–1904/1965). *Slang and its analogues.* New York: Klaus Reprint Corporation.

Graham, A. (1975). The making of a nonsexist dictionary. In B. Thorne & N. Henley (Eds.), *Language and sex: Difference and dominance* (pp. 57–63). Rowley, MA: Newbury House Publishers.

Gregersen, E.A. (1979). Sexual linguistics. In J. Orasanu, M.K. Slater, & L.L. Adler (Eds.), *Language, sex and gender: Does "la difference" make a difference?* (pp. 3–19). New York: New York Academy of Sciences.

Hamilton, M.C. (1985). Linguistic relativity and sex bias in language: Effects of the masculine "generic" on the imagery of the writer and the perceptual discrimination of the reader. *Dissertation Abstracts International, 46,* 1381B. (University Microfilms No. 8513117)

Hamilton, M.C. (1988). Masculine generic terms and misperception of AIDS risk. *Journal of Applied Social Psychology, 18,* 1222–1240.

Hamilton, M.C. (in press). Using masculine generics: Does generic "he" increase male bias in the user's imagery? *Sex Roles.*

Hamilton, M.C., & Henley, N.M. (1988). Sex bias in language. Effects on the reader/hearer's cognitions. Paper submitted for publication.

Harrison L. (1975). Cro-Magnon woman—in eclipse. *Science Teacher, 42* (4), 9–11.

Harrison, L., & Passero, R.N. (1975). Sexism in the language of elementary school textbooks. *Science and Children, 12* (4), 22–25.

Henley, N.M. (1987). *A review of research and theory on the masculine as a generic form in language.* Unpublished manuscript, Department of Psychology, UCLA, Los Angeles.

Henley, N.M., & Dragun, D. (August 1983). *A survey of attitutes toward changing sex-biased language.* Paper presented at the meeting of the American Psychological Association, Anaheim, CA.

Henley, N.M., Gruber, B., & Lerner, L. (1988). Effects of Masculine generic usage on attitudes and self-esteem. Paper submitted for publication.

Hyde, J.S. (1984). Children's understanding of sexist language. *Developmental Psychology, 20,* 697–706.

Kidd, V. (1971). A study of the images produced through the use of the male pronoun as the generic. *Moments in Contemporary Rhetoric and Communication*, *1* (2), 25–30.

Labov, W. (1969). *The study of nonstandard English*. Urbana, IL: National Council of Teachers of English.

Lakoff, R. (1973). Language and woman's place. *Language in Society*, *2*, 45–79.

Levin, M. (1981). Vs. Ms. In M. Vetterling-Braggin (Ed.), *Sexist language: A modern philosophical analysis* (pp. 217–222). Totowa, NJ: Littlefield, Adams.

MacKay, D.G. (1980a). Language, thought and social attitudes, In H. Giles, W.P. Robinson, & P.M. Smith (Eds.), *Language: Social psychological perspectives* (pp. 89–96). Oxford: Pergamon.

MacKay, D.G. (1980b). On the goals, principles, and procedures for prescriptive grammar. *Language in Society*, *9*, 349–367.

MacKay, D.G. (1980c). Psychology, prescriptive grammar and the pronoun problem. *American Psychologist*, *35*, 444–449.

MacKay, D.G., & Fulkerson, D. (1979). On the comprehension and production of pronouns. *Journal of Verbal Learning and Verbal Behavior*, *18*, 661–673.

Markowitz, J. (1984). The impact of the sexist language controversy and regulation on language in university documents. *Psychology of Women Quarterly*, *8*, 337–347.

Martyna, W. (1978). Using and understanding the generic masculine: A social–psychological approach to language and the sexes. *Dissertation Abstracts International*, *39*, 3050B.

Martyna, W. (1983). Beyond the he/man approach: The case for nonsexist language. In B. Thorne, C. Kramarae, & N. Henley (Eds.), *Language, gender and society* (pp. 25–37). Rowley, MA: Newbury House Publishers.

Merriam, E. (1974). Sex and semantics: Some notes on BOMFOG. *New York University Education Quarterly*, *5* (4), 22–24.

Miller, C., & Swift, K. (1976). *Words and women: New language in new times*. Garden City, NY: Doubleday.

Moulton, J., Robinson, G.M., & Elias, C. (1978). Sex bias in language use: "Neutral" pronouns that aren't. *American Psychologist*, *33*, 1032–1036.

Nilsen, A.P. (December 1973). *The correlation between gender and other semantic features in American English*. Paper presented at meetings of the Linguistic Society of America.

Nilsen, A.P. (1977a). Linguistic sexism as a social issue. In A.P. Nilsen, H. Bosmajian, H.L. Gershuny, & J.P. Stanley (Eds.), *Sexism and language* (pp. 1–25). Urbana, IL: National Council of Teachers of English.

Nilsen, A.P. (1977b). Sexism as shown through the English vocabulary. In A.P. Nilsen, H. Bosmajian, H.L. Gershuny, & J.P. Stanley (Eds.), *Sexism and language* (pp. 27–41). Urbana, IL: National Council of Teachers of English.

Nilsen, A.P. (1977c). Sexism in children's books and elementary teaching materials. In A.P. Nilsen, H. Bosmajian, H.L. Gershuny, & J.P. Stanley, *Sexism and language* (pp. 161–179). Urbana, IL: National Council of Teachers of English.

Rosch, E. (1974). Linguistic relativity. In A. Silverstein (Ed.), *Human communication: Theoretical explanations*. Hillsdale, NJ: Erlbaum.

Rosch, E., & Mervis, C.B. (1975). Family resemblances: Studies in the internal structure of categories. *Cognitive Psychology*, *7*, 573–605.

Sapir, E. (1949). *Selected writings of Edward Sapir* (D.G. Mandelbaum, Ed.). Berkeley: University of California Press.

Schneider, J., & Hacker, S. (1973). Sex role imagery and the use of the generic "man" in introductory texts. *American Sociologist, 8* (8), 12–18.

Schneider, M.J., & Foss, K.A. (1977). Thought, sex, and language: The Sapir–Whorf hypothesis in the American women's movement. *Bulletin: Women's Studies in Communication, 1* (1), 1–7.

Schulz, M. (1975). The semantic derogation of women. In B. Thorne & N. Henley (Eds.), *Language and sex: Difference and dominance* (pp. 64–73). Rowley, MA: Newbury House Publishers.

Shimanoff, S.B. (1977). Man = human: Empirical support for the Whorfian hypothesis. *Bulletin: Women's Studies in Communication, 1* (2), 21–27.

Silveira, J. (1978). *Women on the fringes: Generic masculine words and their relation to thinking.* Unpublished manuscript.

Silveira, J. (1980). Generic masculine words and thinking. In C. Kramarae (Ed.), *The voices and words of women and men* (pp. 165–178). Oxford: Pergamon.

Sniezek, J.A., & Jazwinski, C.H. (1986). Gender bias in English: In search of fair language. *Journal of Applied Social Psychology, 16,* 642–662.

Sontag, S. (1973). The third world of women. *Partisan Review, 40,* 180–206.

Stanley, J.P. (1977). Paradigmatic woman: The prostitute. In D.L. Shores & C.P. Hines (Eds.), *Papers in language variation* (pp. 303–321). Tuscaloosa: University of Alabama Press.

Stericker, A. (1981). Does this "he or she" business really make a difference? The effect of masculine pronouns as generics on job attitudes. *Sex Roles, 7,* 637–651.

Stopes, C.C. (1908). *The sphere of "man": In relation to that of "woman" in the Constitution.* London: Unwin.

Veach, S. (April 1979). *Sexism in usage: Intentional, conveyed, or all in the mind?* Paper presented at Conference on Language and Gender, Santa Cruz, CA.

Wallston, B.S., & O'Leary, V.E. (1981). Sex makes a difference: Differential perceptions of women and men. In L. Wheeler (Ed.), *Review of personality and social psychology*, Vol. 2 (pp. 9–41). Beverly Hills: Sage.

Whorf, B.L. (1956). *Language, thought, and reality.* New York: Technology Press of Massachusetts Institute of Technology and John Wiley & Sons.

Wilson, L.C. (1978). Teachers' inclusion of males and females in generic nouns. *Research in the Teaching of English, 12,* 155–161.

4
The Denial of Personal Disadvantage Among You, Me, and All the Other Ostriches

Faye J. Crosby, Ann Pufall, Rebecca Claire Snyder, Marion O'Connell, and Peg Whalen

All throughout America, and in many other parts of the world as well, sex roles appear to be shifting. Medical schools and law schools boast of increasing numbers of female students, and their faculties have begun to hire and sometimes even tenure women. Large corporations have admitted women to the formerly all-male enclaves of executive responsibility, and women are increasingly visible in the lower ranks of corporate life, in the vast cadres of middle management, and in the less glamorous offices of small business. The mass media treat the female penetration of the paid labor force and the male involvement in the family as important news items, and some commentators even speak of the revolution in sex roles.

But if the initial image is one of vigorous change in gender asymmetries, closer scrutiny of both domestic and work life reveals more stasis than change. Look at the division of domestic labor. Virtually every systematic study portrays the traditional imbalance: females perform the bulk of domestic labor and males retain the power to make major family decisions (Pleck, 1983). While the sex differentials diminish somewhat when wives have independent careers, especially careers that produce a lot of income, the actual imbalances persist far more than one would guess from media portraits of the "new husband" or of the "symmetrical family" (Silberstein, 1987; Steil & Turetsky, 1987). If life in the intact family does not benefit women as much as it benefits men, life after divorce usually increases the disparity. Divorce makes women much poorer while making men slightly richer (Weitzman, 1981).

Consider also the facts about the paid labor market. Study after study confirms our fears and disappointments. Unemployment and underemployment plague female workers more than male workers. Then, when women do find employment, they are shunted into a comparatively small number of occupations. Even when women enter professions, the professions tend to splinter (he becomes the corporate lawyer, she becomes the estates lawyer; he becomes the surgeon, she the pediatrician) so that everywhere the sex segregation of the labor market is preserved. Women are also, of course, undercompensated relative to men. Since World War II, females have earned between 59 and 61 cents on the male dollar. (See Kahn & Crosby, 1985, for a review.) Sexual harassment negatively affects female workers far more than male workers (Gutek, 1985). Is this really a revolution in sex roles? Hardly.

Several factors account for the glacial rate of change toward gender equality. As Jacquelynne Eccles demonstrates elsewhere in this volume, it does not suffice to modify people's general attitudes; we must also change specific opinions. Little change will come from convincing people that, generally speaking, males and females are similar in mathematical abilities. More change will come from convincing people that *this* or *that* group of girls should elect *this* or *that* math course. Even if we manage to change some attitudes, we are likely to encounter resistance changing others, especially if the change threatens our deep-seated and generally inaccessible notions of the male as subject and female as object. As Nancy Datan so brilliantly argues in Chapter 8, an oppressive sexist ideology undergirds all parts of contemporary life so that it even manifests itself, albeit covertly, in women's efforts to help other women "reach for recovery."

One additional explanation for the tenaciousness of gender imbalances is that people have a difficult time living their lives in accordance with the trusty feminist slogan "the personal is political." Perhaps one reason for the slow pace of change away from gender injustices is that individuals fail to perceive the personal relevance of facts they know to be true of society (Clayton & Crosby, 1986; Crosby & Clayton, 1986; Stewart & Healy, 1986). Women, as the victims of sex discrimination, tend to imagine, *ostrich-like*, a personal exemption from the rule of general sex bias that they know to operate in society. Those responsible for the effective and just functioning of organizations fall similarly prey to the illusion that aggregate statistics do not relate to the individuals whom they know. The perception of sex discrimination reminds one of fireflies: one can always see the glow from some distance, but bagging the little critters is often an elusive victory.

As long as those who are at a disadvantage—women or minorities—*believe* that they remain unaffected by systemic problems, they may not hasten to correct problems. And as long as women workers think that they are personally and individually untouched by sexism or sex discrimination, they may remain less than maximally effective in devising and helping implement corrective measures. As long as employers and officials believe their own people to be untouched by sex discrimination, *they* may impede the implementation of affirmative action programs.

Too often employers assume that "no news is good news" and that the apparent complacency of workers means that the system operates in a fair way. Assuming that women would complain if the system operated in such a way as to put them at a systematic disadvantage, employers regularly fail to collect systematic and aggregate data that could reveal gender biases in their organizations. Without aggregate knowledge, common but subtle problems can remain invisible, and no change will take place.

The denial of individual disadvantage is the topic of this chapter. Whenever we fail to see that individuals, each and every one, face the same disadvantaged realities that groups face, we engage in the denial of individual disadvantage. Whenever we acknowledge, for instance, that women face employment difficulties and simultaneously ignore that the women we know face such difficulties right this minute, we deny individual disadvantage.

Sometimes the denial of individual disadvantage is a denial of personal disadvantage. Sometimes the individual whose disadvantage we ignore is ourself. By "the denial of personal disadvantage" we mean a difficulty conceiving that the self suffers from a disadvantage suffered by any group to which the self belongs. A woman who thinks herself untouched by the sexism she knows to affect women generally, a black who thinks himself less hampered than other blacks by the racism he recognizes in America, a deaf person who thinks him or herself less stigmatized than other deaf people—all exhibit "the denial of personal disadvantage."

The denial of personal disadvantage took shape as a phenomenon to be investigated in a survey conducted nearly a decade ago in Newton, Massachusetts (Crosby, 1982, 1984). The Newton survey focused on sex discrimination within the work force, matching women and men of equivalent backgrounds and occupational statuses. Salary comparisons revealed systematic imbalances: the 182 men earned significantly more money than the 163 exactly comparable women. Furthermore, sex discrimination was a problem that the employed women in the study acknowledged as a general phenomenon. Yet the women differed not at all from the men on any of the numerous measures of job satisfaction. For some reason, the women were unwilling or unable to see their own personal disadvantage.

Other studies inside and outside the United States have corroborated the findings of the Newton survey and have suggested moreover that the tendency to deny one's own disadvantage is not limited to women. R.P. Abeles (1976) analyzed data from black college activists in the 1960s and found that the best predictor of militancy among the students was the perception that black people in general are unfairly treated. Perceptions about the self were unrelated to militancy or to perceptions about the situation of the group. Guimond and Dube-Simard (1983) found Francophone managers in Quebec to be concerned about the poor treatment of Francophones in Canada but to be unconcerned about their own, personal situations. The individuals in the Canadian study appeared to think themselves personally invulnerable to the general discrimination. More recently, a study of unemployed workers in Australia further confirmed the distinction between resentments felt about one's own personal situation, on the one hand, and resentments about the situation of one's social group on the other hand (Walker & Mann, 1987).

Some of the mechanisms that may account for the denial of personal discrimination have been identified. Certainly emotional factors play a part in the refusal to contemplate unpleasantness. Sigmund Freud is not the only theorist to have observed the human tendency to defend ourselves against unpleasant realities by imagining that reality is not quite so unpleasant or difficult as it may appear to an outsider's objective eye. Our use of the term "denial" is intended to call to mind the involvement of an emotional component. When people fail to recognize disadvantage generally or discrimination specifically, they invest some energy in rendering or keeping themselves blind to disturbing information.

Melvin Lerner (1980) and Morton Deutsch (1985) have both conducted extensive research that documents how people ward off the perception of injustice. Americans, and maybe all Western Europeans (Mikula, 1986; Schwinger, 1986), find the notion of injustice disturbing. Not only do we feel upset at the thought that we cause unjust harm to others—at the thought of ourselves as villains—but we feel upset at the thought of ourselves as suffering injustice. In many instances people are so emotionally threatened by the view of themselves as victims that they refuse to acknowledge their personal disadvantage—even when such recognition serves as a prerequisite for corrective action (Janoff-Bulman & Timko, in press).

Cognitive factors also interfere with the recognition of personal discrimination. It is not always the case, in other words, that emotionally driven denial occurs when people fail to perceive that the political is personal. When people make a determination about whether they are victims of injustice, they tend to compare their own inputs and outcomes with the inputs and outcomes of another individual or set of individuals (Goethals, 1986; Prentice & Crosby, 1987). Aggregate data appear irrelevant to the question of personal discrimination. Yet patterns that reveal sex discrimination can become apparent only with aggregate data.

An example illustrates how simple cognitive factors can impede a recognition of systematic discrimination. Imagine that you are denied promotion and that you are a woman. To determine if the situation is unjust, you would probably compare your qualifications with those of another individual or two who had been promoted recently. Let us consider, for the sake of exposition, that you compare yourself to a man who was promoted last year. Assume that you have been with the organization five years and have a bachelor's degree. The man, you learn, has been with the organization three years but has a master's degree. Is this a case of sex discrimination? It's hard to say. But assume that you look further and can find another department in which a man, a high school graduate with ten years of service, had been promoted while a woman with two years of college and eight years of service had been denied promotion. Now a pattern begins to form. Aggregate data are needed to average away the idiosyncrasies of education, years of service, and so on that are part of individual comparisons.

The importance of aggregate information for the perception of sex discrimination has been demonstrated empirically. In one experiment, subjects read information of the type presented in the example above. When the subjects examined the information in aggregate form, they perceived the discrimination which the materials had been devised to show. But when the same subjects examined the exact same information case by case, they failed to perceive discrimination (Crosby, Clayton, Alksnis, & Hemker, 1986). A subsequent experiment demonstrated that the effect was the same when subjects read affectively neutral materials with no mention of the words "sex discrimination" as when they read the original materials (Twiss, Tabb, & Crosby, 1989).

Given the preliminary indications that people do believe themselves exempt from the disadvantages that they know to be true for other members of their group and given the existence of cognitive and emotional mechanisms that can account for the denial of personal discrimination, the time has come to test the limits of the phenomenon: How widespread is it? Does it apply only to women? Only to those uninvolved in gender politics? What factors tend to guard against the tendency to deny personal disadvantage?

The present chapter has two purposes. First, it aims to present evidence that both attests to the generalizability of the phenomenon of the denial of personal discrimination and shows its limitations. We have conducted two surveys that replicate and extend the Newton survey. One examines the denial of personal discrimination among a group of women with a well-developed consciousness of themselves as a separate group. The other examines the phenomenon among a predominantly working class, rather than middle or professional class, sample. The second study also varies the tacit permission to complain, allowing us to see whether the phenomenon under study is really only a product of polite convention.

The second purpose of the chapter is to discuss the implications of our findings for organizational change and stasis. Women are not the only ones to deny individual disadvantage. Asking women to bear sole responsibility for social change is like blaming the victim; certainly, administrators and other officials must bear a significant portion of the burden of ensuring that organizations operate fairly as well as effectively. The men and women in charge of organizations—not just those affected by the organizations— also need to awaken to the truth that the political is the personal.

Denial of Personal Discrimination Among the Politicized: Survey of Lesbians

There is no basis for thinking that the respondents in the Newton sample had developed a consciousness of themselves as a group of people distinct from the larger American society. Perhaps they had no special identification with the category "working women." But several lines of research suggest that a sense of identification might have facilitated the perception of personal discrimination. Dion (1986) has catalogued the evidence showing a strong association between militancy and the recognition that one is part of an oppressed group of people. In a series of studies of Canadian women and men, Taylor and Dubé (1986) found that one must identify strongly with an oppressed group in order to perceive one's own personal disadvantage. Gurin (1987) has marshalled evidence to show that those who are part of the dominant culture have a hard time being angry about injustices perpetrated in maintenance of the status quo.

To test the generalizability of the Newton findings, we looked for clear evidence of the denial of personal disadvantage among people who see themselves as members of an oppressed group at variance with the dominant culture. More specifically, we used as our test case self-identified ("out of the closet") lesbians living in a liberal community in Massachusetts. It is widely recognized in the community that the self-identified lesbians there have a well-developed, acute (and often astute) ideology. When it comes to issues of gender, the lesbians are highly politicized.

PRELIMINARY STUDY

Would the "politicized" lesbians more readily perceive personal discrimination (as well as group discrimination) than had the predominantly heterosexual women queried in earlier studies? (see Crosby & Herek, 1986.) We hypothesized that lesbians would have a more developed sense of group discrimination than of personal discrimination. We thought lesbians would recognize and feel angry about the discrimination that lesbians generally face while failing to recognize the role of discrimination in their own personal lives. We further hypothesized, on the basis of Taylor and Dubé (1986), that the more a respondent identified with the group "lesbians," the more she would perceive personal discrimination.

We interviewed 15 lesbian career women between the ages of 23 and 47. The predominantly white sample represented a diverse range of occupations. The survey instrument consisted of 38 questions designed to determine the degree of perceived discrimination affecting the woman personally (personal discrimination), the degree of perceived discrimination against lesbians generally (group discrimination), and the degree of personal identification with the group "lesbians."

The results revealed a highly significant difference between perceptions of personal discrimination and perceptions of group discrimination. Participants did perceive themselves as exempt from the discrimination they acknowledged to be true in society at large. We also found that the degree of identification correlated with feelings of personal discrimination ($r = .46$; $p < .05$) and of group discrimination ($r = .45$; $p < .05$). Personal and group discrimination also correlated with each other ($r = .45$; $p < .05$).

Although the data coincided with our expectations, we could not be certain that denial existed. The possibility existed that the lesbians who perceived little personal discrimination were accurately assessing their situations. The community from which we drew the sample was perhaps one in which a lesbian would actually be unlikely to suffer professional disadvantage.

STEP TWO

We therefore decided to conduct a second study in which we would ask the respondents about their own situations and about the situations of other lesbians in the local community as well as other lesbians throughout the country. If the women's feelings about their own situations resembled their feelings about the situation of lesbians in the local community but differed from how they saw lesbians being treated in the country at large, then we would infer that the situation in the local area is, objectively, good for lesbians. If, on the other hand, the women saw themselves as better off than the other local lesbians (and, of course, better off than lesbians nationally), then we would conclude that these women, like respondents in earlier studies, engaged in the denial of personal discrimination.

In the second study, we expected the respondents to perceive more discrimination nationally than locally and more discrimination locally than personally. Extrapolating from Gurin (1987), we also expected, however, that in-group solidarity and the resistance to assimilation would reduce the tendencies toward denial. We hypothesized, more specifically, that the degree of identification (as a lesbian) and the degree of lesbian separatism would positively correlate with the perception of personal discrimination.

METHODS

Respondents

The respondents were 13 employed lesbians between the ages of 22 and 38. Two local lesbian feminists provided the researchers with a list of 15 names. Using a snowball sampling technique, each respondent interviewed was also asked to provide the names of other professional women who were lesbian and who might be willing to be interviewed. Thirteen interviews were arranged and completed. The sample included five professionals working in human services, four computer systems managers, a business coordinator, a consultant, a graphic designer, and a college administrator. All the women lived in Massachusetts in a well-educated and moderately affluent community.

Measures

The interview consisted of 39 close-ended and two open-ended questions, generally arranged according to topics. We asked first about identification, then about perceptions of discrimination, and finally about separatism.

Embedded in the sections on perceived discrimination were questions about the maintenance of a heterosexual facade. The interviews lasted between 30 and 90 minutes.

Scales were created to measure the degree of Personal Discrimination felt by each respondent, the degree of Local Discrimination, and the degree of National Discrimination. The scales were exactly analogous, with minor wording changes to reflect the target of discrimination. Each scale assessed how much discrimination was felt to have been suffered (by self, by lesbians locally, by lesbians nationally) in each of the following categories: overall (one item), work (six items), recreation (three items), home (six items), family of origin (three items), other (one item), and career (one item).

To measure the amount of overall discrimination personally suffered, for example, we asked: "Overall, are you discriminated against on the basis of sexual preference and not simply gender?" and asked for a numerical response between one (not at all) and six (very much). The six items in the question about discrimination suffered at work were job opportunities, choice of profession, salary, promotions and raises, benefits, and informal; and for each item, the respondent rated the amount of discrimination on a scale from 0 (no discrimination) to 6. The interview dealt first with personal discrimination, then with local, and finally with national discrimination.

We also assessed Heterosexual Facade. Respondents rated the extent, on a 7-point scale, of how much they feel they "must maintain a heterosexual facade at work" in terms of appearance, behavior, and conversational topics. Virtually identical questions were asked concerning the local scene and the national scene.

Identification was assessed by asking respondents how much they identified with the lesbian label; how much they identified as a lesbian emotionally, sexually, and socially; how active they were in lesbian events; and how much they supported lesbian activities politically, financially, and socially. From these questions, we created an Identification Scale. Finally, to assess separatism, we measured the respondents' attitudes with ten statements such as "It is very important to get men involved in the feminist movement" (reverse scored) and "Dealing with men is a waste of energy that could be better used to further the feminist movement."

RESULTS

Preliminary Results

The scales were all internally reliable. Alpha levels for Personal Discrimination, Local Discrimination, and National Discrimination were 0.82, 0.91, and 0.93, respectively. Each of the discrimination scales was decomposed into subscales concerning work, recreation, housing, and family matters. Again, internal consistencies were high, ranging from $\alpha = 0.63$ to $\alpha = 0.93$. The facade scales also appeared internally consistent ($\alpha = 0.95$

for Personal Facade; $\alpha = 0.98$ for Local Facade; and $\alpha = 0.88$ for National Facade), as did the Identification Scale ($\alpha = 0.87$) and the Separatism Scale ($\alpha = 0.82$).

Denial

The data confirmed our hypothesis that the lesbians would perceive less discrimination in their own lives than in the lives of lesbians locally or nationally. A one-way repeated measures analysis of variance (ANOVA) proved significant ($F [2,24] = 63.11$; $p < .0001$). Additional analyses showed that respondents perceived significantly less discrimination personally than locally ($F = 75.49$; $p < .0001$) and significantly less discrimination locally than nationally ($F = 43.07$; $p < .0001$). The mean scores were 2.6, 3.6, and 4.7, respectively, for personal, local, and national discrimination (on a scale where 0 = no discrimination and 6 = maximum discrimination).

When we considered individually the four subscales of discrimination, similar patterns emerged. More specifically, the respondents perceived significantly more national than local discrimination and significantly more local than personal discrimination on the Work Subscale and the Housing Subscale. On the Recreation Subscale, respondents perceived significantly less discrimination locally than nationally, but the difference between local and personal was not significant. Only for the Family of Origin Subscale was there no pattern of denial.

Analyses of the questions on heterosexual facade also confirmed the basic hypothesis about the denial of personal discrimination. A one-way repeated measures ANOVA was statistically significant ($F [2,24] = 10.99$; $p < .0001$). Specific comparisons showed that the respondents thought that lesbians throughout the nation needed to keep up a heterosexual facade more than lesbians in the local environment needed to ($F = 33.64$; $p = < .0001$) and also distinguished between their own personal situation and the local situation ($F = 4.87$; $p < .05$). The mean scores were 3.42, 3.62, and 5.05 for personal, local, and national facade questions, respectively.

Neutralizing Denial

We expected two factors to mitigate the tendency to deny personal discrimination. The first was identification as a lesbian. The data confirmed this expectation. The more identified a woman was as a lesbian, the greater was her sense of personal discrimination generally ($r = .56$, $p < .02$) and specifically in terms of work ($r = .49$, $p < .05$). Scores on the Identification Scale also correlated with scores on the Local Discrimination Scale ($r = .63$, $p < .01$) and with scores on the Work Subscale for local lesbians ($r = .75$, $p < .002$). Identification was unrelated to the perception of national discrimination.

Our expectations concerning separatism were not confirmed. Separatism did not correlate with perceptions of personal discrimination, local discrimination, or national discrimination.

DISCUSSION

The results of our survey generally replicate the findings of earlier studies. Members of a disadvantaged group were less likely to perceive the presence of discrimination in their own personal lives than in the lives of others, even when these others lived in the same community as themselves. The findings held true not only for overall discrimination but also for discrimination at work and in housing.

Not all respondents were equally likely to deny the existence of discrimination in their own lives. The more a respondent identified with the disadvantaged reference group—in this case, lesbians—the more likely was she to recognize her own personal disadvantage. This finding is consistent with Gurin's (1987) analyses of political identification among women.

Do feelings of distance or separation from the dominant group act in the same way as positive feelings of in-group solidarity? Based on Gurin's (1987) analysis of how assimilation thwarts the development of group identification and inhibits discontent, we had expected to find an inverse relation between the denial of personal discrimination and separatism. Among our sample, contrary to our expectations, perceptions of discrimination were unrelated to the lesbians' feelings about remaining separate from men.

Nor were the women in our sample especially likely to perceive discrimination if they could hold someone responsible. Crosby (1984) has theorized about the importance of having someone to blame for the disadvantage of an individual. According to Crosby, it is psychologically easy to recognize how a *group* can be disadvantaged by social forces but difficult (in our culture) to imagine how an *individual* is disadvantaged by social forces. Having someone to blame should therefore facilitate the recognition that one is personally disadvantaged. Such was not the case in the survey of lesbians.

Further Extensions: Success and the Denial of Disadvantage Among the Working Class

While the lesbian study convinced us that even ideologically sophisticated women can succumb to the tendency to deny personal disadvantage, it left us wondering about other factors that could inhibit or promote the denial of personal disadvantage. The women in the lesbian study were employed in middle-class and professional occupations. Would less privileged people also deny discrimination? Some evidence suggests that people in many walks of life like to see themselves as better off than similar others. In the Newton survey women in low-prestige occupations (e.g., waitresses and sales clerks) denied their own disadvantage as much as did women in high-prestige occupations (e.g., lawyers and physicians). An extensive study of black lesbians across the nation, furthermore, showed that the women thought themselves to have suffered little, if at all, from discrimination on the basis of sex, sexual preference, or race (Mays & Cochran, 1986). While most of the 450 black lesbians classified themselves as "middle class," they varied in their levels of education, their incomes, and their occupations.

We wished to have direct evidence about the denial of personal disadvantage among people with a working class background to supplement the indirect evidence of the earlier studies. To obtain the desired information, we conducted a study at a community college in Springfield, Massachusetts. The students at the college generally see themselves and are seen by others as upwardly mobile people coming from nonprivileged families. Many minority students attend the college.

We also designed the Springfield study to test whether we could reduce people's tendency to deny their own disadvantage, relative to their reference group, by giving people tacit permission to complain. Perhaps the women and men in earlier studies, including the Newton study and the survey of lesbians, had thought it would be impolite or otherwise gauche to complain about their personal situation. Society has long frowned on the office crabs, nitpickers, whistle blowers, Cassandras, and screaming hags. Especially unattractive to some eyes is the complaining woman. What would happen, we wondered, if we encouraged half of the people in the study to complain? Would they present themselves as less advantaged, relative to their reference group, than others who had no such encouragement?

Finally, we constructed the instrument for the Springfield study in such a way as to probe one last question: we wondered if it would be possible to distinguish between discrimination and disadvantage. "Discrimination" is an emotionally loaded word. It seemed plausible that people may acknowledge their own disadvantage but shy away from a recognition that they, personally and individually, have suffered due to discrimination. Alternatively, people may feel more comfortable admitting that they personally have encountered discrimination than admitting that they are or have been "downed" (or disadvantaged) by the discrimination. Indeed, it may even be a matter of pride for some to think how well they have met the challenges of life in our imperfect society.

METHODS

Participants

Students were recruited at a community college in Springfield, Massachusetts and asked to fill out a questionnaire during class time. The participants included 106 caucasian women, 80 caucasian men, 24 minority women, and 12 minority men. Of approximately 250 questionnaires distributed, 217 were complete and therefore usable. Only after data had been collected from all participants did any learn of the purposes of the study.

Instrument

The 9-page questionnaire existed in two versions. Both contained an informed consent request and a set of demographic questions. For a randomly selected half of the subjects, the second page read: "The following questionnaire will assist in a further understanding of events which surround discrimination. With due consideration, please answer each of the questions carefully." The other half of the subjects encountered a second page that was designed to give implicit permission to see oneself as the victim of discrimination without the need to lower one's self-esteem. The passage began with a general observation ("Discrimination has become a fact in society and permeates our lives. If we seriously examine almost any situation, we can usually find evidence of some unequal disadvantage.") and proceeded to give a long series of examples. The passage ended, 162 words later: "Whatever your financial, educational or physical status, age, gender, race or religion, you may have experienced some similar or otherwise unique personal or group discrimination which placed you in a situation of unfair disadvantage. With due consideration. . . ." Thus, half of the subjects were in the permission condition and half in the no-permission condition. Approximately equal numbers of minority and caucasian men and women were in each cell.

Measures

We measured perceived discrimination with a set of scales composed of close-ended questions, similar to the ones used in the survey of lesbians, and with a version of Cantril's ladder (Cantril, 1965). Four pages of the questionnaire asked the participant to rate on a scale from 1 (no, never) to 5 (yes, a lot) how much discrimination had been encountered in terms of education (four items), employment (four items), recreation (four items), and housing (three items). The items about housing were dropped from the analyses when we discovered that approximately half of the participants still lived with their families of origin.

We varied the time frame (last year, ever) and also the focus (self, family) of the questions. One page instructed the participant to complete the questions as they applied to herself or himself personally and within the last twelve months; another as they applied to herself or himself personally and ever in her or his life; a third as they applied to her or his family in the last twelve months; and finally as they applied to her or his family ever. We had thus four Likert-formatted measures of discrimination: (1) self in the last year, (2) self ever, (3) family in the last year, and (4) family ever. For each measure, the possible range of scores was from 12 (never encountered discrimination) to 60 (encountered a lot). Comparing the discrimination scores of the self with those of the family constituted one test of the denial of personal disadvantage.

Cantril's ladder shows a ladder with eleven rungs. Participants were asked to imagine that one end of the ladder represented "a life which is free of discrimination" while the other end represented "a life which is full of discrimination." They were instructed to place themselves, their families, their ethnic-racial groups, most men as a group, and most women as a group on the ladder. We could observe whether the participant saw herself or himself as having a life that was more free or less free of discrimination than other comparison people.

A second Cantril's ladder allowed us to measure disadvantage as distinct from discrimination. Participants were told: "This diagram of a ladder represents your chances for a successful life. The top rung is the best possible life in our society and the bottom is the worst." Participants were instructed to place on the ladder themselves, their families, their racial-ethnic groups, men as a group, and women as a group.

RESULTS

Preliminary

The discrimination scales, derived from the Likert-type questions, were internally reliable. Alpha levels for the measures of (1) self in the last year, (2) self ever, (3) family in the last year, and (4) family ever were 0.80, 0.80, 0.86, and 0.84, respectively.

Discrimination

We used a set of five-way repeated measures analyses of variance (ANO-VAs) to examine variations in perceived discrimination generally and separately for education, employment, and recreation. We treated the following as independent variables in the analyses: sex (male, female), ethnic group (caucasian, minority), experimental condition (tacit permission to complain, no-permission), time frame (ever, last year), and focus (self, family). The only variables to prove statistically significant were time frame and sex. All categories of participants reported much more discrimination "ever" than "in the last twelve months" ($F = 50.23$; $p < .001$), as indeed is logical. The interaction between gender and time frame was statistically significant ($F = 9.01$; $p < .01$) with women reporting significantly more discrimination "ever" than men. Women did not report more discrimination than men within the last year.

The permission and focus variables produced no significant effects. People's willingness to admit how much they have suffered from discrimination did not depend on being given tacit permission to complain, and they did not report that they suffered less discrimination than their families. Thus the Likert-type questions showed no evidence of any denial of personal discrimination.

Cantril's ladder for discrimination yielded more surprising results. Most participants rated themselves as suffering *more* discrimination than other people, not less. Of 74 men locating both the self and "men as a group" on the discrimination ladder, 73% saw themselves as suffering more discrimination than most men. How did the men see themselves relative to women as a group? Of the 81 men who placed both self and women, 26% saw themselves as suffering less discrimination than women, 28% as suffering the same, and 46% as suffering more discrimination than women.

Women's ratings paralleled the men's. Approximately 20% of the women thought they suffered less discrimination than most women; 20% said the same; and 60% said they suffered more discrimination than most women. Only 4% of the women said they suffered less discrimination than most men, and 8% said the same amount. Eighty-eight percent of the women saw themselves as suffering more discrimination than most men.

Neither permission to complain nor ethnic group affected this pattern. Contrary to our expectations, our participants all exhibited the same tendency to see the self as having suffered more discrimination than comparison groups.

Chances for Success

Curiously, examination of the other Cantril ladder showed that the people in Springfield, like people in previous studies, thought themselves to be better off than others in their own groups. Figure 4.1 depicts the percentages of women and men who claim to have less good, equal, or better chances for a good life in our society than do women or men as a group. Of special interest are the women's ratings. Nearly a quarter of the women see themselves as better off than most men. Nearly three-quarters of the women see themselves as better off than most women.

DISCUSSION

The Springfield study helps define the limits of the denial phenomenon and suggests new questions for research. The fact that our experimental manipulation—tacit permission to complain—did not affect people's responses suggests that it is not simply politeness that accounts for people's greater willingness to voice discontent on behalf of their groups than on behalf of themselves.

The Springfield participants did not differentiate in their responses between their own personal situations and the situations of their families. At a minimum, this finding suggests that people do not see themselves as exempt from the problems that have affected their families. Combined with

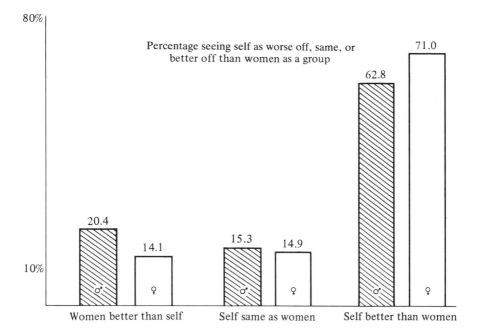

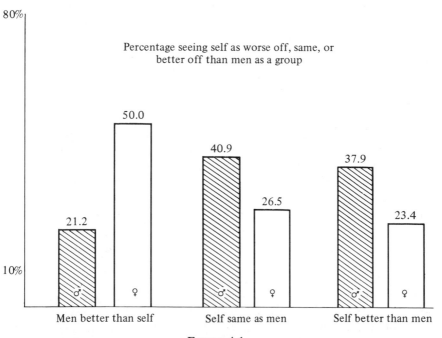

FIGURE 4.1.

the information obtained by assessing discrimination with Cantril's ladder, the results suggest more. The aspirant working class, represented in the Springfield sample, may have more willingness than the middle-class and professional people of earlier surveys to acknowledge that they have suffered as many hard knocks as have others in their reference group.

The sample's willingness to admit personal tribulations makes all the more interesting their unwillingness to admit personal disadvantage—as distinct from discrimination. It seems as if the participants in the Springfield study are saying in effect: "Yes, I have suffered as much—even more—than others like me; but I'm unusually skilled at coping!" People apparently like to think of themselves as fighters against the odds. As Nancy Datan so eloquently expresses it (see Chapter 8), we have much to gain by seeing ourselves as warriors and not as victims. But perhaps too we lose something if our pride in coping blinds us to continued disadvantages.

The Other Side of the Coin

The lesbians in our first study, like people in earlier samples (e.g., women in Newton, Francophones in Canada) may deny the extent to which they are discriminated against because, essentially, they have made their peace with their social world. The people in Springfield, in contrast, may be in the process of changing their personal situations, and specifically of bettering their lot in life through education. Would people who wish neither to settle for the current situation nor to change the current situation in wholly personalistic ways also see themselves as coping better than their reference group? Only future research can tell us.

In the meantime, some lessons are already clear. The most important implication of the current line of research is that we must not measure the need for social reform by how upset people feel with their personal situations in life. Karl Marx was right about false consciousness: those who are oppressed or disadvantaged rarely have a well-developed sense of their own disadvantage.

Interestingly, precisely the opposite conclusion was recently reached by an economist publishing in the prestigious *American Economic Review* (Kuhn, 1987). The economist, Peter Kuhn, conducted elaborate secondary analyses of national probability survey data collected in 1977 by researchers at the University of Michigan (Quinn & Staines, 1979) and of a similar Canadian data set. The surveys contained objective measures of earnings and of earning-relevant qualifications as well as measures of people's (subjective) sense of grievance. The women were asked specifically if they had suffered sex discrimination. Kuhn found that only 9.9% of the women in the United States and 15.4% of the women in Canada perceived their own disadvantage, despite large wage differentials between women and men in both samples. He further found low correlations between the objective measures of discimination (derived from the earnings and earning-relevant qualifications) and the subjective measures.

Kuhn suggested that the women in the surveys did not feel aggrieved because they knew that they were less qualified than men on factors relevant to earnings but unmeasured by the survey researchers. He futher speculated that the low correlations between actual and perceived discrimination were caused by the greater probability that women with a lot of education and training work in male-dominated fields where they might select men as their referents in determining the fairness of their own earnings. Then, rather than concluding, as we have done, that women's sense of grievance offers but a poor measure of their true disadvantage, Kuhn concluded that the objective data must be flawed. In the abstract of his article, Kuhn baldly states: "Statistical [meaning objective] evidence is found to be less important than other, 'nonstatistical' evidence" (Kuhn, 1987, p. 567). Less important, indeed!

If a trained economist, publishing in one of the best journals, can make such mistakes, would it be any wonder that administrators with less statistical sophistication regularly underestimate the existence of sex bias in their own organizations? Obviously not. The question then arises about whether administrators who are sympathetic to women's causes might be more able than others to analyze correctly information relevant to sex discrimination. Feminists have sometimes assumed that administrative blindness to sex discrimination results from blatant or latent misogyny and have assumed, furthermore, that those with politically correct attitudes will see the sex discrimination that eludes the view of others.

Such assumptions do not appear warranted. Administrators are probably no more talented than anyone else at bridging the gap between aggregate and individual data or at discerning patterns from the individual instances of relevant data that they perceive around them. Administrators are human beings and as such make the same mistakes as other human beings in the processing of information. People—including administrators —tend to assume congruence of cause and effect (Einhorn & Hogarth, 1986), for example, and may therefore think that when an individual suffers, it is because another individual or set of individuals (purposely) caused the suffering. The administrators may then believe that because no woman or man whom they know seems to be causing this or that target woman to suffer, the target does not suffer.

Should the administrator's vision be clearer than that of the victimized woman simply because the administrator may, in some cases, be impartial? The answer unfortunately is no. Empirical evidence shows that impartial observers, even those largely indifferent to issues of gender equity, are extremely unskilled in inferring overall patterns from bits of data that they encounter. In one experiment (Crosby, Clayton, Alksnis, & Hemker, 1986) male undergraduates at an elite university were presented with information about a hypothetical company which was concerned about sex inequalities in pay. The young men received detailed information about the factors that were relevant to salary in the company and information on the specific qualifications of "an average" woman and "an average" man from each of the company's ten departments. Half of the time the information was presented serially, department by department, and half of the time it was presented on a single sheet, arranged so that the aggregate picture was visible at a glance. All the subjects received both types of information—half of the time in one order (aggregate, then individual) and half of the time in the other (individual, then aggregate). The information was contrived so that, for the company as a whole, there was pronounced sex discrimination: the women and men in the hypothetical company had exactly equal qualifications, on average, but the women earned much less than the men.

When the subjects saw the information in aggregate form, they judged that sex discrimination was both likely and serious. They saw discrimination as much less of a problem when they saw the information department by department. The subjects' self-reported attitudes about feminism bore no relation to their perceptions. Self-described feminists were no more likely to see discrimination in the materials than were others, and everyone made the error of underestimating discrimination when they encountered the relevant information piecemeal and serially.

A follow-up experiment (Twiss, Tabb, & Crosby, 1989) added more evidence that the failure to perceive discrimination can result simply from cognitive functioning and not from emotional or attitudinal factors. One problem with the basic study was that it used the words "sex discrimination" and thus might have aroused in the subjects some emotional responses that might then have clouded their clear vision. The follow-up study included the original materials (in the sex-discrimination conditions) and also an exact analog of the original materials that described not men and women but rather the workers in Plant A and Plant B of the company (the latter being the plant conditions). Subjects in the sex-discrimination conditions reported their interest in participating in the experiment, while the subjects in the plant conditions reported (and showed in their comportment) that they found the experiment tedious. But in all other respects the emotionally neutral materials produced exactly the same results as the original materials. Once again, subjects proved unable to see the forest for the trees.

One final experiment reversed the materials so that discrimination appeared, by illusion, to be present in the aggregate data but was only sometimes present in fact in the actual individual data (Crosby, Burris, Censor, & MacKethan, 1986). The materials were constructed not because they map everyday reality—indeed, it took three people one week to contrive a case where discrimination appeared in aggregate form but not in the detailed case-by-case comparisons—but because we wished to demonstrate the transitive or bidirectional nature of the phenomenon. Once again, the data showed that subjects process information differently when they encounter it in summary form than when they encounter it bit by bit.

For those who wish to assure the fair distribution of rewards in their organizations, these data carry a clear message. The lesson is this: do not trust your own impressions any more than you trust the impressions of the women in your organization. Women may be motivated to deny their own disadvantage; but nobody—no matter what the level of emotional involvement or detachment—should trust to conclusions based on unaggregated figures. Only by bringing all the data together can one see patterns.

David Funder (1987) has recently distinguished between errors and mistakes. Errors occur in the laboratory when, for example, people incorrectly assume congruence between cause and effect. Mistakes, in contrast, have social relevance. The denial of individual disadvantage, growing from identified errors in reasoning, constitutes an important mistake. Women are mistaken in believing the self to be invulnerable to the discrimination that exists all around. Administrators are mistaken to think they can detect discrimination without systematic and aggregate data.

Compounding the first set of mistakes is a second set. Both feminists and reactionaries tend, mistakenly, to assume that distorted visions correspond to poor attitudes. The feminists start with the observation that many institutions operate in a sex-biased way and conclude that the administrators harbor misogynist opinions. The administrators start with the observation that they harbor no misogynist opinions and conclude that their institutions operate in sex-neutral ways. Both camps are wrong.

Attitudes and intentions do not matter in the firefly phenomenon. One's opinions about modern art have no effect on one's susceptibility to optical illusions; most illusions work the same for everyone, no matter what the person's aesthetic tastes. In just the same way, everyone—no matter what the sociopolitical persuasion—has difficulty seeing the operation of sex bias in individual cases. When once we understand how very impersonal the process is, we can stop hurling accusations of misogyny and of masochism at each other.

The injustices of society may diminish if we can all extract our heads from the sand and see how the system operates in the lives of individuals, ourselves and others whom we know. Let us devote our efforts to correction, not retribution. We shall all be blind and toothless before we finish taking an eye for an eye and a tooth for a tooth. And perhaps the best form of correction is to work together, women and men, to bring about a world with fewer categorical disadvantages for all.

Acknowledgments. We would like to thank Barbara Nesto and Karla Stormo as well as Karen Dwyer, Karen Elefterakis, Susan Smith, Fletcher Blanchard, and Vickie Mays.

REFERENCES

Abeles, R.P. (1976). Relative deprivation, rising expectations, and black militancy. *Journal of Social Issues*, *32* (3), 119–137.

Cantril, H. (1965). *The pattern of human concerns.* New Brunswick, NJ: Rutgers University Press.

Clayton, S., & Crosby, F. (1986). Postscipt: The nature of connections. *Journal of Social Issues*, *42* (2), 189–194.

Crosby, F. (1982). *Relative deprivation and working women.* New York: Oxford University Press.

Crosby, F. (1984). Relative deprivation in organizational settings. In B. Staw & L.L. Cummings (Eds.), *Research in organizational behavior* (Vol. 6, pp. 51–93). Greenwich, CT: JAI Press.

Crosby, F., Burris, L., Censor, C., & MacKethan, E.R. (1986). Two rotten apples spoil the justice barrel. In H. Bierhoff, R. Cohen, & J. Greenberg (Eds.), *Justice in social relations* (pp. 267–281). New York: Plenum.

Crosby, F., & Clayton, S. (1986). Introduction: The search for connections. *Journal of Social Issues*, *42* (2), 1–10.

Crosby, F., Clayton, S., Alksnis, O., & Hemker, K. (1986). Cognitive biases in the perception of discrimination: The importance of format. *Sex Roles*, *14*, 637–646.

Crosby, F., & Herek, G.M. (1986). Male sympathy with the situation of women: Does personal experience make a difference? *Journal of Social Issues*, *42* (2), 55–66.

Deutsch, M. (1985). *Distributive justice: A social psychological perspective.* New Haven: Yale University Press.

Dion, K.L. (1986). Responses to perceived discrimination and relative deprivation. In J.M. Olson, C.P. Herman, & M.P. Zanna (Eds.), *Relative deprivation and social comparison. The Ontario Symposium* (Vol. 4, pp. 159–179). Hillsdale, NJ: Erlbaum.

Einhorn, H.J., & Hogarth, M. (1986). Judging probable cause. *Psychological Bulletin*, *99*, 3–19.

Funder, D.C. (1987). Errors and mistakes: Evaluating the accuracy of social judgments. *Psychological Bulletin*, *101*, 75–90.

Goethals, G.R. (1986). Social comparison theory: Psychology from the lost and found. *Personality and Social Psychology Bulletin*, *12*, 261–278.

Guimond, S., & Dubé-Simard, L. (1983). Relative deprivation theory and the Quebec nationalist movement: The cognition–emotion distinction and the personal–group deprivation issue. *Journal of Personality and Social Psychology*, *44*, 526–535.

Gurin, P. (1987). The political implications of women's statuses. In F. Crosby (Ed.), *Spouse, parent, worker. On gender and multiple roles* (pp. 165–196). New Haven: Yale University Press.

Gutek, B. (1985). *Sex and the workplace: The impact of sexual behavior and harassment on women, men, and organizations.* San Francisco: Jossey-Bass.

Janoff-Bulman, R., & Timko, C. (in press). Coping with traumatic life events: The role of denial in light of people's assumptive worlds. In C.R. Snyder & C. Ford (Eds.), *Coping with negative life events: Clinical and social psychological perspectives.* New York: Plenum.

Kahn, W., & Crosby, F. (1985). Change and stasis: Discriminating between attitudes and discriminatory behavior. In L. Larwood, B.A. Gutek, & A.H. Stromberg (Eds.), *Women and work, an annual review* (Vol. 1, pp. 215–238). Beverly Hills: Sage.

Kuhn, P. (1987). Sex discrimination in labor markets: The role of statistical evidence. *American Economic Review*, 77, 567–583.

Lerner, M. (1980). *The belief in a just world. A fundamental delusion.* New York: Plenum.

Mays, V., & Cochran, S. (1986). *Relationship experiences and the perception of discrimination of black lesbians.* Paper presented at the American Psychological Association annual convention, Washington, DC.

Mikula, G. (1986). The experience of injustice: Toward a better understanding of its phenomenology. In H.W. Bierhoff, R.L. Cohen, & J. Greenberg (Eds.), *Justice in social relations* (pp. 103–124). New York: Plenum.

Pleck, J.H. (1983). Husband's paid work and family roles: Current research issues. In H. Lopata & J.H. Pleck (Eds.), *Research in the interweave of social roles: Families and jobs* (Vol. 3. pp. 251–333). Greenwich, CT: JAI Press.

Prentice, D., & Crosby, F. (1987). The importance of context for assessing deservingness. In J.C. Masters & W.P. Smith (Eds.), *Social comparison, social justice and relative deprivation. Theoretical, empirical, and policy perspectives* (pp. 165–182). Hillsdale, NJ: Erlbaum.

Quinn, R., & Staines, G. (1979). *Quality of employment survey, 1977: Cross section.* Ann Arbor, MI: Inter-University Consortium for Political and Social Research.

Schwinger, T. (1986). The need principle of distributive justice. In H.W. Bierhoff, R.L. Cohen, & J. Greenberg (Eds.), *Justice in social relations* (pp. 211–226). New York: Plenum.

Silberstein, L. (1987). *The dual-career marriage. A system in transition.* Unpublished doctoral dissertation, Yale University.

Steil, J.M., & Turetsky, B.A. (1987). Marital influence levels and symptomatology among wives. In F. Crosby (Ed.), *Spouse, parent, worker. On gender and multiple roles* (pp. 74–90). New Haven, CT: Yale University Press.

Stewart, A.J., & Healy, J.M. Jr. (1986). The role of personality development and experience in shaping political commitment: An illustrative case. *Journal of Social Issues*, 42 (2), 11–32.

Taylor, D.M., & Dubé, L. (1986). Two faces of identity: The "I" and "we". *Journal of Social Issues*, 42 (2), 81–98.

Twiss, C., Tabb, S., & Crosby, F. (1989). Affirmative action and aggregate data: The importance of patterns in the perception of discrimination. In F. Blanchard & F. Crosby (Eds.), *Affirmative action in perspective* (pp. 159–167). New York: Springer-Verlag.

Walker, I., & Mann, L. (1987). Unemployment, relative deprivation, and social protest. *Personality and Social Psychology Bulletin*, 13, 275–283.

Weitzman, L.J. (1981). *The marriage contract.* New York: Free Press.

5
Gender and Thought: The Role of the Self-Concept

Hazel Markus and Daphna Oyserman

In the continuing analysis of sex and gender differences, there is a growing awareness of the possibility of fundamental differences in how women and men perceive themselves and their worlds, in how they take meaning, and in how they come to know or reason (e.g., Belenky, Clinchy, Goldberger, & Tarule, 1986; Block, 1984; Cantor & Kihlstrom, 1987; Chodorow, 1987; Gilligan, 1982; Miller, 1986; Ruddick, 1980). The nature of these differences and the psychological structures and mechanisms that mediate them are not well understood. Such differences are likely to be subtle and not easily isolated but when closely analyzed may prove powerful. Our goal is to examine the divergent theories of the self that can be held by men and women and to explore how they may influence basic perceptual and cognitive processes.

This chapter has its origins in several general assumptions that derive from psychology's two basic paradigms–the person as constructor of external reality and the person as constructed by external reality (see Chapter 1 in this volume). From our perspective, the self-concept governs one's perception of reality. It is an important mediator and regulator of thoughts, feelings and actions. Furthermore, both the structure and the function of the self-concept will vary according to the nature of the social environment. The nature of the social environment is determined by its structural features and also by the theories and assumptions of the individuals (including the individual herself or himself) who create this environment.

Overview of the Approach

Our view is that men and women are typically encouraged to make the great divide—the self/nonself divide—in very different ways. This divergence comes as a consequence of the different patterns of social interaction and interpersonal experience that are likely to characterize men and women from their earliest experience and throughout their lives. More specifically, men and women will construct different types of structures about the self and as a consequence their thought processes may diverge both in content and in form.

Building on the ideas of a number of theorists (Chodorow, 1978; Erikson, 1968; Gilligan, 1982; Miller, 1986; Sampson, 1988; Stewart & Lykes, 1985), we suggest that women are more likely than men to have what can be called a "collectivist," "sociocentric," "ensembled," "communal," or "connected" schema for the self. A schema here is an affective/cognitive structure that is created to lend meaning and coherence to one's experience. In a connectedness schema, relations with others are the basic elements. In contrast, men are relatively more likely to have what can be called an "individualist," "egocentric," "separate," "independent," or "autonomous" schema of the self. Other individuals are represented not as part of the self but as separate and distinct from it.

We assume that connectedness and separateness self-schemas influence thinking, not just about the *self* but about *all* objects, events, and situations. This assumption is compatible with a variety of theoretical perspectives (Baldwin, 1902; Erikson, 1968; Fast, 1985; Jacobson, 1964; Kernberg, 1976) yet it seldom finds expression in studies of social cognition. While infants quickly achieve a diversity of representations of their experience, our perspective assumes that the self/nonself distinction affords a particularly meaningful categorization and integration of these representations. The self/other distinction is made repeatedly and in a variety of ways in the course of development. The typical degree of separation from or connection to the interpersonal context that characterizes it, however, will provide a model for the representation of all objects, events, and situations.

A sense of self as separate, individuated, and autonomous gives rise to the normative task of knowing, expressing, or realizing this "true" or unique inner self regardless of the constraints of the current social environment. Conversely, a sense of self as interdependent, embedded, and continuous with others is linked with the normative task of being carefully attuned to the immediate social environment and of coming to know and understand the other (for further discussion of the importance of normative life tasks, see Cantor & Kihlstrom, 1987; Erikson, 1968; Veroff, 1983).

Neither of these views of the self should be considered more developed or more productive than the other. Rather, they reflect divergent views of "who am I" and what it means to a "self." Self-schemata deriving from a sense of self as connected have a different structure and determine different patterns of perception and thought than those deriving from a sense of self as separate. Connected selves should not be viewed as less "good" because they are responsive to the social environment. Many treatments of sex differences in self-structure (Aries & Olver, 1985; Mahler, Pine, &

Bergman, 1975) begin with the assumption that the lack of a sense of self as separate from others must always comprise a difficulty or a conflict for women, one that must be overcome if a woman is to become a complete or developed individual. From our view, believing one's self to be functioning autonomously as an isolated individual is only one approach to selfhood, and one that has at least as many complications and limitations as an approach that focuses on connectedness (Hare-Mustin & Marecek, 1986).

There are at least three aspects to our frankly speculative argument. The first aspect is based on the idea that the characteristically different experiences of men and women with other people will result in differing conceptions of self and other. These divergent self/other conceptions can arise for a variety of reasons. Chodorow (1978) proposes that mothers and daughters, unlike mothers and sons, experience a sense of similarity and continuity with one another. As a result, in defining themselves, women learn to focus on and value relationships more so than do men. Similarly, Miller (1986) claims that relations to others are central to women's sense of self. She arrives at this point by analyzing women's relatively powerless position in society. As subordinates in a culture dominated by men, women must be constantly attuned to and responsive to others because it is these others who control their future.

The second aspect of our argument derives from the growing literature on culture and selfhood (Geertz, 1975; Harding, 1987; Heelas, 1980; Kelly, 1987; Marsella, De Vos, & Hsu, 1985; Shweder & Levine, 1984). This literature claims that different cultures or different social environments may well create and foster the development of divergent idioms and bedrock assumptions about the nature of the self and the nature of others. From this literature comes the idea that individuals can be mutually dependent and that this interdependence or sense of community with others can be a central organizing reality. Individuals thus can develop self-structures in which the primary referent is not the individual himself or herself, but instead the self-in-interpersonal relationships.

The third aspect of the argument comes from research on cognitive approaches to self and personality. This literature claims that the nature of the self-structure determines how information about the self and others is processed. Markus and her colleagues, for example, suggest that individuals develop a system of distinct self-schemata. These schemata are theories about the self derived from the repeated categorizations and evaluation of behavior by oneself and by others (Markus, 1977; Markus, Crane, Bernstein, & Siladi, 1982; Markus, Smith, & Moreland, 1985). These self-schemata enable perceivers to detect features and higher-order thematic structure in their own behavior and in that of others to which they otherwise would be insensitive. These schemata are focally active in the interpretation and comprehension of the social world (for a review of schema functioning, see Markus & Zajonc, 1985). Notions about the general cognitive consequences of self-structures can also be found in Bowlby's

(1980) attachment theory and in objects relations theory (Greenberg & Mitchell, 1983).

From an integration of these three sets of ideas, we suggest that the self-definitional project is quite different for men and women and that, as a result, they will develop different types of self-schemata. In the following sections we first detail the nature of separateness and connectedness self-schemata, discuss the possible developmental origins of these divergent self-schemata, and finally explore the ways that these self-schemata may influence thought.

The Nature of Connectedness and Separateness Self-Schemata

All individuals establish some structure in which they conceptualize the self as distinct from others (Hallowell, 1955). An understanding of how the self is different from others (i.e., of one's "individuality") is assumed to be essential to healthy functioning. One's understanding of and participation in the social world depends on this differentiation. Yet people can individuate themselves and experience themselves as distinct in a variety of ways. Thus, although people everywhere will ask "who am I?" (see Shweder & Levine, 1984), we reason that not everyone will construct the same answer to the question.

Specifically for females, a first and core self-schema is likely to establish the self as "interdependent or connected" (see Figure 5.1). This is the first answer to the "who am I?" question. This schema roughly parallels the "contextual" or "relational" structures (Hamaguchi, 1985) that are thought to characterize individuals in many non-Western societies, such as Japan. Such structures do not imply a merging of self and others or a lack of individuation. Rather, they emphasize the importance of others in defining the self. One's individuality or uniqueness is thus a result of one's configuration of relationships. Furthermore, interaction and interpersonal relationships are important as ends in themselves.

For males, a first and core self-schema is likely to establish the self as "autonomous or separate" (see Figure 5.1). In this self-schema, the self is viewed as discrete and as separate from the individual's situation or context. Individuality is achieved through delineation of the boundaries between self and other individuals. Such a schema is characterized by what Geertz (1975) has called the "Western conception of the person," which assumes that the individual is a "bounded, unique, more or less integrated motivational and cognitive universe . . . a distinctive whole set contrastively against other such wholes and against a social and natural background" (p. 225). The bounded self is seen as relatively independent of social roles or relationships. Relationships are important primarily as a means of affirming, verifying, or defending the self.

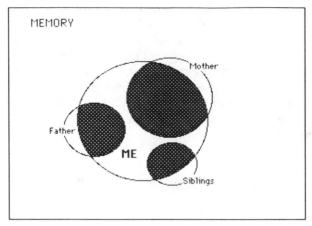

ME AS CONNECTED

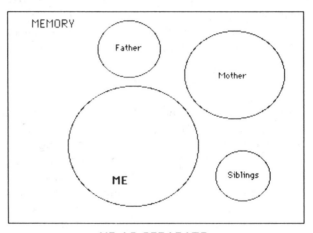

ME AS SEPARATE

FIGURE 1. Two possible representations of self and other in memory.

REFINING THE CORE SELF-SCHEMATA

With development the basic connectedness self-schema is likely to become differentiated into multiple domain-specific self-schemata. A girl may begin with a general sense of herself-as-interdependent with others and with further social experience refine and specify the diverse nature of this interdependence. Exactly which self-schemata will be constructed depends on the meaning that is given to the normative tasks of connecting with or separating from others. How these tasks are personalized and assume specific self-relevant form is a function of individuals' unique social and developmental history (Cantor & Kihlstrom, 1987). It is unlikely that individuals will articulate or become aware of a connectedness schema per se. Yet the tendency to connect to others through affection, commitment, dependency, obligation, and responsibility that is the hallmark of the schema will underlie many of the other more specific self-schemata.

Some women will elaborate schemata that derive in a fairly straightforward fashion from their sense of themselves as connected. They will develop schemata of themselves as understanding and caring, as loving and nurturant, or as responsible, considerate, conscientious, or sensitive. Others may create a more general gender schema, defining themselves primarily in terms of their social roles (for a discussion of gender schemata and other specific attribute-based schemata, see Bem, 1981, and Markus, 1977). All these self-schemata, however, will have as their referent the self-in-relation with another. One cannot manifest one's responsibility, conscientiousness, or sensitivity without an actual or implied other to receive one's actions. Women may, of course, also develop schemata of themselves as autonomous or separate in nature, that is, themselves as independent, creative, or competent. Yet when these latter self-schemata are developed within a context of basic connectedness or interdependence they may also implicate or depend on the reactions and evaluations of others.

With development, the basic separateness self-schema is likely to become the foundation for more specific self-schemata of independence, assertiveness, instrumentality, and competitiveness. These schemata have as their referent not the self in relation with another, but the self in contrast or comparison with another. To make these comparisons, the self must be separated from others. Men may also develop schemata of themselves as connected, but if these schemata are developed against a backdrop of separateness they may assume a somewhat different form. For example, when viewing the self as connected, the connection will involve an exchange between two separate entities rather than the interdependence of these entities.

CULTURAL VARIATIONS IN SELF-SCHEMATA

The recent literature on culture and personhood contains extensive discussions about the nature of self. This literature can be useful in drawing out the phenomenological experience of having a self that begins in connection or one that begins, instead, in separation. These theoretical discussions (Dumont, 1970; Geertz, 1973; Schneider, 1976; Shweder & Bourne, 1984; White & Kirkpatrick, 1985) underscore an important point: differences in cognition should *not* be viewed as deficits among the group possessing the least Western, individualist, or masculine orientation. Furthermore, it should not be assumed that the less Western groups will naturally develop with education and modernization toward a more Western mode of thought. Instead, recent theorists of selfhood stress the influence of culture on perception and thought, where culture is defined as a shared set of meanings that structure one's perception of the self and the world (for recent discussions, see Cousins, 1987; Miller, 1984; Shweder & Bourne, 1984). From this view, "self" can have multiple conceptual representations depending on the assumptions that are used to create it.

In the perspective we have developed here, we assume that the representations of self typically constructed by girls and boys will be somewhat different because girls and boys inhabit different interpersonal environments, *and* because different assumptions are immediately brought to bear in their development as they are perceived as male or female.

The distinction between the self-as-connected and the self-as-separate maps roughly onto the distinction between individualist and collectivist selves and onto the difference between Western and Eastern selves. Examples of collectivist selves are the Japanese, the Chinese, the Indians, the Africans, and many people of the Pacific. The distinction is an old one and it has been given a number of other labels—egocentric versus sociocentric, individualized versus contextualized, or individual centered versus situation centered. The general difference highlighted in these distinctions seems to capture at least some of the important differences between the self-structure of Western women and men.

For example, to the Japanese self, interdependence is everything (Lebra, 1976; Marsella et al., 1985). One's self-esteem and one's future are tied always to one's social relationships with others. Lebra (1976) defines the essence of Japanese cultures as an "ethos of social relativism" that translates into a constant concern for belongingness, dependency, empathy, occupying one's proper place, and reciprocity. She quotes the Japanese proverb "The nail that stands out gets pounded down." According to many analyses of Japanese culture, the Japanese feel most fully human in the company of others. The goal is not one of functioning autonomously, but rather one of functioning interdependently.

For the individualist self, however, it is the independent, nonconforming, assertive self that is the desired future self. Its exemplary proverb is quite different: "It's the squeaky wheel that gets the grease." Rather than being essential to the self-definition, interpersonal relations are important to the extent that they allow one to realize and express his or her separate and unique potential. Freedom from a concern with how people think and feel is often the highest goal. Independence is everything (Marsella et al., 1985).

Similarly, Dixon (1976) presents a paradigm of the African world view as contrasted with a European world view. He cites evidence that Europeans separate the self from the other, perceiving the self as in contrast to and separate from all else. Africans, on the other hand, are said not to create such a gap between the self and the world. The world, and the others in it, are viewed as an extension of one another. Dixon argues that with such a sense of self, the immediate social environment cannot be escaped; the individual must respond in terms of the needs of immediate environment because they are experienced as needs of the self. A defining feature of a Western self is freedom from environmental control, and thus it can choose to manipulate, act on, or defer environmental demands. An African self is experienced as part of the environment. Such differences in the conceptualization of the self/other divide have implications for the way information about the world is processed.

In analyses of how the collectivist and individualist theories of personhood may influence thinking, Shweder and Bourne (1984) asked respondents in India and America to describe a number of close acquaintances. They found the descriptions of the Indians to be more concrete and extensively qualified according to the context of the relationship. Yet on an independent test of abstract cognitive skills that included a variety of labeling and sorting tasks, they found no differences among the two groups. Similarly, Miller (1984) asked Indian Hindus and Americans for their patterns of attribution about hypothetical events. Hindus explained most actions in terms of features of the situation, while Americans used many more global traits and internal dispositions to explain behavior. Again, no differences were found between the two groups in tests of abstract cognitive skills. Instead, the difference in attribution seemed best explained in terms of differences in the individualistic and sociocentric theories of the person.

In a recent study, Cousins (1987) examined the impact of these two divergent theories on the perception of the self. He used two different free-response formats, the TST (Twenty Statements Test) and a questionnaire asking subjects to describe themselves in several situations (me at home, with friends, at school). On the TST the Japanese descriptions were more concrete and role specific ("I play tennis on the week-end"), while the American descriptions included more global psychological characterizations ("I am optimistic"). When the social context was provided for the self-descriptions, however, this pattern of results was reversed: the Japanese scored higher on global psychological characterizations of themselves than did Americans. Once a particular interpersonal context was specified, the Japanese also described themselves in abstract terms.

We have reviewed these studies primarily because they suggest that those with sociocentric theories of themselves and the world are not appropriately characterized as having either undifferentiated, submerged views of the self, or as having some type of cognitive deficit. For those with sociocentric selves, like those with connected selves, the most natural and readily accessible modes of perception and thought are those that stress the importance of the immediate interpersonal situation, context, or experience. In addition, these studies represent initial forays into how divergent theories of the self may influence thought. We are not suggesting these differences across cultures map exactly onto the differences between Western men and women. Futhermore, the differences discussed here are global differences thought to generalize across men and women within any given culture. We suggest, however, that self-schemata of connectedness and separateness are divergent theories of the self and that they influence not just self-description and explanations for behavior, but a wide array of other perceptual and cognitive tendencies as well.

We reason then that all individuals in Western cultures will experience a powerful press to become "autonomous centers" and to develop and express their own essential uniqueness. This is the imperative that accompanies a belief in individualism. As a result, there should be a great deal of similarity in the general content of the self-concept of women and men in Western cultures and this will be increasingly so in the urban elite subcultures. Still there may be subtle but powerful differences in the nature of the self-concepts that are constructed by women and men because of the relatively greater tendencies of women to automatically focus on and incorporate *others* into their self-structure.

Origins of the Connectedness and Separateness Self-Schemata

We are proposing that differences in the structure and functioning of the self-concept derive from multiple sources. Following on Chodorow's (1978), Dinnerstein's (1977), and Miller's (1986) basic notions, one very important difference between men and women may be in their types of relations with others and in the meaning of these relations.

From Chodorow's perspective, one of the key features of the first important social environment (the child and the mother) for girls, as opposed to boys, is that of gender similarity. As children begin to individuate themselves and wonder "who am I?," girls are afforded a readily accessible answer—"I am like my mother." This answer is often encouraged directly by mothers and others in the social environment. Sons are not provided with the same experience of similarity and continuity with their mothers; a key feature of their social environment is the difference from their mothers. According to Chodorow (1978), the mother experiences the son as more of an "other," as an "external object," and thus the mother encourages the son to view himself as distinct and separate from the mother. An initial answer to the "who am I" question would then be "I am not like my mother." Chodorow assumes that gender is made salient enough to young children that they can use it in making similarity/difference distinctions.

Block (1984) also argues that male children experience a major discontinuity and sense of separation not experienced by female children as the mother, after about 18 months, automatically begins to disengage from the son. From this perspective, however, mothers begin distancing because they are consciously or unconsciously attempting to foster appropriate gender-role definitions. Such distancing between mother and son is also noted in the primate world where males are pushed into the outside world sooner than females and are essentially "peripheralized" (Nash & Ransom, 1971).

From Miller's (1986) perspective, the basic gender issue is not an issue of continuity versus distinctness from mother but a more global issue of the societal power differential between men and women. Women must learn to relate to others and be carefully attuned to others if they are to survive in male-dominated society. "Subordinates, then, know much more about the dominants than vice versa. They have to. They become highly attuned to the dominants, able to predict their reactions of pleasure and displeasure. . . . If a large part of your fate depends on accommodating to and pleasing the dominants, you concentrate on them" (pp. 10–11).

A more general social learning perspective provides yet another framework for understanding the development of different core schemata in males and females. Within this framework, maleness and femaleness are modeled by same-sex parents and significant others who foster and encourage identification by providing examples and reinforcing appropriate behavior. Males model autonomy and sharp self–other boundaries while females model connectedness and interdependence in relationships. Once established these sex-linked differences in self-definition will thus tend to perpetuate themselves.

Parents provide conceptions of how the child should be now, but they also provide a vision of the child's future. As the daughter tries to comprehend the roles worth imagining (Erikson, 1968), the mother is readily available, and in most cases, a willing model. As a result, the daughter will attend closely to the mother for in the mother is the outline of a future possible self (Markus & Nurius, 1986). To the extent that the mother models a subordinate social role for her daughter, however, the daughter's sense of the possible will be limited. As a son attempts to imagine his future, the mother typically does not offer herself as a model. The son is provided a model through his father. If the father models a dominant role, he may experience a relatively more expansive set of possibilities for the future.

A basic assumption common to these varied perspectives is that all individuals need to define themselves and will naturally look to their ongoing experiences for self-definitions. Where these perspectives differ is in which aspects of the social environment they claim as critical or essential for self-definition. However, self-definition in all these frameworks involves some assessment of similarity with others and difference from others.

A focus on difference with others is a natural extension of a normative task of discovering a unique self and then defending it from influence. A focus on continuity with or similarity with others follows from a normative task of attending to and knowing about others. Within the first normative task, a bounded, "true" self must be protected and concerns about differences between this internal truth and the presented social self naturally arise. When the normative task focuses on knowing and being attuned to the environment, the "true" self is the social, connected self. Concerns about differences between the true internal self and a presented external self are decidedly less relevant from the perspective of the connected self.

A consequence of the fact that the self-definition process normally occurs within a framework of continuity and similarity for daughters and discontinuity and differences for sons is that a view of the self as self-in-relation—the core of the connectedness self-schema—is fostered in daughters. From this sense of continuity comes the sense that to know about herself, the daughter must know about another. From very early on, learning about the self then involves a careful attention to and analysis of another. The daughter learns in this way that attention to others is critical and that others are a powerful source of self-relevant information.

A pattern of focusing on and attending to others is heavily reinforced by societal beliefs about what a woman should do to be a "good self." Continual practice in this mode provides girls with the opportunity to become exquisitely skilled in being sensitive to others—in hearing them, in sharing their internal states, in empathizing with them, and in learning from them. With increasing elaboration of this self-schema, girls become " experts" in knowing what others are thinking, in feeling what they are feeling. As a result of this expertise, they will feel relatively comfortable relying on such knowledge about themselves and others as a basis for action. In contrast, a separateness self-schema will focus boys' attention on their own skills, attributes, and talents. Others will be used as reference points for comparison. Rather than learning about the self in relationship with others, the autonomous self learns by comparing self with others.

How the Connectedness and Separateness Self-Schemata May Influence Thought

DIFFERENCES IN THE CONTENT AND STRUCTURE OF CONNECTEDNESS AND SEPARATENESS SELF-SCHEMATA

We have suggested that connectedness and separateness self-schemata can differ in their content, their structure, and their function. Our basic assertion is that, for women, relations with others will be especially significant in their self-definition. Thus women will be particularly sensitive and responsive to others, and they will have well-elaborated knowledge and understanding of others. From extensive studies in cognitive personality and social psychology, we know that cognitive structures influence thought in specific and systematic ways (see Fiske & Taylor, 1984; Markus & Zajonc, 1985).

Building on this work we can assume that individuals with connectedness self-schemata and their derivatives are especially sensitive and responsive to information that is potentially revealing of this aspect of self. These schemata summarize and integrate information that is relevant to their view of self. Furthermore, these schemata process information efficiently and retain it well. Given the attention to others that is essential for self-schemata based in connectedness, individuals will develop considerable expertise in interpersonal domains. In contrast, a separateness self-schema is sensitive to a very different type of information. These schemata are comprised of the integration of representations of the self-as-separate, and they privilege the processing of information that is relevant to this view. Individuals with such schemata will be especially responsive to stimulus configurations that are potentially informative of separateness, both their own and others.

A further claim of our approach and one that is much more difficult to evaluate is that the schemata of men and women differ not only in their content but in their structure as well. This difference in structure has a variety of consequences. The first is that the experience of reality for those with a connectedness self-schema may often be a shared reality such that what is experienced is a result of the synthesis of the individual's own experience *and* what she believes or infers the others' experience to be. In this sense, knowledge of others is used in shaping one's experience and a shared or negotiated understanding is an end in itself.

More specifically, given the proposed structure of the connectedness self-schema, when those aspects of the self that articulate its connectedness are active (see Figure 5.1), some of the representations of the others (e.g., mother, father, siblings) to which it is connected are necessarily active as well. Moreover, when schemata of important others are active, the self, or some aspects of it, will also be active because some of the representations of important others are representations of that person in relation to the self. Others are thus partially represented *within* the self-schema of connectedness.

Block (1984) has suggested that women are particularly facile at fitting or assimilating information into their existing structures. Men, in contrast, are likely to accommodate and change their structures as a result of incoming information, experiencing greater difficulty finding similarity in apparently disparate elements. She attributes this difference to the experience of male children in responding to change and discontinuity in their environment as a result of the mother pulling away at an early age. Similarly, in a provocative discussion of "maternal thinking," Ruddick (1980) suggests that mothers must preserve life, but most importantly, they must encourage growth and welcome change. The mother must be prepared for a child that changes continually and finally moves away. She argues that a mother's conceptual schema for herself, her child, and the world must necessarily be open and responsive. Her structures must be easily able to respond and assimilate children who are "irregular, unpredictable, often mysterious" (p. 352).

DIFFERENCES IN STYLE OR MODE OF THINKING

The difference in content and structure that have been outlined above have direct consequences for the way one thinks. The activation of the connectedness self-schema occasions a mode of processing in which one is particularly sensitive to the surrounding social environment. Such attention to others is necessitated by the structure of the connectedness self-schema. Representations of others are not included in separateness self-schemata and the reactions of others are not focal for such a schema. For those with a separateness self-schema, precisely mapping the interpersonal domain is less important because relatively less information is needed from it.

A further consequence of difference in the structure of separateness and connectedness self-schemata is that women, in contrast to men, will have a style or mode of perceiving and thinking that can be characterized as more connected in that the surrounding context is incorporated into the representation of the focal person or object. As a result of this pervasive tendency to include self when representing other, and to include other when representing self, it may seem unnatural and relatively difficult for those with a preponderance of connectedness self-schemata to extract the self from the perceptual and cognitive process at any time. As a result, for those with a predominance of connectedness-based schemata, extracting the self and realizing the state of so-called objectivity, in many cases, is not a meaningful process.

A mode of processing in which one is sensitive to the interpersonal environment may be related to what Belenky et al. (1986) have referred to as "women's way of knowing." Connected knowers, they argue, begin with an interest in other people and they learn through empathy with these others. In so doing they are characterized by a nonjudgmental stance and by struggling to see if they have understood the other's perspective before giving a judgment. Starting with a premise of connection with others, they avoid disagreeing, arguing or making negative judgments because such behavior would seem to violate the assumption of connection and may endanger the connection. They suggest that connected knowers then are more inclined "to believe" than "to doubt" because doubting the other may also threaten the connection. Here, as always, it is the connection with others that is self-affirming and that is the ultimate reality.

Essential to separate knowing as described by Belenky et al. (1986) is critical thinking or doubting (see also Elbow, 1973). Doubters, unlike be-lievers, do not worry about a lack of connection. Separate knowers can pull themselves away from an argument or an idea and look for something wrong—an error or a contradiction. The very goal for a separate knower is to keep the self out of the discourse, to be objective, to respond only to the arguments. This goal is completely inconsistent with a self-schema of con-nectedness. Connected knowers, Belenky et al. (1986) propose, are more comfortable with what is pejoratively labelled gossip. "Gossip concerns the personal, the particular, . . . but it does not follow that it is a trivial activ-ity" (p. 116). Based on an analysis of gossip by Spacks (1982), they argue that gossipers give each other information, but most importantly they tell each other about themselves and they create a mutual reality through the interpretations they make of the information. As Spacks says, "response to news matters more than news itself" (p. 28).

In a recent analysis, Bruner (1985) draws a similar distinction to that of separate and connected knowers. He distinguishes between "paradigma-tic" and "narrative" modes of thought. He argues that the first is the mode that characterizes science and logic, while the second is imaginative and constructive and tries to search for "the meaning of historical and personal events in their full comprehensive richness" (p. 101).

A Selective Review of Gender Differences

In this section we attempt to organize a wide array of literature that has examined gender differences in some aspects of thinking. It is important to acknowledge at the outset that this body of research is unsystematic, large-ly atheoretical, and the gender-related differences obtained are usually small. However, these data may still be useful for an initial assessment of some of our claims. Our goal is to determine if a variety of puzzling and unrelated gender differences can be organized and somewhat better under-stood by assuming that individuals' core self-schemata and their domain-specific derivatives differ in content and structure, and that these schemata can influence many aspects of thinking. Necessarily, this review is not meant to be exhaustive.

SPATIAL ABILITIES

Reports of differences between men and women in spatial abilities have intrigued researchers for over 30 years. Spatial ability tasks are thought to be comprised of at least two separate factors (Halpern, 1986). One is a visualization factor that emphasizes the ability to imagine how objects will appear when they are rotated or transformed in some way. A current and commonly used test is the Shepard–Metzler Mental Rotation test (Vandenberg & Kuse, 1978), which requires subjects to keep a complex form in memory while deciding what it would look like after it is rotated in three-dimensional space.

A second spatial ability factor is orientation, which emphasizes the ability to detect relationships and perceive patterns. A classic test of orientation is the rod-and-frame test, which requires that subjects position a rod to the vertical within a tilted frame (Witkin, Dyk, Faterson, Goodenough, & Karp, 1962). This test is said to assess "the extent to which the person perceives part of a field as discrete from the surrounding field as a whole, rather than embedded in the field" (Witkin, Moore, Goodenough, & Cox, 1977, pp. 6–7). Witkin et al. (1962) found that individuals classified as egotistical personalities could also be called egotistical in their perceptions. These people were field independent such that their perception was not influenced by the visual framework. Other studies showed a relationship between field dependence and characteristics indicating a sensitivity and receptivity to social context. Witkin and Goodenough (1977) wrote that a field-dependent person is "interested in people, wants to help others, has a concern for people, has wide acquaintanceship, knows many people, and is known to many people" (p. 672).

Although differences between men and women in field dependence and in spatial abilities have received more attention than all other gender differences together, the meaning of these differences remains unclear (see Burnett, 1986; Caplan, MacPherson & Tobin, 1985; Halpern, 1986; Sanders, Cohen, & Soares, 1986). The current picture suggests that men are consistently better than women at some spatial relations tasks. These differences between men and women in spatial abilities, although often small, are important because they are thought to underly substantial differences in math ability and perhaps in math interest as well. Most recent explanations center on brain-based differences such as sex-related differences in brain lateralization. Building on the early suggestion that these differences are probably best interpreted as a reflection of individual differences in cognitive style, we suggest that differences in how men and women represent themselves is another causal factor worthy of serious consideration.

Many spatial tasks seem to require the ability to decontextualize the self, that is, to remove the self from the present perspective in the environment and to assume instead an alternative perspective. Keeping a three-dimensional object in memory while rotating it requires mentally removing one's self from the initial viewing perspective and rapidly tracking the object's movement from a detached or separated perspective. Having a sense of self as separate, bounded, or noninterrelated may, facilitate performance on spatial tasks.

With a connectedness schema, women may have more difficulty in assuming the detached, separated perspective that is helpful to this task. The context is vitally important to a connected self. Those with connected selves will thus be relatively less familiar with removing the self from the current perspective. As a result, they are more wedded to the perspective or the orientation suggested by their initial perception of a figure. Tasks involving spatial manipulations can be solved by visualizing the self as constant and manipulating an internal image of the object or, alternatively, by visualizing the object as constant and then mentally envisioning the self moving to another perspective on the object. In either case a separate and bounded self will be easier to manipulate. And this is especially the case if the bounded self is visually or spatially represented.

We have argued earlier that boys at a relatively early age are encouraged —perhaps forced—to create a separate sense of self, a self that does not include the mother. In making this separation, they must necessarily rely on their preverbal visual/spatial skills as these are the means most available to them at this age. The early self-structure of separateness may thus be grounded in visual, spatial, or other somatic representations of the self-as-separate in space, and as detached from the environment and the context. As the separateness self-schema develops and is confirmed through interactions with the mother, these representations are repeatedly employed and further elaborated and may continue to comprise the core of the separateness self-schema.

Since girls are not pushed to differentiate from the mother as early as boys, they are likely to have some verbal capacities to bring to bear on the task when differentiation becomes necessary. Moreover, girls are often verbally precocious and able to employ a verbal mode of representation considerably earlier than boys (e.g., Maccoby & Jacklin, 1974). As a result, when beginning to individuate the self and to create a representation of the self, girls may be more likely to use verbal representations. Furthermore, the representation of self-as-connected, as in-relation, or as interdependent may lend itself more easily to verbal representation than nonverbal representation.

Because of their experience with representing the most important object in the environment—the self—in visual and spatial terms, this mode of rep-

Because of their experience with representing the most important object in the environment—the self in visual and spatial terms, this mode of representation may become especially well-elaborated and finely tuned for men. They will then have an advantage with problems that can be solved by using a visual representation (Johnson, 1984). Furthermore, when problems require a separation of self from the problem space, males may also have an advantage because of their tendency to separate the self from the environment in the service of self-definition. The male advantage in spatial tasks has been thought to emerge most clearly in adolescence (Maccoby & Jacklin, 1974). Recent work, however, suggests that when carefully tracked differences in spatial ability can be seen at a much earlier age (Johnson & Meade, 1987).

SOCIAL SENSITIVITY, EMPATHY

If males have an advantage when tasks require nonverbal and decontextualized representations of objects, females should have an advantage when tasks afford or require a verbal representation, and an appreciation of the interdependence or connection among separate objects and events. Lewis (1985) claims that interaction with humans as opposed to things requires a vicarious experience of the other's feelings and thus necessitates a self with permeable boundaries. Unfortunately, there has been much less systematic attention to defining interpersonal or social sensitivity and to formulating tasks to assess abilities of this sort or to compare differences in this ability. Most hypotheses about the greater sensitivity of women are derived from studies in which sensitivity is inferred as a mediating mechanism. For example, a recent review of interpersonal processes in close relationships (Clark & Reis, 1988) suggests that women are disturbed by relationships in which they receive more than they give, while this form of inequity does not appear to bother men. Such a finding can be used to suggest that women are more sensitive to the needs and feelings of the other.

As connectedness self-schemata become active and begin to exert their selective and directive influences on thought, individuals will automatically attend to and encode a diverse array of information—information about the self and information about the others to whom the self is connected. As one consequence of the operation of these complex connected self-schemata, females may have a greater capacity for empathy. Empathy is defined here as a vicarious affective or cognitive responding to another's state of mind. In the connectedness self-schema, important others are represented as part of the self, and thus perceivers may be as sensitive to stimuli relevant to these others as they will be to what appears as more purely self-relevant stimuli. In this sense information about these others *is* self-relevant information. As a consequence, empathic responding is almost an unavoidable response.

The literature on empathy is as fraught with controversy as the literature on spatial abilities. The review by Maccoby and Jacklin (1974) concluded that there was no evidence of sex differences in empathy, but more recent reviews have forced a reexamination of these ideas. As with spatial abilities, it is the definition of and measurement of empathy that creates challenge and confusion in this field. However, Hoffman (1977) (reviewing primarily studies with children) found that females were significantly more empathic than males. In a more recent meta-analysis, Eisenberg and Lennon (1983) found large sex differences in favor of females when measures of self-report were used, but fewer differences when physiological measures of one's reaction to another's state are compared.

From our perspective, more empathic responding should be expected when the others involved are importantly self-defining. The argument is that those with a separateness self-schema can also respond vicariously in the required manner, but that, in most cases, the response will require effort as opposed to being relatively automatic. For those with a connectedness self-schema, information about others is self-defining, and responses from these others are essential for completing the self. As indirect support of this idea, many general surveys report that women are much more likely than men to claim the well-being of their parents, children, or spouses as important sources of concern (Brody, 1981; Campbell, Converse, & Rodgers, 1976). Such concern over others may be almost inevitable for those with connectedness self-schemata. In contrast, when information about others is safely compartmentalized into separate structures relevant to these others (see Figure 5.1), such automatic activation or intrusion can be controlled by focusing on the self.

It is well documented that women experience a significantly higher level of psychological distress than men (Al-Issa, 1982). Recent analyses suggest that this distress may come not from a deficit in effective coping skills, but from a much greater involvement by women in the lives of those around them (Dohrenwend, 1977; Kessler & McLeod, 1984). Dohrenwend, for example, found that women considered a much greater variety of events to be stressful than did men. The additional events not typically considered stressful by males included life crises that occurred to the respondents' family, friends, and neighbors. Kessler and McLeod (1984) found that men are as distressed as women by serious crises that befall their children or spouses. However, men showed much less concern with the diversity of events that occur to members of the extended family, friends, and coworkers. We suggest that because of their connected self-schemata, women are automatically sensitive and responsive to information about the troubles of others. Furthermore, due to the greater complexity of their connectedness schemata, such information receives a more elaborate encoding and subsequently is easily remembered and highly accessible in working memory. Even without an explicit belief or decision that one should be concerned about another, the processes of attention and concern may be underway.

Other than studies of empathy, there are few studies that explore sensitivity to social cues (see Maccoby & Jacklin, 1974). Based on the reasoning that attending to others is the basis of self-definition and self-validation, we would expect women to reveal a genuine expertise on tasks that require careful, subtle, or quick attention to and analysis of others. The choice of tasks examined to reveal this difference is critical here, however, because men and women alike must be relatively expert in the social domain (Lykes, 1985). Without such skills it is impossible for anyone to function effectively. There are a handful of findings, however, suggestive of women's expertise in social sensitivity. Hall (1978), for example, in a review of 75 studies finds that females are significantly better than males in decoding or interpreting visual and auditory cues about another's affective state.

MEMORY

Although most people believe than men and women remember different kinds of information, there is little empirical work to document gender differences in memory (Crawford, Herrmann, Vaughan, & Robbins, 1987). While there is no reason to expect differences in digit span, for example, there is every reason to anticipate, based on the reasoning outlined above, that women may remember interpersonally relevant material more efficiently than men. The self-in-relation schema occasions more complex or elaborate encodings of such material. A meta-analysis of facial identification studies (Shapiro & Penrod, 1986) suggests that women are indeed superior at recognition memory for faces, and that this result holds true particularly when the stimuli are faces of women. Such a finding suggests that, as with empathy, gender differences may reveal themselves most clearly in ambiguous situations where the stimuli are impoverished or where quick or difficult judgments are required.

Other approaches to gender and memory suggest that women provide the collective memory and that they are the keepers of stories and myths. Such accounts often imply that women remember because it is their role to help preserve and strengthen cultural tradition. Our view suggests that women may remember interpersonal events and social experiences because with their connected self-schemata they cannot do otherwise.

INTUITION

Throughout the literature, there are references to women's "intuition" or to a special "sixth sense." Deutsch (1944) referred to the intuition of women and their ability to directly understand or perceive reality without the apparent contribution of any explicit or conscious reasoning processing. Intuition is frequently used to refer to strongly held, but unanalyzable, hunches about what is happening in a given social situation. Rather than anything mysterious, such apparent intuition may be a product of the automatic activation of connectedness self-schemata that immediately make accessible a great deal of information about the self and the other, and about their relation. Similarly, Miller (1986) suggests that this sixth sense probably develops as the subordinates learn to pay very careful attention to the dominants.

The expertise that we have suggested characterizes women in the interpersonal domain may allow them to survey a problem and then to "know" exactly what to do. In this process, they would not necessarily have access to the rapid appraisal and multiple inferences that gave rise to this "immediate" understanding. Moreover, attempts to specify them could interfere with performance. In theory, experts have different types of knowledge representation in which the elements are unitized and thus can be activated immediately as a whole. Experts can do a number of things better than novices: recognize when input information is relevant to the domain of their expertise; integrate this information with previously acquired information; and make greater use of contextual cues to improve recall (Chase & Simon, 1973; Spilich, Vesonder, Chiesi, & Voss, 1979). Such qualities of thought in women may give rise to what appears as pure, non-inferential knowledge in the interpersonal domain.

MORAL REASONING

Gilligan's (1982) groundbreaking work on moral development is directly related to the ideas we have outlined. Drawing on Chodorow's (1978) theorizing, she argues that there are two very different approaches to morality. One, the masculine approach, is born of separation and individuation; the other, the feminine approach, is focused on attachment and caring.

An overriding concern with relationships follows from an appreciation of one's fundamental relatedness and the extent to which the core self is constituted by relations with others. The reluctance to judge others and a tendency to accept others' points of view result from a desire to preserve the connection to these others. In an extension of Gilligan's (1982) work, Lyons (1983) asked subjects to describe themselves and then coded their responses for mentions of relations with others or concern for others. Those who mentioned having relationships and/or concern with others in characterizing themselves were more likely to consider the response of the others in their moral judgments. Conversely, those who described relationships in instrumental terms or referred to their skills in interacting with others more frequently used a consideration of rights in their moral judgments.

Gilligan's work has been criticized for providing a simple dichotomy and for focusing on difference instead of exploring the issue of morality more broadly (Harding, 1987). Furthermore, recent studies claim that it is factors related to gender such as level of college education or amount of work experience outside the home that is related to the individual's moral stance rather than gender per se (cf. Walker, de Vries, & Trevethan, 1987; Sher, 1987; for a summary of studies up to 1983, see Lifton, 1985). Other findings indicate that, depending on the task at hand, both men and women can be characterized as utilizing various degrees of each moral stance. This critical examination of Gilligan's work is directly relevant to our framework as well. We propose that it is the way men and women are socialized and the way they take meaning from this socialization that contributes to differences in how they make the self/nonself distinction. As men's and women's typical patterns of social interaction and interpersonal experience change, so too will their structures for organizing this experience.

Concluding Comments

We have argued that individuals with divergent schemata of the self—me-as-connected to others (a connectedness self-schema) and me-as-separate from others (a separateness self-schema)—are likely to differ in both the form and content of their basic perceptual and cognitive processes.

We began our analysis with a discussion of the probable nature of the basic connectedness or separateness self-schemata. In the course of attempting to describe these critical mediating structures, a number of important questions have been raised. Because the view of the self-as-separate, bounded, and autonomous has been the model for the ideal self in virtually all of Western psychology (Lykes, 1985), it is relatively easy to characterize this model and to speculate about the nature of self-as-separate representations. Much less consideration, however, has been given to the form of the interdependent self or to the nature of self-as-connected representations. Are relational schemata somehow more open and more flexible because they require input from the social environment before they are instantiated? Is a self-concept that is rooted in connectedness a more variable or a more complex self because its precise nature depends on relations with diverse others? And, in general, what does it mean to say that representations are shared or joint, or to say that some representations include the self together with the other?

Recently, theorists such as Hamaguchi (1985) have written insightfully about the nature of Asian selves. He describes the Japanese self as being constantly redefined and as including one's share of the lifespace that is commonly shared by both oneself and other actors. In this theory of "relational" selves, as in all analyses of non-Western selves, however, no separate attention is given to describing the self-structures of women. Moreover, it is important to keep in mind that the connected selves that Western women are developing are constructed within a culture that is the world's most extreme in terms of its press for autonomy and unfettered individualism. The development of a conception of self takes place within a cultural and a historical context. This means that developing a self-schema requires an integration of the general cultural view of the self and the specific view presented as gender appropriate within this context. The finding of general differences between Western and non-Western conceptions of self that cut across men and women in these cultures suggests that the cultural world view asserts a strong influence on all members of the culture. This is not to say that men and women do not differ within a given cultural framework, but it implies that the self-schemata of women from different cultures may differ markedly. The form these differences may take has yet to be charted.

Throughout the chapter we have speculated about the various developmental origins of connectedness and separateness self-schemata. We have argued that these core self-schemata develop early in life and are repeatedly reinforced by early socialization experiences. How these self-schemata influence later experience depends on the nature of the interaction between the early socialization and the current situational demand (Deaux & Major, 1987). To the extent that men and women are placed in situations that differentially reinforce their sense of themselves as connected and autonomous, their early tendencies and strategies will be accentuated. Furthermore, following Sedney's (1987) analysis of the development of gender identity over the lifespan, we anticipate that the specific forms taken by the connectedness and separateness schemata may well change during the course of maturation.

The last section of the chapter was devoted to hypothesizing about how connectedness and separateness self-schemata may influence perceptual and cognitive processes. We have argued that the nature of one's core self-schema may shape not just self-perception but perception and cognition generally. In attempting to assess these ideas, we briefly reviewed a variety of research areas that focus more or less directly on thinking. The findings are generally consistent with the idea that divergent theories of the self differentially constrain thinking. While a more systematic review of the research is clearly indicated, this initial analysis suggests that by focusing on the structure and function of the self-concept, we may be able to organize and at least partially explain a diverse array of sex and gender differences, ranging from differences in the rotation of three-dimensional figures to differences in capacity for empathy and susceptibility to social influence.

What remains now to be done is a careful analysis of which aspects of perception and cognition are the most likely to be systematically influenced by the nature of the self-schema and to explore the persuasiveness of this influence. It follows, for example, that those with a connectedness self-schema and those with a separateness self-schema will have somewhat different strategies for scanning or charting the terrain of the social environment. In addition, there is a diverse array of additional cognitive phenomena that may be influenced by the nature of these core self-schemata. For example, because of their expertise in interpersonal domains, will women reveal less pluralistic ignorance and also be less susceptible to the false consensus bias in which people assume that other people think, feel, and act as they do? Is it the case that women with different "ways of knowing" will be interested in different problems than men and will frame them in divergent ways? Will some problems be inherently more compelling to women because they involve seeking similarity, interdependence, integration, or convergence? One can also speculate about gender differences in other areas that imply a connection or relation between the self and other. These include social comparison, social facilitation, vicarious learning, imitation, suggestibility, and hypnosis. In the process of answering these questions, the hope is that we can further understand the precise way in which the self-system actively mediates, regulates, and constructs the individual's thoughts, feelings, and actions.

Acknowledgment. While preparing this chapter, the first author was supported by a National Science Foundation grant (BNS #84–08057).

REFERENCES

Al-Issa, I. (1982). Gender and adult psychopathology. In I. Al-Issa (Ed.), *Gender and psychopathology* (pp. 84–103). New York: Academic.

Aries, E.J., & Olver, R.R. (1985). Sex differences in the development of a separate sense of self during infancy: Directions for future research. *Psychology of Women Quarterly, 9*, 515–532.

Baldwin, J.M. (1902). *Social and ethical interpretations in mental development.* New York: Macmillan.

Belenky, M.F., Clinchy, B.M., Goldberger, N.R., & Tarule, J.M. (1986). *Women's ways of knowing: The development of self, voice, and mind.* New York: Basic Books.

Bem, S.L. (1981). Gender schema theory: A cognitive account of sex typing. *Psychological Review, 88*, 354–364.

Block, J.H. (1973). Conceptions of sex role: Some cross cultural and longitudinal perspectives. *American Psychologist, 28*, 512–526.

Block, J.H. (1984). How gender differences affect children's orientations to the world. In *Sex role identity and ego development.* San Francisco: Jossey-Bass.

Bowlby, J. (1980). *Attachment and loss*, Vol. III. New York: Basic Books.

Brody, E.M. (1981). Women in the middle and family help to older people. *The Gerontologist, 21*, 471–480.

Brody, E.M. (1985). Gender differences in emotional development: A review of theories and research. In A.J. Stewart & M.B. Lykes (Eds.), *Gender and personality: Current perspectives on theory and research.* Durham, NC: Duke University Press.

Brooks, J., & Lewis, M. (1974). The effect of time on attachment as measured in a free play situation. *Child Development, 45*, 311–316.

Bruner, J.S. (1985). Narrative and paradigmatic modes of thought. In *Learning and teaching the ways of knowing. 84th yearbook of the National Society for the Study of Education* (pp. 97–115). Chicago: University of Chicago Press.

Burnett, S.A. (1986). Sex-related differences in spatial ability: Are they trivial? *American Psychologist, 41*, 1012–1014.

Campbell, A., Converse, P., & Rodgers, W. (1976). *The quality of American life: Perceptions, evaluations, and satisfactions.* New York: Russell Sage.

Cantor, N., & Kihlstrom, J.F. (1987). *Personality and social intelligence.* Englewood Cliffs, NJ: Prentice-Hall.

Caplan, P.J., MacPherson, G.M., & Tobin, P. (1985). Do sex-related differences in spatial abilities exist?: A multilevel critique with new data. *American Psychologist, 40* (7), 786–799.

Chase, W.G., & Simon, H.A. (1973). Perception and chess. *Cognitive Psychology, 4*, 55–81.

Chodorow, N. (1978). *The reproduction of mothering: Psychoanalysis and the sociology of gender.* Berkeley: University of California Press.

Clark, M.S., & Reis, H.T. (1988). Interpersonal processes in close relationships. *Annual Review of Psychology, 39,* 609–672.

Clarke-Stewart, K.A., & Hevey, C.M. (1981). Longitudinal relations in repeated observations of mother–child interaction from one to two and one-half years. *Developmental Psychology, 17,* 127–145.

Clarke-Stewart, K.A., VanderStoep, L.P., & Killian, G.A. (1979). Analysis and replication of mother and child relations at two years of age. *Child Development, 50,* 777–793.

Cousins, S. (1989). *Culture and selfhood in Japan and the U.S. Journal of Personality and Social Psychology,* in press.

Crawford, M., Herrmann, D.J., Vaughan, J., & Robbins, D. (1987). *Gender and beliefs about memory.* Paper presented at meeting of the Eastern Psychological Association, Arlington VA, April.

Deaux, K., & Major, B. (1987). Putting gender into context: An interactive model of gender-related behavior. *Psychological Review, 94* (3), 369–389.

Deutsch, H. (1944). *The psychology of women: A psychoanalytic interpretation.* New York: Grune & Stratton.

Dinnerstein, D. (1977). *The mermaid and the minotaur.* New York: Harper & Row.

Dixon, V. (1976). World views and research methodology. In L.M. King, V. Dixon, & W.W. Nobles (Eds.), *African philosophy: Assumptions and paradigms for research on black persons.* Los Angeles: Fanon Center Publication, Charles R. Drew Postgraduate Medical School.

Dohrenwend, B.S. (1977). Social status and stressful life events. *Journal of Personality and Social Psychology, 9,* 203–214.

Dumont, L. (1970). *Homo hierarchicus.* Chicago: University of Chicago Press.

Eisenberg, N., & Lennon R. (1983). Sex differences in empathy and related capacities. *Psychological Bulletin, 94,* 100–131.

Elbow, P. (1973). *Writing without teachers.* London: Oxford University Press.

Erikson, E.H. (1968). *Identity, youth and crisis.* New York: Norton.

Fagot, B.I. (1974). Sex differences in toddlers' behavior and parental reaction. *Developmental Psychology, 10,* 554–558.

Fast, I. (1985). *Event theory: A Piaget–Freud integration.* Hillsdale, NJ: Erlbaum.

Fiske, S.T., & Taylor, S.E. (1984). *Social cognition.* Reading, MA: Addison-Wesley.

Geertz, C. (1973). *The interpretation of cultures.* New York: Basic Books.

Geertz, C. (1975). On the nature of anthropological understanding. *American Scientist, 63,* 47–53.

Gilligan, C. (1982). *In a different voice: Psychological theory and women's development.* Cambridge, MA: Harvard University Press.

Goldberg, S., & Lewis, M. (1969). Play behavior in the year-old infant: Early sex differences. *Child Development, 40,* 21–31.

Greenberg, J.R., & Mitchell, S.A. (1983). *Object relations in psychoanalytic theory.* Cambridge, MA: Harvard University Press.

Gunnar, M.G., & Donahue, M. (1980). Sex differences in social responsiveness between six months and twelve months. *Child Development, 51,* 262–265.

Hall, J.A. (1978). Gender effects in decoding nonverbal cues. *Psychological Bulle-*

tin, *85*, 845–858.

Hallowell, I. (1955). The self and its behavioral environment. *Culture and experience*. Philadelphia, University of Pennsylvania Press.

Halpern, D.F. (1986). A different answer to the question, "Do sex-related differences in spatial abilities exist?" *American Psychologist*, *41*, 1014–1015.

Hamaguchi, E. (1985). A contextual model of the Japanese: Toward a methodological innovation in Japanese studies. *Journal of Japanese Studies*, *11*, 289–321.

Harding, S. (1987). The curious coincidence of feminine and African moralities: Challenges for feminist theory. In E.F. Kittay & D.T. Meyers (Eds.), *Women and moral thought*. Totowa, NJ: Rowman & Littlefield.

Hare-Mustin, R.I., & Marecek, J. (1986). Autonomy and gender: Some questions for therapists. *Psychotherapy*, *23*, 205–212.

Haviland, J.J., & Malatesta, C.Z. (1981). The development of sex differences in nonverbal signals: Fallacies, facts and fantasies. In C. Mayo & N. Henley (Eds.), *Gender and nonverbal behavior*. New York: Springer-Verlag.

Heelas, P. (1980). The model applied: Anthropology and indigenous psychologies. In P. Heelas & A. Lock, (Eds.), *Indigenous psychologies: The anthropology of the self*. New York: Academic.

Hoffman, M.L. (1977). Sex differences in empathy and related behaviors. *Psychological Bulletin*, *54*, 712–722.

Jacobson, E. (1964). *The self and the object world*. New York: International Universities Press.

Johnson, E.S. (1984). Sex differences in problem solving. *Journal of Educational Psychology*, *76*, 1359–1371.

Johnson, E.S., & Meade, A.C. (1987). Developmental patterns of spatial ability: An early sex difference. *Child Development*, *58*, 725–740.

Kelly, P. (1976). The relation of infant's temperament and mother's psychopathology to interactions in early infancy. In K.F. Riegel & J.A. Meacham (Eds.), *The developing individual in a changing world* (Vol. II, pp. 664–675). Chicago: Aldine.

Kelly, W. (1987). *The taut and the empathic: Antinomies of Japanese personhood*. Unpublished manuscript.

Kernberg, O. (1976). *Object relations theory and clinical psychoanalysis*. New York: Jason Aronson.

Kessler, R.C., & McLeod, J.D. (1984). Sex differences in vulnerability to undesirable life events. *American Sociological Review*, *49*, 620–631.

Klein, R.P., & Durefee, J.J. (1978). Effect of sex and birth order on infant social behavior. *Infant Behavior and Development*, *1*, 106–117.

Korner, A. (1969). Neonatal startles, smiles, erections, and reflex sucks as related to state, age, and individuality. *Child Development*, *40*, 1039–1053.

Lebra, T.S. (1976). *Japanese patterns of behavior*. Honolulu: University of Hawaii Press.

Lewis, H.B. (1985). Depression vs. paranoia: Why are there sex differences in mental illness? In A.J. Stewart & M.B. Lykes (Eds.), *Gender and personality: Current perspectives on theory and research*. Durham, NC: Duke University Press.

Lewis, M. (1969). Infants' responses to facial stimuli during the first year of life. *Developmental Psychology*, *1*, 75–86.

Lewis, M. (1972). State as an infant–environment interaction: An analysis of mother–infant interaction as a function of sex. *Merrill-Palmer Quarterly, 18,* 95–121.

Lewis, M., Kagan, J., & Kalafat, E. (1966). Patterns of fixation in the young infant. *Child Development, 37,* 331–341.

Lewis, M., & Weintraub, M. (1974). Sex of parent, sex of child: Socioemotional development. In R.C. Friedman, R.M. Richard, & R.L. Van de Wiele (Eds.), *Sex differences in behavior.* New York: Wiley.

Lifton, P. (1985). Individual differences in moral development: The relation of sex, gender, and personality to morality. In A.J. Stewart & M.B. Lykes (Eds.), *Gender and personality: Current perspectives on theory and research.* Durham, NC: Duke University Press.

Lykes, M.B. (1985). Gender and individualistic vs. collectivist bases for notions about the self. In A.J. Stewart & M.B. Lykes (Eds.), *Gender and personality: Current perspectives on theory and research.* Durham, NC: Duke University Press.

Lyons, N. (1983). Two perspectives on self, relationships and morality. *Harvard Educational Review, 53,* 125–145.

Maccoby, E.E., & Jacklin, C.N. (1974). *The psychology of sex differences.* Stanford, CA: Stanford University Press.

Maccoby, E.E., & Jacklin, C.N. (1980). Sex differences in aggression: A rejoinder and reprise. *Child Development, 51,* 964–980.

Mahler, M., Pine, F., & Bergman, A. (1975). *The psychological birth of the human infant: Symbiosis and individuation.* New York: Basic Books.

Margolin, G., & Patterson, G.R. (1975). Differential consequences provided by mothers and fathers for their sons and daughters. *Developmental Psychology, 11,* 537–538.

Markus, H. (1977). Self-schemata and processing information about the self. *Journal of Personality and Social Psychology, 35,* 63–78.

Markus, H., Crane, M., Bernstein, S., & Siladi, M. (1982). Self-schemas and gender. *Journal of Personality and Social Psychology, 42,* 38–50.

Markus, H., & Nurius, P. (1986). Possible selves. *American Psychologist, 41,* 954–969.

Markus, H., Smith, J., & Moreland, R.L. (1985). The role of the self-concept in the perception of others. *Journal of Personality and Social Psychology, 49,* 1494–1512.

Markus, H., & Zajonc, R.B. (1985). The cognitive perspective in social psychology. In G. Lindzey & E. Aronson (Eds.), *The handbook of social psychology* (Vol. I, pp. 137–230). New York: Random House.

Marsella, A., De Vos, G., & Hsu, F. (1985). *Culture and self.* London: Tavistock.

Messer, S.B., & Lewis, M. (1982). Social class and sex differences in the attachment and play behavior of the year-old infant. *Merrill-Palmer Quarterly, 18,* 295–306.

Miller, J.G. (1984). Culture and the development of everyday social explanation. *Journal of Personality and Social Psychology, 46,* 961–978.

Miller, J.B. (1986). *Toward a new psychology of women,* 2nd ed. Boston: Beacon Press.

Moss, H. (1984). Early sex differences in the mother–infant interaction. In R.

Friedman, R. Reichert, & R. Vande Weile (Eds.), *Sex differences in behavior.* New York: Wiley.

Murphy, L.B., & Moriarty, A.E. (1976). Vulnerability, coping, and growth. New Haven, CT: Yale University Press.

Nash, L., & Ransom, T. (1971). *Socialization in baboons at the Gombi Stream National Park, Tanzania.* Paper presented at meeting of the American Anthropological Association, New York, September.

Ruddick, S. (1980). Maternal thinking. *Feminist Studies, 6,* 70–96. Reprinted in A. Cafagna, R. Peterson, & C. Staudenbaur (Eds.), *Child nurturance: Volume 1, Philosophy, children and the family.* New York: Plenum Press, 1982.

Sampson, E.E. (1988). The debate on individualism: Indigenous psychologies of the individual and their role in personal and societal functioning. *American Psychologist, 43,* 15–22.

Sanders, B., Cohen, M.R., & Soares, M.P. (1986). The sex difference in spatial ability: A rejoinder. *American Psychologist, 41,* 1015–1016.

Schneider, D. (1976). Notes toward a theory of culture. In K. Basso & H. Selby (Eds.), *Meaning in anthropology* (pp. 197–220). Albuquerque: University of New Mexico Press.

Sedney, M.A. (1987). Development of androgyny: Parental influences. *Psychology of Women Quarterly, 11,* 311–326.

Shapiro, P., & Penrod, S. (1986). Meta-analysis of facial identification studies. *Psychological Bulletin, 100,* 139–156.

Sher, G. (1987). Other voices, other rooms? Women's psychology and moral theory. In E.F. Kittay & D.T. Meyers (Eds.), *Women and moral theory.* Totowa, NJ: Rowman & Littlefield.

Shweder, R.A., & Bourne, E.J. (1984). Does the concept of the person vary cross-culturally? In R.A. Shweder & R.A. Levine (Eds.), *Culture theory: Essays on mind, self, and emotion* (pp. 158–199). New York: Cambridge University Press.

Shweder, R.A., & Levine, R.A. (1984). *Culture theory.* New York: Cambridge University Press.

Spacks, P. (1982). In praise of gossip. *Hudson Review, 35,* 19–38.

Spilich, G.J., Vesonder, G.T., Chiesi, H.L., & Voss, J.F. (1979). Text processing of domain-related information for individuals with high and low domain knowledge. *Journal of Verbal Learning and Verbal Behavior, 18,* 275–290.

Stewart, A.J., & Lykes, M.B. (1985). Conceptualizing gender in personality theory and research. In A.J. Stewart & M.B. Lykes (Eds.), *Gender and personality: Current perspectives on theory and research.* Durham, NC: Duke University Press.

Vandenberg, S., & Kuse, A.R. (1978). Mental rotations: A group test of three-dimensional spatial visualization. *Perceptual and Motor Skills, 47,* 599–604.

Veroff, J. (1983). Contexual determinants of personality. *Personality and Social Psychology Bulletin, 9,* 331–344.

Walker, L.J., de Vries, B., & Treventhan, S.D. (1987). Moral stages and moral orientations in real-life and hypothetical dilemmas. *Child Development, 58,* 842–858.

Walraven, M. (1974). *Mother and infant cardiac responses during breast and bottle feeding.* Unpublished dissertation, Michigan State University, Lansing.

White, G.M., & Kirkpatick, J. (Eds.) (1985). *Person, self, and experience: Exploring Pacific ethnopsychologies.* Los Angeles: University of California Press.

Witkin, H.A., Dyk, R.B., Faterson, H.F., Goodenough, D.R., & Karp, S.A. (1962). *Psychological differentiation: Studies of development.* New York: Wiley.

Witkin, H.A., & Goodenough, D.R. (1977). Field dependence and interpersonal behavior. *Psychological Bulletin, 84,* 661–689.

Witkin, H.A., Moore, C.A., Goodenough, D.R., & Cox, P.W. (1977). Field-dependent and field-independent cognitive styles and their educational implications. *Review of Educational Research, 47,* 1–64.

6
Agreeing to Differ: Feminist Epistemologies and Women's Ways of Knowing

Mary Crawford

"The Brain: His and Hers;" "The Truth About Sex Differences;" "Just How the Sexes Differ;" "She and He: Different Brains?" and "The Gender Factor in Math: A New Study Says Males May Be Naturally Abler Than Females"—all are titles of recent features in mass-circulation magazines. When the popular press reports psychological research on sex differences, the message is that psychologists have discovered universal, fundamental differences that explain the behavior and social positions of women and men. Most of these "discoveries" are announced with no mention of the existence of contradictory evidence or diverse viewpoints within the field (Beckwith, 1984). But the extent and meaning of sex differences in personality, cognitive abilities, and behavior have been divisive issues among psychologists.

Feminist psychologists have a long tradition of skepticism about sex differences. Many of the first generation of women in the field devoted their research careers to demolishing their male colleagues' empirically indefensible beliefs about cognitive sex differences (Rosenberg, 1982). Their contemporary counterparts have, for the most part, maintained that research on sex differences should not be a major project for psychology and have characterized the literature as inconsistent, atheoretical, and inconclusive (Deaux, 1984; Sherif, 1979; Unger, 1979).

Recently, however, new claims have been made about modes of moral reasoning (Gilligan, 1982) and thinking (Belenky, Clinchy, Goldberger, & Tarule, 1986) more characteristic of women than men. These research projects, which are informed by feminist values, have been acclaimed as groundbreaking, revolutionary, and celebratory of women's strengths. How can the new claims of difference best be evaluated? If masculinist values have undermined the validity of past sex difference research, do feminist values lead to more valid research or merely substitute a different set of biases? Given the long-standing minimization of difference in feminist psychology, can these new differences be accommodated? Can feminist psychologists agree on the question of difference, or must we agree to disagree?

Although the minimization and maximization of difference exist side by side in current feminist theorizing on the psychology of women (Hare-Mustin & Marecek, 1988), they have rarely been compared directly. Partly this is because most maximizing analyses are based on psychodynamically derived clinical evidence and most minimizing ones originate in quantitatively oriented experimental psychology. Outside psychology, the more impressionistic and qualitative models are often very influential. Witness, for example, the rapid acceptance and continuing influence in women's studies of Chodorow's (1978) *The Reproduction of Mothering*. Within psychology, however, proponents of each approach tend to dismiss the other. Debates among psychologists about the empirical validity of the work of Chodorow (1978) and Miller (1976), for example, often center on whether the verbal statements of clients as interpreted by their therapists constitute acceptable evidence about normal developmental processes (Rossi, 1981).

The question of how to evaluate claims of difference is complicated by the changes in research methods and values brought about by feminist scholarship. As in other disciplines, placing women at the center of inquiry has led to questioning fundamental assumptions underlying the theories and practices that define the discipline (McIntosh, 1983). In psychology, questioning has included the concept of objectivity, the assumption that methods are value-free (Crawford & Marecek, 1988; Sherif, 1979), and the utility of various epistemological stances (see Chapter 1 in this volume).

In this chapter I examine research on "women's ways of knowing" (Belenky et al., 1986) from two epistemological stances (Harding, 1986). The first is a *feminist empiricist* view, which argues that sex bias in scientific research can be corrected by stricter adherence to rules of good research design and norms of correct interpretation. The second is a *feminist standpoint* view, which maintains that women's experiences as members of a subjugated group provide them with unique perspectives for understanding social relations. The two stances lead to very different judgments of the validity of *Women's Ways of Knowing* and its usefulness for women. Finally, I consider the popularization of the idea that there are uniquely feminine modes of thought, showing that difference takes on a third set of meanings when it leaves the academy and enters popular media.

Ways of Knowing Women's Ways of Knowing

In their book, Mary Belenky and her colleagues Blythe Clinchy, Nancy Goldberger, and Jill Tarule used structured interviews of 135 women to assess women's "ways of knowing:" that is, "perspectives from which women view reality and draw conclusions about truth, knowledge, and authority" (p. 3). Their interviewees were a diverse group of 90 selected students in six heterogeneous academic institutions (25 of whom had been interviewed earlier for a different research project) and 45 mothers who were clients in helping agencies (15 of whom were interviewed again a year after the initial contact).

The conceptual scheme used for classifying the women's responses built on the work of Perry (1970). Perry used a sequence of four yearly interviews with Harvard undergraduates of the 1950s and 1960s to describe how students' epistemological stances and understanding of themselves as knowers changed during the undergraduate years. (Perry believed that the Radcliffe women he tested followed the same developmental pattern as the Harvard men, and he did not report their results separately.)

Belenky et al. discerned five major epistemological positions in their interviewees: *silence*, in which women experience themselves as "mindless and voiceless and subject to the whims of external authority;" *received knowledge*, in which women perceive themselves as capable of taking in knowledge from external authorities but incapable of original thought; *subjective knowledge*, in which truth is perceived as personal and intuitive; *procedural knowledge*, in which women focus on applying objective procedures for learning and communicating; and *constructed knowledge*, in which all knowledge is seen as contextual and women value both objective and subjective ways of knowing, seeing themselves as creators as well as receivers of knowledge. Within the procedural category, the authors distinguish between *connected* and *separate* modes; the terms are taken from Gilligan (1982) and Lyons (1983) and are used to describe knowledge established through care and intimacy versus impersonal procedures.

Rather than quantitative or statistical analyses of their interview material, Belenky et al. relied on a qualitative content analysis. The number of women who held each perspective is not specified. The "silence" and "constructed knowledge" positions were rare, with not more than two or three women (about 2% of the sample) classified in each. "Almost half" of the women were subjectivists; younger women were the majority of received knowers, and college students the majority of procedural knowers.

How do the methods and modes of interpretation of *Women's Ways of Knowing* fare when judged by the criteria feminist empiricist researchers have applied to masculinist claims of difference? How do they fare when judged as examples of feminist standpoint research? I now turn to a critical examination of *Women's Ways of Knowing* from these two contrasting epistemological perspectives.

Beyond "Sentimental Rot and Drivel:" Feminist Empiricism and Sex Difference Research

An important contribution of feminist psychology from its inception has been to expose the exaggeration of sex difference in scientific research. The first generation of scientifically trained women devoted much research effort to challenging accepted wisdom about the extent and nature of differences. Helen Thompson Wooley, for example, conducted the first experimental laboratory study of sex differences in mental traits, using a variety of innovative measures. In interpreting her results she stressed the overall similarity of the sexes and the environmental determinants of observed differences, remarking acerbically in a 1910 *Psychological Bulletin* article that "there is perhaps no field aspiring to be scientific where flagrant personal bias, logic martyred in the cause of supporting a prejudice, unfounded assertions, and even sentimental rot and drivel, have run riot to such an extent as here" (p. 340). Among the women inspired by her work was Leta Stetter Hollingworth, who challenged the Darwinian view that women are innately less variable (and therefore less likely to be highly creative or intelligent) (Shields, 1982). The work of these women was influential in undermining biological determinism in psychology, opening the way for critical empirical research to replace unexamined assumptions about women's "natural" limitations (Rosenberg, 1982).

But an increase in the amount and sophistication of empirical research did not guarantee a less biased approach to the question of difference. Critics have again found it necessary to point out that the vast but atheoretical literature on sex differences resists coherent interpretation (Deaux, 1984; Maccoby & Jacklin, 1974; Unger, 1979) and have again charged that "psychology is replete with inconsequential, accidental, and incidental findings of 'sex differences'" that often are distorted, exaggerated, and miscited (Grady, 1981, pp. 632–633). Like their intellectual foremothers, they have concentrated on exposing both faulty methods and masculinist values and on showing how the two interact. Even recent advances in techniques for meta-analysis (Eagly, 1987; Hyde & Linn, 1986), which provide improved ways of aggregating and interpreting data from large numbers of studies, cannot wholly compensate for the biases in the original studies or ensure "objective" interpretation (Unger & Crawford, in press).

In reaction to the exaggeration and politicization of sex differences in research, the project of feminist empiricism has been to show that with better (less biased and more sophisticated) research methods, sex differences diminish in frequency, reliability, and predictive power. It has claimed that the documentation of more such differences is far less interesting and important than other lines of research. At best, it claims, the reporting of sex differences is merely descriptive, not explanatory (Deaux, 1984; Unger, 1979). At worst, it is a fundamentally misguided attempt to justify the existence of unequal social categories. This work has had a great deal of conceptual and practical impact. It has not only demonstrated once again the exaggeration of sex difference in the scientific literature, it has delineated the methods and mechanisms of exaggeration.

The feminist empiricist critique of sex-biased methods has been nicely summarized by Jacklin (1981), who enumerated ten "ubiquitous" methodological flaws in difference research:

The methodological issues in the study of sex-related differences include: 1) conceptualization of the term "difference," 2) failure to distinguish the significance of an effect from the size of an effect, 3) bias toward positive findings in the publishing . . . and reprinting of results, 4) confusion of within-sex differences with between-sex differences, 5) assuming that all sex-related differences are expressions of genetic or innate differences, 6) confusion of sex-of-stimuli effects with sex-of-subject effects, 7) interaction of sex-of-experimenter effects with sex-of-subject effects, 8) disregard of systematic differences in self-report of males and females, 9) reliance upon a narrow data base in terms of subject characteristics from which most sex-related differences are generalized, 10) the number of variables confounded with sex which make comparisons of sex difficult.

Though feminist psychologists have focused on claims of difference articulated by men (or people whose values were judged masculinist), the tools of this perspective can also be applied to women's (and feminists') claims. Has *Women's Ways of Knowing* succeeded in avoiding the "ubiquitous methodological problems" described by Jacklin (1981)? On the contrary, several of the logical and conceptual flaws Jacklin described are apparent in *Women's Ways of Knowing* and, from this perspective, are very probably the source of the spurious "difference" it discovers.

To begin with, it is impossible to demonstrate a sex difference (or a sex similarity) if only one sex is studied (the fourth error in Jacklin's list). Characterizing this error as "glaring, but common," Jacklin gives examples of studies that measured behaviors of only one sex and erroneously drew conclusions about differences between the sexes—for example, measuring the relationship between hormonal levels and mood only in women and concluding that only women show such relationships. Yet the claims of sex difference in *Women's Ways of Knowing* are based on exactly this approach, studying people of one sex and speculating about how people of the other sex might or might not differ if they had also been studied. Whether men hold the epistemological positions characterized as "women's" ways of knowing remains an empirical question.

Perhaps Belenky et al. intended only to add information about women to already existing information about men, or to compare theoretical constructs about ways of thinking, regardless of gender, rather than to claim that their women's ways of knowing were in any way different from men's. But their analysis is based specifically on the premise that women's experience is different from men's and produces the differences between their sample and Perry's. Detailed comparisons with the men in Perry's (1970) study (and other research on male intellectual development) are made throughout the book, and although other factors, such as social class, are considered as possibly accounting for difference, sex itself is seen as central. Thus the study uses research on one sex to make claims about sex difference and then views the created difference as explainable by sex (cf. Unger, 1979).

This limitation is most clear when Belenky et al. (1986) explain the origins of differences in ways of knowing. Focusing on a male-oriented (competitive and individualistic) educational system, they conclude that women are uniquely and in their totality different from men in being harmed by competition and requiring a supportive environment. But differences in class size, teacher sex, and other factors may be as important in influencing classroom interaction as whether the student is female or male (Crawford & MacLeod, 1988). And, as Jacquelynne Eccles (Chapter 2) and others (e.g., Johnson & Johnson, 1987) have documented, highly competitive classrooms benefit a small minority even among white males.

Deciding what constitutes an appropriately comparable sample of women and men is another methodological problem. Jacklin (1981) maintains that the number of variables that are confounded with sex (error 10) is "the most pervasive problem in sex-related research." Even when a researcher makes a determined attempt to measure comparable males and females in the same study, it is often unclear what characteristics should be matched and which are irrelevant. Male and female college students who are matched on level of formal education will have very different backgrounds in mathematics, science, and the humanities, starting in high school (see Chapter 2) and will be concentrated in different courses of study in college. These differences may be irrelevant to some research questions but crucial to others. The comparisons made by Belenky et al. (1986) of their sample of women with Perry's (1970) sample of men are even more problematic than typical college-student comparisons because the two groups differed in many nontrivial ways. Perry's men were all Harvard undergraduates, a much more homogeneous group than Belenky et al.'s women in social class, age, ethnicity, and educational level. They were also part of a different age cohort. If one imagines a diverse 1970s sample of men including welfare clients, students at junior colleges and elite liberal arts colleges, older returning students, minority people, and victims of child abuse—that is, a male sample comparable to Belenky et al.'s females—the possible impact of factors other than gender can be conceptualized. Would any researcher expect such a sample to share the exact epistemological stances of 1950s Harvard undergraduates?

This is not to argue that researchers should study only Harvard undergraduates, or that women's and men's experiences in our culture are identical, even when they are "matched" by researchers. But the understanding of differences attributable to sex and gender is not served by indirect comparisons that confound sex and gender with many other variables.

A similar argument applies to claims about differences among women. Although the Belenky et al. sample of women differed in age, ethnicity, and class, these were not varied systematically, and therefore their contribution to the differences obtained *among women* cannot be assessed. The fact that all the "silenced" women were poor, most of the "subjectivists" young, and all the "procedural knowers" college students is uninterpretable. Whether these differences are class-related, age-related, dependent on level of formal schooling, or due to situational or methodological factors (e.g., students and nonstudents were given different forms of the interview schedule) is impossible to determine.

Other methodological confounds are evident in *Women's Ways of Knowing*. In comparing their women interviewees with Perry's men, the researchers recognize but discount the importance of the fact that the two groups were asked different questions in the context of different interview schedules. This bears some similarity to Jacklin's error (#6) of comparing males and females who are given "feminine" and "masculine" versions of a test, respectively. In addition, Perry's men were interviewed over four years, allowing a developmental picture to emerge for each individual. Although *Women's Ways of Knowing* is subtitled *The development of self, voice, and mind*, its authors acknowledge that it is not a developmental study. Most of the women were interviewed only once, making comparisons with Perry's men problematic on this dimension as well.

Finally, Jacklin (1981) notes that there is a sex-related difference in responding to self-report measures. Females are more willing or able to disclose personal feelings. She notes that "self-report may be the only possible way to study many aspects of adult feelings and behavior, but concern for the bias that this type of data collection produces must be taken into account. We should either attempt to estimate the defensiveness of subjects or attempt to validate the self-report measures more carefully than has been done" (pp. 270–271). Because Belenky and her colleagues developed an original questionnaire for their study, none of the traditional measures of validity and reliability are available.

The work of Gilligan (1982) has also been criticized from the feminist empiricist standpoint; some of those criticisms are relevant here because Gilligan's research provided a conceptual background for *Women's Ways of Knowing*. The two studies share the problem of having deduced sex differences from indirect comparisons. Gilligan's claim that women have a unique orientation of care and connectedness in moral decisionmaking is based largely on her study of real-life moral reasoning of women facing the crisis of an unwanted pregnancy. Studying a small sample of women, she compared their responses to those of men solving hypothetical moral dilemmas in earlier research by Kohlberg. The women in Gilligan's study should have been compared with men facing real-life dilemmas; for example, the men responsible for the unwanted pregnancies could have been questioned and their responses compared to those of the women (Colby & Damon, 1983). Unless similar women and men are compared in similar situations, claims of difference cannot be logically sustained. When direct comparisons are made, and occupational/educational background controlled, gender differences in ethical orientation and moral reasoning disappear (Walker, 1984). Thus the better controlled a study is the less likely it is to find "sex" differences (Jacklin, 1981).

By empiricist criteria then, *Women's Ways of Knowing* has methodological flaws and inadequacies that compromise its scientific validity. But un-covering methodological inadequacy in research done by feminist psycho-logists also uncovers epistemological contradictions and paradoxes in the feminist empiricist perspective. The implicit claim of this perspective is that, since androcentric values make for sexism in methods and the result is "bad science," feminists can remove bias and create "good science" by substituting a different set of researchers and a different set of values. Thus *Women's Ways of Knowing* and *In a Different Voice* can be seen as attempts to add a female (or feminist) perspective to scientific knowledge. But the empiricist argument that scientific methods, when properly ap-plied, are value-neutral and capable of discovering objective facts about reality conflicts with the claim that women (or feminists) *as a group* pro-duce better science than men (or nonfeminists). "Thus, feminist attempts to reform what is perceived as bad science bring to our attention deep logical incoherences and what, paradoxically, we can call empirical inade-quacies in empiricist epistemologies" (Harding, 1986, p. 26).

"Hand, Brain, and Heart:" Feminist Standpoint Epistemologies and Sex Difference Research

Feminist standpoint theorists maintain that scientists working from within women's unique position in social life can provide understandings of the natural and social world that are not possible from within men's social position. Although different theorists emphasize different aspects of women's experience as crucial in providing the basis for a distinctive episte-mological stance, their theories all originate in the idea that "men's domi-nating position in social life results in partial and perverse understanding, whereas women's subjugated position provides the possibility of more complete and less perverse understanding" (Harding, 1986, p. 26). Hilary Rose (1983), for example, stresses the division of labor. Women's tradi-tional work, she argues, is characterized by a unity of mental, emotional, and physical activity. When women bring their characteristic "caring labor" practices to scientific inquiry, they challenge the masculinist (and capitalist) division of scientific labor into classes of people who "do" (tech-nicians, research assistants, custodians) and those who "think" (the scien-tists who generate and direct research projects). Rose also argues that a feminist epistemology must be grounded in the goals and practices of the women's movement. The goal of a science fully informed by feminism would be to increase women's knowledge and control of their own minds and bodies. Thus, according to Rose, a distinctive feminist standpoint emerges in the work of feminist researchers in areas of inquiry where work can be organized as "craft labor."

More generally, Fee (1986) defines feminist science in terms of three characteristics. First, it places women at the center of inquiry. Feminist psychologists have long criticized the discipline for overreliance on males as objects of study and for asking only masculinist questions (e.g., Sherif, 1979). Second, it reduces or eliminates the boundary between the knower and the object of study. In psychology, this would mean relinquishing the belief that only the "subject" is emotionally involved in the outcome of the research and is incapable of understanding her or his own experience without the aid of the "objective" experimenter. Third, it employs knowledge in order to liberate women, not to dominate or control them. Like Rose, Fee maintains that women (or feminists) make better scientists than men (or nonfeminists).

The feminist values orientation underlying the research by Belenky and her colleagues is clearly articulated in their book. They justify the study of women by maintaining that women's experience differs systematically from men's experience because women's position in society determines the social relations and activities in which women engage. Therefore the epistemological perspectives articulated by men do not represent the human experience but the male experience. To obtain complete and undistorted knowledge, women must be the focus of inquiry:

In our study we chose to listen only to women. The male experience has been so powerfully articulated that we believed we would hear the patterns in women's voices more clearly if we held at bay the powerful templates men have etched in the literature and in our minds. (p. 9)

The study of women who vary in ethnicity, age, and social class also reflects feminist values of seeking to understand not only sexism but other forms of oppression:

Including women from different ethnic backgrounds and a broad range of social classes enabled us to begin to examine and see beyond our own prejudices. It also allowed us to examine the injustices of the society by comparing women who were challenged and stimulated by the most elaborate of educations with women who were essentially uneducated. (pp. 13–14)

The researchers reflected practices of the women's movement in undertaking the task collectively, reaching conclusions by consensus and sharing authorship equally:

During our work together, the four of us developed among ourselves an intimacy and collaboration which we have come to prize. We believe that the collaborative, egalitarian spirit so often shared by women should be more carefully nurtured in the work lives of all men and women. . . .

In collaborating on writing this book we searched for a single voice—a way of submerging our individual perspectives for the sake of the collective "we." Not that we denied our individual convictions or squelched our objections to one another's points of view—we argued, tried to persuade, even cried at times when we reached an impasse of understanding—but we learned to listen to each other, to build on each others' insights, and eventually to arrive at a way of communicating as a collective what we believe. (p. ix)

The project also exemplifies Rose's conceptualization of feminist science as "craft labor" involving hand, brain, and heart (Rose, 1983). Belenky and her colleagues conducted the lengthy interviews themselves and devised a laborious method of content analysis. They describe this method as providing a qualitative, involved understanding of the phenomenological world of the interviewees rather than a distanced, pseudo-objective one.

From a feminist standpoint perspective then, *Women's Ways of Knowing* has strengths that are obscured by an empiricist perspective. In contrast to the minimization of difference that has characterized most feminist empiricism, feminist standpoint theorists seek out differences. Unlike masculinist claims about "women's natures," their claims of difference are based on values of respect for women's experience. *Women's Ways of Knowing*, as well as other claims of significant differences between women and men in personality structure (Chodorow, 1978; Miller, 1976), moral reasoning, and ethical orientation (Gilligan, 1982), is cast in a positive light when viewed as an example of a new, feminist approach to science.

Still, it is puzzling why the authors of *Women's Ways of Knowing* repeatedly compare the responses of their interviewees to Perry's. From a feminist standpoint perspective, their research project is not concerned with sex difference at all, but rather with illuminating *women's* experience. Comparisons with men should be superfluous. Moreover, it would only be expected that, as women and as feminists, Belenky, Clinchy, Goldberger, and Tarule would have looked for and found different "ways of knowing" than Perry and his interviewers, even if they had interviewed the same people. Differences between the two groups of respondents may be due to the interviewers as much as the interviewees. Can research define "women's experience" without defining it against men's experience? Are there limits to the importance of the researcher's social identity in determining the form and content of the data? These remain relatively unexplored questions for feminist standpoint theorists.

Feminist standpoint epistemologies also raise the question of what constitutes the basis for a standpoint. Can a universalized "women's" standpoint exist when women differ by age, class, race, sexual preference, and ethnicity? Or must theorists allow for the existence of multiple standpoints, those "hyphenated feminisms" such as black-lesbian or older-working-class women's perspectives? Can a woman ever legitimately study or write about women whose standpoints differ from hers? These issues are real ones in contemporary feminist discourse. For example, Mohanty (1988) criticized the concept of global feminism as based in mistaken attempts to describe the lives of Third World women of color from the perspective of white, middle-class American sociologists.

Feminist empiricism seeks to remediate sex bias by improving empirical research, while the feminist standpoint approach attempts to develop a uniquely feminist way of doing science (Harding, 1986). I have illustrated the incompatibility of the two epistemologies, and some of their limitations, by applying criteria derived from each to a feminist research project.

However, there is more to consider than epistemological stance when assessing the usefulness of research for women. In our individualistic culture, psychology has a popular appeal unique among academic disciplines. And because our culture is also androcentric, psychological research that demonstrates sex differences is likely to be interpreted as demonstrating new sources of biological deficiency in women. In the interpretation and popularization of research, the social processes by which difference becomes a rationale for oppression can be observed.

Women's Natures: The Pop-Psych Construction of Reality

In the case of gender research, only a few discoveries reach the public at all (Beckwith, 1984). When they do, a predictable set of events takes place, one that researchers themselves can do little to control. A sex difference typically will be interpreted as a deficiency or problem *of women*. It will be *dichotomized* and *universalized*—seen as characteristic of *all* women and no men. It will be *essentialized*, or seen as having origins in women's essential (biological) natures. These processes, visible in the history of difference research, can be expected to recur with feminist difference research. In this final section I discuss the popularization of research on women's thinking and show how the processes of dichotomizing, universalizing, and essentializing occur.

That women have a different way of knowing seems on its way to becoming an established pop-psychological "fact," or, at the least, a "conceptual bandwagon" (Mednick, 1987). It is instructive to compare the media acceptance and endorsement of *In a Different Voice* and *Women's Ways of Knowing* with that of the most recent Hite report, *Women and Love* (Hite, 1987). (It should be noted that there are important differences in these projects. Hite is not a trained social scientist, and she used a mail survey rather than in-depth interviewing. However, her work bears at least superficial similarity to the others in its use of qualitative analysis of self-reports from nonrepresentative samples of women). Gilligan's work was lionized (e.g., Van Gelder, 1984), and *Ms. Magazine* pronounced her Woman of the Year. *Women's Ways of Knowing* was described as "a rich supply of resources for feminist analysis, public policy—and for theoretical and political struggles—for years to come" (Harding, 1987) and praised for its systematic, empirical approach (Hoffman, 1986) by feminist reviewers. It has also been awarded a Distinguished Publication Award from the Association for Women in Psychology. Its reception in the popular press has been positive. To one reviewer, the authors were "Joans of Arc guided by the sounds of women's voices" (Neustatdtl, 1986). To date, no reviewer has raised methodological issues. *Women and Love*, which was critical of men's behavior, was widely attacked as unscientific, methodogically flawed, murky and muddled, statistically deficient, and completely unrepresentative of "most women" (Hochschild, 1987; Shapiro, 1987; Wallis, 1987). Hite has been denigrated as an emotionally disturbed "pop-culture demagogue" (Barol & Brailsford, 1987).

Should feminists be concerned about the popular reception of *Women's Ways of Knowing?* One reason for its popularity may be that women find its ideas empowering (Mahlstedt, 1988). But even though the ideas are appealing from a feminist standpoint perspective, they may be distorted as they are disseminated. The culture will most readily authorize scientific research when it can be most easily enlisted to maintain male dominance (Mednick, 1987). Female superiority will not be authorized because the power to define "superior" and "inferior" remains with the dominant group (Bleier, 1984; Unger, 1987). The dangers of extolling feminine virtues were apparent to many of the pioneers of modern feminist psychology (Rosenberg, 1982). Difference—even though originally conceptualized as female strength, superiority, or virtue—is almost always transformed into "deficiency" for women. Because Western culture has long evaluated "masculine" reason and abstraction as inherently superior to "feminine" intuition and connection, the claim of "women's ways of knowing" is likely to be interpreted as further confirmation that rational thought is "male" (Hare-Mustin & Marecek, 1988).

Arguing that "difference" has long been both a way of construing the meaning of gender and a source of justification for the oppression of women, some feminist theorists propose that gender as difference and as deficiency may be inseparable (Hare-Mustin & Marecek, 1988; Unger, 1979). In each of the oppositional pairs that constitute the building blocks of western thought—mind/body, fact/value, reason/emotion, culture/nature, and of course, masculine/feminine—the pole associated with men is more highly valued (Fee, 1986). At the individual level, the polarization and evaluation of oppositional pairs can readily be demonstrated with psychological techniques (Osgood & Richards, 1973). At the social level, there is abundant evidence that processes of social judgment lead to the equating of "male" with "superior" and "female" with "inferior." As Unger (1979) stated: "In sex, as in race, there are no separate but equal social categories" (p. 1092).

Once a category of behavior or personality becomes "gendered," it is increasingly seen as exclusively the property of one sex or the other. Gilligan's (1982) book is frequently cited, despite her disclaimers, in dichotomous terms—for example, as having "exploded on the psychological world with its clear argument explaining how women make moral judgments differently from men" (Neustatdtl, 1986, p. 38). Evidence that the two orientations described by Gilligan are *not* gender-related (Brabeck, 1983; Ford & Lowery, 1986; Walker, 1984) receives no media coverage. Similarly, the study by Belenky et al. is described as demonstrating a sex difference: "Even if they were glossed over (in the past), there are gender differences in the quest for knowledge, to finding self" according to the *Los Angeles Times* (Kovacs, 1986). And the difference is seen as separating all women from all men: "Just as the voice of conscience says different things to women than it does to men" (a reference to Gilligan's work), "the authors found that a different voice speaks to women when they ask themselves what it is they know," reports the *New York Times Book Review* (Neustatdtl, 1986). In *Women's Ways of Knowing*, dichotomizing is encouraged when the authors overgeneralize from their sample to all women (and from Perry's sample to all men) and when they fail to systematically examine variables other than sex. For example, they claim that women as a group have been harmed by a competitive educational system:

Our interviews have convinced us that every woman, regardless of age, social class, ethnicity, and academic achievement, needs to know that she is capable of intelligent thought, and she needs to know it right away. Perhaps men learn this lesson before going to college, or perhaps they can wait until they have proved themselves to hear it. (p. 193)

This generalization is unwarranted without systematically separating sex from class, ethnicity, and other variables related to similarity between women and men. Feminist critics have pointed out that Gilligan (1982) also discounts factors such as class and religion, attributing all observed differences in moral reasoning to sex (Auerbach, Blum, Smith, & Williams, 1985; Lott, 1986). Yet ethnicity and class are important factors in moral reasoning. Research on black Americans, although not directly comparable to Gilligan's, suggests that women and men frame moral choices similarly (Stack, 1986). Several theorists have suggested that apparent sex differences in moral reasoning may reflect women's subordinate social position and lack of power (Tronto, 1987). This view implies that the "ethic of care" will be expressed by powerless people generally rather than being characteristic of women (Hare-Mustin & Marecek, 1988).

Dichotomization has different consequences for men and women as groups. Men continue to be viewed as individuals and in terms of many possible social groupings, while women are viewed as women (Hare-Mustin & Marecek, 1988). Universalizing women tends to downplay the importance of immediate situational determinants of their behavior (McCullough, 1987). But much of gendered behavior is created in ongoing social interaction where not only gender but other factors come into play (Deaux & Major, 1987; Unger, Chapter 1 & 1987; West & Zimmerman, 1987). Global conclusions about women and competition, for example, beg the question of how women, and only women, could develop profound doubts about their abilities in an educational system in which most teachers are women, or how and why some women seek out and thrive in some competitive situations.

Do people move from one "way of knowing" to another as they respond to the novelty or difficulty of a learning situation, their status as members of a majority or minority group in the setting, the immediate behavior of higher status persons in a particular context, their expectations for themselves, or other factors? Would a student trained in mathematics and logic express the same epistemological position in describing her approach to math as in relating her attempts to solve a conflict with her parents? Might a poet be temporarily "silenced" on his first encounter with computer programming? Whether people would maintain consistent epistemological positions across situations such as these cannot, of course, be addressed by the retrospective report methods of Belenky et al., and it is not an appropriate question to ask of their data. One strength of the analysis in *Women's Ways of Knowing* is that it shows a diversity of approaches to knowledge. But if women are seen as holding particular epistemological positions *as women*, universalized questions about women become easy to ask (cf. on designing an education for women, Belenky et al. propose to start with the question "What does a woman know?" p. 198). Other questions, such as those that specify "Which women?" and "In what situations?" become more difficult to ask.

Once a sex difference is seen as categorically distinguishing the genders, it becomes "only natural" to assume that it is biologically based (Jacklin, 1981). Popular press accounts of sex differences in mathematics performance stress "math genes" and a male "hormonal edge" (Beckwith, 1984; Eccles & Jacobs, 1986). Even differences that are originally conceptualized as stemming from socially constructed experience become essentialized (Bleier, 1984; Unger, 1979) and seen as immutable. Chodorow (1978), for example, is explicit in rejecting Freud's notions of the biological origins of gendered personalities, and yet her work has frequently been misinterpreted as an essentialist account (Marecek, 1983). In *Women's Ways of Knowing* the endorsement of environmental causes of difference is undermined by references to the "naturalness" of some differences. For example, "women seem to take *naturally* to a nonjudgmental stance . . . when someone said something they disagreed with or disapproved of , their *instinct* was not to argue" (pp. 116–117, emphasis added); or "many women take *naturally* to connected knowing" (p. 121, emphasis added). The more judgmental and analytical style attributed to men is not justified as natural or instinctive. Thus the way is opened for essentialist accounts of women's—and only women's—thinking.

These issues take on immediate practical importance when public policy may be based on presumed differences. Belenky et al., for example, suggest that educational systems be changed to meet what they see as women's unique needs for connected, noncompetitive, and nonhierarchical educational settings. But Fausto-Sterling (1985) argues that educational reforms emphasizing the special needs of women (based on differences in men's and women's thinking) have historically occurred whenever women are a majority in educational settings. Such reforms have functioned to segregate women and maintain power imbalances.

The operation of a sex and gender system can be seen in the popularization of research on women. Research that reports new ways that women differ from men or have special "women's" problems receives a great deal of attention (Crawford & Marecek, 1988). Research that reports similarities between women and men receives little. When a much-publicized difference fails to replicate in further investigations, either the new information is not reported or the argument for profound and immutable differences simply shifts to another ground (Shields, 1982; Unger, 1979).

Perhaps the paradox is inherent: in challenging a system of subordination by gender, feminist psychologists have attempted to remediate sex bias in research and to demonstrate a uniquely feminine experience. But construing gender as a property of individuals, rather than as a set of interactive processes that form a system of subordination, leads back to the questions about the nature and meaning of difference that have preoccupied feminist psychology for so long.

Acknowledgments. Friends and colleagues helped me write this chapter by reading my first attempts and discussing the ideas with me. I thank Roger Chaffin, Rachel Hare-Mustin, Carol Farley Kessler, Deborah Mahlstedt, Mary McCullough, Pat Manfredi, Pat O'Neill, Donna Summerfield, and Rhoda Unger.

References

Auerbach, J., Blum, L., Smith, V., & Williams, C. (1985). On Gilligan's *In a different voice. Feminist Studies, 11*, 149–161.

Barol, B., & Brailsford, K. (1987). Men aren't her only problem. *Newsweek*, Nov. 23, p. 76.

Beckwith, B. (1984) How magazines cover sex differences research. *Science for the People, 16*, 18–23.

Belenky, M.F., Clinchy, B.M., Goldberger, N.R., & Tarule, J.M. (1986). *Women's ways of knowing: The development of self, voice, and mind*. New York: Basic Books.

Bleier, R. (1984). *Science and gender: A critique of biology and its theories on women*. New York: Pergamon.

Brabeck, M. (1983). Moral judgment: Theory and research on differences between males and females. *Developmental Review, 3*, 274–291.

Chodorow, N. (1978). *The reproduction of mothering*. Berkeley: University of California Press.

Colby, A., & Damon, W. (1983). Listening to a different voice: A review of Gilligan's *In a different voice. Merrill-Palmer Quarterly, 29*, 473–481.

Crawford, M., & MacLeod, M. (1988). *Sex roles in the college classroom: An assessment of the "chilly climate" for women*. Manuscript submitted for publication.

Crawford, M., & Marecek, J. (1988). *Psychology reconstructs the female: 1971–1988*. Paper presented at the Nags Head Conference on Sex and Gender, Nags Head, NC.

Deaux, K. (1984). From individual differences to social categories: Analysis of a decade's research on gender. *American Psychologist, 39*, 105–116.

Deaux, K., & Major, B. (1987). Putting gender into context: An interactive model of gender-related behavior. *Psychological Review, 94*, 369–389.

Eagly, A.H. (1987). *Sex differences in social behavior: A social role interpretation*. Hillsdale, NJ: Erlbaum.

Eccles, J.S., & Jacobs, J.E. (1986). Social forces shape math attitudes and performace. *Signs: Journal of Women in Culture and Society, 11*, 367–389.

Fausto-Sterling, A. (1985). *Myths of gender: Biological theoies about women and men*. New York: Basic Books.

Fee, E. (1986). Critiques of modern science: The relationship of feminism to other redical epistemologies. In R. Bleier (Ed.), *Feminist approaches to science*. New York: Pergamon.

Ford, M.R., & Lowery, C.R. (1986). Gender differences in moral reasoning: A comparison of the use of justice and care orientations. *Journal of Personality and Social Psychology, 50*, 777–783.

Gilligan, C. (1982). *In a different voice*. Cambridge: Harvard University Press.

Grady, K.E. (1981). Sex bias in research design. *Psychology of Women Quarterly, 5*, 628–636.

Harding, S. (1986). *The science question in feminism*. Ithaca, NY: Cornell University Press.

Hare-Mustin, R., & Marecek, J. (1988). The meaning of difference: Gender theory, postmodernism, and psychology. *American Psychologist, 43*, 455–464.

Hite, S. (1987). *The Hite report: Women and love. A cultural revolution in progress*. New York: Knopf.

Hochschild, A.R. (1987). Why can't man be more like a woman? *New York Times Book Review*, Nov. 15, pp. 3, 32.

Hoffman, N.J. (1986). Feminist scholarship and women's studies. *Harvard Educational Review, 56*, 511–519.

Hyde, J.S., & Linn, M.C. (Eds.) (1986). *The psychology of gender: Advances through meta-analysis*. Baltimore: Johns Hopkins University Press.

Jacklin, C.N. (1981). Methodological issues in the study of sex-related differences. *Developmental Review, 1*, 266–273.

Johnson, D.W., & Johnson, R.T. (1987). *Learning together and alone: Cooperative, competitive, and individualistic learning*. Englewood Cliffs, NJ: Prentice-Hall.

Kovacs, D. (1986). Review of *Women's ways of knowing*. *Los Angeles Times*, Sept. 7, p.10.

Lott, B. (1986). *Women's lives: Themes and variations in gender learning*. Monterey, CA: Brooks/Cole.

Lyons, N. (1983). Two perspectives on self, relationships, and morality. *Harvard Educational Review, 53*, 125–145.

Maccoby, E., & Jacklin, C. (1974). *The psychology of sex differences*. Stanford, CA: Stanford University Press.

Mahlstedt, D. (1988). Personal communication, May 25.

Marecek, J. (1983). *Identity and individualism in feminist psychology*. Paper presented at the Penn Women's Studies Conference, Philadelphia.

McCullough, M. (1987). *Analysis of "Feminist theory: From margin to center."* Unpublished manuscript.

McIntosh, P. (1983). *Interactive phases of curricular revision: A feminist perspective.* Working paper no. 124. Wellesley, MA: Wellesley College Center for Research on Women.

Mednick, M. (1987). *On the politics of psychological constructs: Stop the bandwagon, I want to get off.* Paper presented at Third International Interdisciplinary Conference on Women, Dublin, Ireland.

Miller, J.B. (1976). *Toward a new psychology of women.* Boston: Beacon Press.

Mohanty, C. (1988). Global feminism and its territories: Boundaries of politics and method. Presented at Feminist Thought for the Year 2000 Conference, Hamilton College, April 9.

Neustratdtl, S. (1986). They hear different vocies. *New York Times Book Review,* Oct. 5, p. 38.

Osgood, C.E., & Richards, M.M. (1973). From yang and yin to *and* or *but. Language, 49,* 380–412.

Perry, W.G. (1970). *Forms of intellectual and ethical development in the college years.* New York: Holt, Rinehart, & Winston.

Rose, H. (1983). Hand, brain, and heart: A feminist epistemology for the natural sciences. *Signs: Journal of Women in Culture and Society, 9,* 73–90.

Rosenberg, R. (1982). *Beyond separate spheres: Intellectual origins of modern feminism.* New Haven, CT: Yale University Press.

Rossi, A.S. (1981). On the reproduction of mothering: A methodological debate. *Signs: Journal of Women in Culture and Society, 6,* 492–500.

Scarborough, E., & Furumoto, L. (1987) *Untold lives: The first generation of American women psychologists.* New York: Columbia University Press.

Shapiro, L. (1987). Eavesdropping on women. *Newsweek,* Oct. 19, p. 86.

Sherif, C.W. (1979). Bias in psychology. In J.A. Sherman & E.T. Beck (Eds.) *The prism of sex: Essays in the sociology of knowledge.* Madison: University of Wisconsin Press.

Shields, S.A. (1982). The variability hypothesis: The history of a biological model of sex difference in intelligence. *Signs: Journal of Women in Culture and Society, 7,* 769–797.

Stack, C.B. (1986). The culture of gender: Women and men of color. *Signs: Journal of Women in Culture and Society, 11,* 321–324.

Tronto, J.C. (1987). Beyond gender difference to a theory of care. *Signs: Journal of Women in Culture and Society, 12,* 644–663.

Unger, R.K. (1979). Toward a redefinition of sex and gender. *American Psychologist, 34,* 1085–1094.

Unger, R.K. (August, 1987). The social construction of gender: Contradictions and conundrums. *Paper presented at the meeting of the American Psychological Association, New York.*

Unger, R.K., & Crawford, M. (in press). Methods and values in decisions about gender differences: Review of Alice H. Eagly, *Sex differences in social behavior: A social role interpretation. Contemporary Psychology.*

Van Gelder, L. (1984). Carol Gilligan: Leader for a different kind of future. *Ms.,* Jan., pp. 37–40, 101.

Walker, L. (1984). Sex differences in the development of moral reasoning: A critical review. *Child Development*, *55*, 667–691.

Wallis, C. (1987). Back off, buddy. *Time*, Oct. 12, pp. 68–73.

West, C., & Zimmerman, D.H. (1987). Doing gender. *Gender & Society*, *1*, 125–151.

Wooley, H.T. (1910). Psychological literature: A review of the recent literature on the psychology of sex. *Psychological Bulletin*, *7*, 335–342.

7
Feminist Transformations of/Despite Psychology

Michelle Fine and Susan Merle Gordon

The field of psychology has long enjoyed an internal debate about women (Crawford & Marecek, 1988; Hare-Mustin & Marecek, 1987). Traditionally, we have been the *objects* of these conversations, however, and not their subjects. With due respect to our foremothers, feminist psychologies have developed institutionally only over the past two decades. Now generating critique, reclaiming the topics of girls and women, and creating novel methods for exploring gender as noun and verb (Unger, 1983; West & Zimmerman, 1987), this work is rich and interdisciplinary, but not always recognizable as psychology.

Finding and representing a powerful, coherent, and sustained set of feminist voices within the discipline is no easy task (see Walsh, 1987, on current controversies). Many interrogate gender differences. Some explore girls and women alone. Still others struggle over the dialectics of gender with race/ethnicity (Amaro & Russo, 1987; Espin, 1987; Ladner, 1972; Lykes, 1986; Rodgers-Rose, 1980; Smith & Stuart, 1983), social class (Rubin, 1976), sexual orientation (Boston Lesbian Psychologies Collective, 1987; Brown, 1987), disability (Fine and Asch, 1988), and/or age (Huddy & Goodchilds, 1985). We exist at moments, at the margins and among ourselves. Whether or not we have transformed the discipline of psychology, and whether or not we would like to, remain empirical and political questions (see Grady, 1981; Parlee, 1979; Shields, 1975; Unger, 1983; Wallston, 1981; Witting, 1985, for critique).

At the level of theory, methods, politics, and activism, it is safe to say that feminist psychology has interrupted the discipline. And yet many of us have left our disciplinary homes. Some have literally exited the academy to work with activist organizations (Vanderslice, in press), conducting research, practice, and/or evaluations. Others remain academy bound but scattered throughout schools of education, social work, communications and law, in women's studies or Afro-American studies, working at the interdisciplinary fringes, trying to articulate feminist epistemologies, theories, methods, and politics through the world of the university (Mayo, 1982). Some survive inside traditional psychology departments, writing within the mainstream, while a few seek audience and collaboration among friends, students, and colleagues who have abandoned or been tossed out of the mainstream of psychology. If many of the critical daughters of psychology have left home and others remain "in the kitchen" doing the dirty work of critique, transformation, and creativity (e.g. Caplan & Hall-McCorquodale, 1985), perhaps we need to reflect on where feminist psychologies and psychologists have gone, where we are going, and whether or not we want to reclaim the discipline.

In this chapter we explore the question: Is feminist psychology an inherent contradiction? Are psychology's obsessions compatible with notions of feminist epistemology (see Flax, 1987; Harding, 1987; Hartsock, 1987)? These obsessions include notions of experimental control; explicit distance separating researcher from researched; conversion of subjects into objects; "universal laws" that render race/ethnicity, gender, and social class to be "noise;" a romance with sterile environments called laboratories in which human behavior can be perverted and then studied as if "natural" and "uncontaminated;" a commitment to generalizability which turns "real" social contexts into intrusions on science; and a fetish with imposed categories, comparisons, hierarchies, and stages. In the first half of this chapter we consider how these contradictions (de)form the scholarship we call psychology of women/gender, and in the second half we imagine the contours of a project of political feminist psychology.

Feminist Transformations of Psychology

Women who have investigated the question of feminist influence on psychology have typically been quite generous to our forefathers, foremothers, and colleagues, measuring the "challenge" over the past twenty years in the broadest possible terms. Maxine Bernstein and Nancy Russo (1974), Brinton Lykes and Abbey Stewart (1986), Mary Parlee (1979), Mary Roth Walsh (1987), and others document feminist influence in the increase of numbers of women published as authors, listed as editors, footnoted by authors, and included as "subjects;" the diminished proportions of male-only studies; the increased proportions of studies in which females are compared to males; and in the use of methods and contexts broadened far beyond the laboratory into the realms of lived experience.

Building on this scholarship, we propose a more precisely defined set of criteria. If feminism has had a transformative impact on psychology, we would expect that psychologists who interrogate gender would do so with the following a priori understandings (Harding, 1987):

1. *Power asymmetries* structure gender relations.
2. Gender always braids with social class, race/ethnicity, age, disability (or not), and sexual orientation, as well as social context to produce *socially and historically constituted subjectivities*.

3. The *meanings* of a social experience *as expressed by women* must be unraveled if that experience is to be fully analyzed.
4. *Contextualized research* is necessary to unearth women's psychologies as they reflect, reproduce, resist, and transform social contexts, hegemonic beliefs, and personal relationships.

With these criteria, dare we note that the transformation of psychology by feminism has been modest. Psychology, like other oppressive social institutions, has been relatively immune to the transformative power of feminism (and other civil rights movements).

Sociologists and psychologists today conclude that, while the feminism of the 1960s to 1980s has systematically affected women's consciousness, the traditional division of domestic labor, the organization of paid work, and the national distribution of wealth, income, and poverty have been relatively untouched. In the United States women still do the housework (91% of married women), tend to children, make the dinners, care for the elderly, and live in disproportionate poverty—even while we may feel more "liberated" than twenty years ago. Girls and women across classes, racial and ethnic groups *have* changed, but the structures around us remain relatively intact. The discipline of psychology, like marriage, work, and parenting practices, has basically retained its shape, its boundaries, and its resistance to disruption in the eye of the feminist storm.

It is true that today more women are published, included as "subjects" and quantitatively compared to male subjects. These criteria, however, should be considered wholly inadequate to render psychological research feminist. While a vibrant strain of feminist psychology survives and flourishes, and while psychology of women courses are offered widely and enjoy extreme popularity, mainstream psychological research remains basically unchanged. For main/male stream psychology to display proudly its feminist heritage, gender, race/ethnicity, class, and other social dimensions of what feel like "personal experiences" would have to be placed squarely within the context of power. On this dimension the transformative impact of feminism has been sorely lacking.

THE EVIDENCE ON TRANSFORMATION: KEEPING OUR MOUTHS SHUT

A student recently informed me that a friend, new to both marriage and motherhood, now lectures her single women friends: "If you're married and want to stay that way, you learn to keep your mouth shut." Perhaps (academic) psychologists interested in gender have learned (or anticipated) this lesson in their "marriage" with the discipline of psychology. With significant exceptions, feminist psychologists basically keep our mouths shut within the discipline. We ask relatively nice questions (given the depth of oppression against women); we do not stray from gender into race/ ethnicity, sexuality, disability, or class, and we ask our questions in a relatively tame manner. Below we examine how feminist psychologists conduct our public/published selves. By traveling inside the pages of *Psychology of Women Quarterly*, and then within more mainstream journals, we note a *disciplinary reluctance* to engage gender/women at all, but also a *feminist reluctance* to represent gender as an issue of power.

In 1985, Brinton Lykes and Abbey Stewart compared articles in *Psychology of Women Quarterly* to those in *Journal of Personality and Social Psychology*. They learned that *PWQ* more often analyzed data between males and females and included adults as "subjects." Moreover, only 15% of its studies were experiments, as compared with more than 50% in *JSP*. They concluded that a feminist challenge to psychology has been felt, but not in the mainstream. We decided to expand the Lykes–Stewart analysis to study the feminist transformation of psychology through an assessment of what we decided to call the "penetration index," the "ovulation index," and the "transformative index."

The *penetration index* (PI) measures the extent to which mainstream journals in psychology cite articles from feminist journals. Drawing on three major psychological journals, *Developmental Psychology*, *Journal of Personality and Social Psychology*, and *Psychology of Women Quarterly*, we measured the frequency of citation of articles published in the seven feminist journals indexed in the *Social Science Citation Index* (*Feminist Studies, International Journal of Women's Studies, Psychology of Women Quarterly, Sex Roles, Signs, Women's Health*, and *Women's Studies International Forum* represented 0.005 of the 1413 journals indexed in 1986).

Tracking the three psychological journals from 1981 through 1986, we found that *Developmental Psychology's* citations referred to a feminist journal article in a ratio of 0.03 (in 1981) and 0.02 (1986); *Journal of Personality and Social Psychology* referred to a feminist journal article in a ratio of 0.04 (in 1981) and 0.03 (1986); and *Psychology of Women Quarterly's* citations referred to a feminist journal article in a ratio of 0.32 (in 1981) and 0.37 (1986). Thus, on this first measure of *penetration*, we see a slow leak of feminist scholarship into the mainstream, little change over historic time, and a persistent community of co-citers among feminist scholars.

A second index of penetration measures the ratio by which studies from *PWQ* are cited in explicitly feminist versus other journals. That is, what share of the feminist citation pie is accounted for historically by feminist publications? Here we have more evidence of both the growing community of co-citers and the resistance to feminism within the mainstream. In 1981, 9% of the 1035 *PWQ* cites were located in feminist journals, with 91% in other journals. By 1986, whereas the total number of citations had dropped by 10% to 932, we find that 23% are in feminist journals and 77% are not. Feminists cite feminists more than they did five years ago, while others cite them less.

Since we developed a penetration index we were politically obligated to develop an *ovulation index* (OI). The OI measures the frequency of articles published in the mainstream and periodically released, which deal with gender and race. The data on the OI are disturbingly slim and disturbingly consistent from 1980 through 1986. Reviewing *American Psychologist, Developmental Psychology, Journal of Counseling Psychology*, and *Journal of Personality and Social Psychology*, we find that the percentage of studies (except in *American Psychologist* where we relied on articles) dealing specifically with gender in 1980 ranged from 10% to 17% and in 1986 from 10% to 16%. Articles on race were even less frequent, ranging in 1980 from 2% to 5%, and in 1986 from 1.5% to 9%. Across these years and journals, only one article could be found which explicitly analyzed for social class differences and that was in 1980; sexual preference emerged in 1986 *Developmental Psychology* and *JPSP* articles at a frequency of 1% each; and disability showed up as a researched topic in 1986 in 2–4% of the articles reviewed. The interactions of these variables were entirely absent from the volumes studied. In terms of ovulation, the flow is regular, slow, and relatively uneventful across studies of gender, race, social class, sexuality and disability.

Finally, we come to the *Transformative index* (TI), which turns our analyses away from the mainstream and onto feminist psychology itself. We examined *Psychology of Women Quarterly* volumes of 1985 and 1986 to establish a baseline of what feminist psychologists do methodologically, discursively, and politically that would/could/should transform the "malestream" (Hartsock, 1987) of psychology. Our results were again disappointing. When feminism and psychology mate, feminism seems to bear only recessive genes.

Before launching into the transformative index for 1985–1986 we digress for a moment to consider the findings of a similar review conducted by one of us (Fine, 1985) on *PWQ* articles published from 1978 through 1981. Of this earlier cohort of articles, it was found that 51% reported college women as their respondents with 9% mentioning nonwhite respondents. A full 71% examined only *individual* attributes and 21% studied *interpersonal* relationships. Problematic themes wove through the conclusions: (1) authors ended their pieces on a note of *progressive progress*, with unchecked optimism about women in the future; (2) authors *psychologized the structural forces* that construct women's lives by offering *internal explanations for social conditions*; and (3) through the *promotion of individualistic change strategies* authors invited women to alter some aspect of *self* in order to transform social arrangements. That analysis concluded with a caution about the creeping conservatism of the times and the discipline:

If we do not resist what I assume will be a concerted effort to undermine our advance, feminist psychology may assimilate to the powerful traditions of psychology. (1985, p. 181).

Turning to *PWQ* for 1985–1986, we note the persistence of individualism and conservatism, but a substantial diversification of samples studied. In 1985, of 42 *PWQ* articles, 37 reported studies of which 18 (52%) included college student subjects and 9 (24%) mentioned "diverse" populations (not only white, middle-class, heterosexual and non-disabled). A full 86% (32) studied individuals rather than pairs, groups, collectives, relationships, or structures; and 24% of the studies' conclusions referred to some notion of *change*. In only 8% of these studies, however, was this change social, as opposed to individual. A year later, in 1986, there were 34 articles and of these 27 were studies. A third of the studies reported samples of college student subjects, with 41% describing samples selected for their diversity (by race/ethnicity and sexual orientation). One-third relied on women subjects only, and the remaining two-thirds compared females to males. Eighty one percent (22) studied individuals, and an equal proportion concluded their essays with summarizing descriptions of the data. One-fifth attributed outcomes to gender differences, whereas 80% explained findings based on contextual or historic factors. Nineteen percent referred to change, and 7% offered thoughts on the relationship of the study to social change.

Feminist psychology published within *our* representative divisional journal does reform the samples, methods, and questions of psychology as well as broaden the scope of interpretation. But we also reproduce the individualism and conservatism of the larger discipline. Most feminist psychologists have yet to declare questions of power primary; to establish white, heterosexual, patriarchal control as central to relations and representations of gender; and to take seriously the spaces that women create as retreats, as celebrations, as moments of resistance, and as the closets for our social transformation. Even among ourselves, feminist psychologists, by necessity or desire, appear to be playing to a male psychological audience. In our attempts to bring feminism to psychology we have perhaps undermined the politics and scholarship of feminism, refused questions of power asymmetry, and defaulted to the benign study of gender differences.

REFUSING POWER AND STUDYING DIFFERENCES: A POLITICAL COMPROMISE ON GENDER

Rachel Hare-Mustin and Jeanne Marecek (1987) argue that to the extent that psychology (feminist and not) "does" gender at all, it "does" gender as difference. In this formulation, they describe two "biases." The "alpha bias" occurs when gender differences are exaggerated, and the "beta bias" occurs when differences are minimized. Drawing on the Hare-Mustin–Marecek compelling meta-view of gender inside psychology, we argue that this almost exclusive construction of gender-as-difference functions inside psychology as a political and scientific diversion away from questions of power, social context, meaning, and braided subjectivities.

Psychological researchers interested in gender typically rely on the simple and essential notion of "differences." Within our culture and particularly our discipline, these empirical "differences" are then transformed into *either* hierarchy (see Chapter 6 in this volume) or a dualistic complementarity (as in the androgyny literature). To test male subjects only and then generalize to the human species is considered politically incorrect—even if still practiced regularly. To rely on female subjects only is to do a study on a "special interest group." But to incorporate both genders and divide by two is to conduct "good, nonsexist" psychology (see McHugh, Koeske, and Frieze 1986, for nonsexist guidelines).

We *as psychologists* do not typically study gender as power. We *as feminists* may "do" power between the genders but not within (with important exceptions see Collins, 1988; Fine & Asch, 1988; Golden, 1987; Joseph and Lewis, 1981; Smith and Stewart, 1983) and remain ever reluctant to study that which interferes with feminist notions of sisterhood, communality, relational orientation, and cooperation (see Dill, 1987; Fine & Asch, 1988; Miner and Longino, 1987; Rollins, 1985). Perhaps, in the relatively unexciting space in which we compare women to men and call the results gender differences, we offer a political compromise satisfying minimally the Right and the Left.

The perversion of gender into the dominant study of gender differences may represent a safe, political compromise for feminist and nonfeminist scholars. But the consequences of that compromise are intellectually and politically serious. By drawing on a difference argument, not only do we deploy and legitimate essentialist understandings of gender (Chodorow, 1978; see Chapter 6 in this volume), but we reproduce a series of dualistic beliefs about gender, sexuality, and race/ethnicity. Psychologists fetishize gender differences, as they do other differences, by flattening, normalizing, and making "scientific" those aspects of "personal" experience which are ideologically constructed and born of inequality. Theresa de Laurentis (1987) writes that a focus on sex differences keeps us in an "always already . . . political consciousness . . . of dominant cultural discourses." By posing universal oppositions, we are "imprisoned in the master's house" (pp. 2–3).

We want to make three points about the unexamined gender difference research frame. First, a focus on between-gender differences as the primary design for gender research creates, as it legitimates, a powerful and unarticulated commitment to heterosexuality as the frame for social research on gender. In Jungian terms, that which is masculine complements and completes that which is feminine. The androgyny literature is replete with this assumption (Bem, 1974). To the extent that males and females bring distinct strengths and deficits to their lived experiences, their merger makes good sense and constitutes that which is *normal*.

Further obscured by the gender difference formulation is the political and/or psychoanalytic insight that to be male or masculine in our culture is to *not* be female or feminine. The former requires the eclipsing of the latter (Chodorow, 1978; de Laurentis, 1987; Harding, 1987). And yet a gender difference frame implies the inherent compatibility of the two "roles." The frame fails to challenge the construction of social arrangements/ relationships in which the processes and structures of gendering artificially biologize and then split off that which is conceived of as "male" and that which is conceived of as "female." A gender difference analysis simply reproduces the false splitting of the masculine from the feminine, camouflages oppressive structures that split and then "naturalize" gender differences and compulsory heterosexuality (Rich, 1980; Rubin, 1984), and renders invisible and unnatural a more full menu of human sexualities.

Third, and finally, the gender difference research frame renders the study of *differences among and intimacy between women* as either irrelevant to social theory or plainly bad science. We know from feminist scholarship and politics (Weitz, 1984) that women alone—defined without men—always embody social danger. Whether lesbian, nun, prostitute, widow, single mother, or just a woman alone, she activates social anxieties, signals social dangers, and inherits social degradation. A threat automatically converted into an object of deprecation, she inherits disdain. Inside the discipline of psychology, we find that the study of women alone—without a comparison group of men—is typically disparaged as inadequate research. Whether it is a dissertation proposal of which colleagues may say, "You need to include men to compare these women to" or a review of the psychological literature in which females, if included at all, are typically compared to males, the assumption prevails that this comparison is necessary. When men are studied alone, they produce data on "human behavior." When women are studied alone, they produce barely credible data. The obsession with gender differences forces women's "subjugated knowledges" substantially underground (Belenky, Clinchy, Goldberger, & Tarule, 1986; Foucault, 1972).

By pitting that which is supposed to be male against that which is supposed to be female, psychologists mask all that we can learn about the construction and politics "in-between" (Poovey, 1988) and within the genders. Indeed, we need new language, for we are not actually speaking here about the study of *sex* as biology, or even *gender* as the social correlate of biological attributes. We are speaking of the study of the *politics* of *sex/ gender* relations, which organize and reproduce, as they resist, and transform oppressive social arrangements (Flax, 1987; Rubin, 1984; Scott, 1985). We are speaking of what may feel biological or psychological but is dialectically entwined with politics. In the absence of such research, we are saturated with studies of gender differences. And most psychologists maintain—implicitly if not explicitly—that with respect to gender, our theories, methods, and politics are inherently neutral.

THE DISTORTION OF GENDER IN THE GUISE OF NEUTRALITY

If psychology has generated two primary positions in response to the "gender question," with the first arguing for gender differences, the second represents psychology as inherently gender (and power) neutral. The search for "truth" can be navigated through questions of gender, like all other questions. Gender presumably represents a dichotomous variable that can be examined within a laboratory, in a survey, through observations, or with an interview. Absent from the formulation is gender as a relational concept, knitted with power, context, and intimate meanings (see Chapter 1). We reflect now on these methodological scenes of ostensible neutrality.

What academic psychologists do well are experiments in laboratories. In 1980 this method accounted for 71% of studies reported in major social psychological journals. In 1985, it accounted for 78%. Psychologists typically generate theory and evidence from accessible populations—white, college-aged, privileged male undergraduates (Sears, 1986) and write about that evidence as "human behavior." In 1980, 75% of reviewed social psychological studies were conducted with students. In 1985, this profile accounted for 83% of studies. David Sears concludes his review of social psychology with some distress, noting that the prestige of social psychological research seems to be linked to the inclusion of college students as subjects, and to the location of a study inside experimental laboratories.

The experimental laboratory indeed distinguishes psychology from other social sciences. It is heralded as sterile, neutral, and fully appropriate for eliciting "objective" phenomena while holding the "noise" of social context and background variables silent. When I (Michelle Fine) was an undergraduate, gender was still considered "noise" in social psychological studies. That is, women were considered "noisy" because our data did not conform to male patterns (sometimes called universal laws) and so women were typically excluded from these studies. Today we are back in the lab. Removed from social relationships, interaction in the lab is typically limited to a "subject" and a white (often male) experimenter. There may be some strangers present, who are euphemistically called group members. Defining features of this context include a lack of trust, longevity, and connection. In caricature, this sounds like a scene designed for Clint Eastwood (a prototypic if not real male), and a scene that would drive women mad. Given the ambiguity of the circumstances, the absence of relationships and the anonymity, it is, for instance, a scene in which racist behaviors by white "subjects" may be most likely to be enacted (as long as they could be concealed) (Gaertner & Dovidio, 1981). So much for the study of "objective" phenomena in "uncontaminated" spaces.

The ostensible sterility and neutrality of the lab mean only that hegemonic beliefs can be imported but not disrupted; that the social relationships and contexts in which women weave their lives are excluded as if irrelevant; that the ways in which women operate as community "glue" and as the institutionalized other are rendered invisible. What we have in these scenes are female "subjects" who are actually turned into "objects" of the experimenter. Whereas feminist theorists have worked hard to distinguish the biological *sex* from the social *gender* (Unger, 1983), the experimental laboratory removes women from their social contexts, so as not to reveal much about sex or gender. The subject is a product of the laboratory, gendered by what she imports into the lab and gender-perverted by the laboratory that extracts her from the context of her identity. This is no opportunity for the "untainted" display of sex or gender, and certainly no test of the political aspects of the *sex/gender* system and its implications for individual or collective psychologies (Rubin, 1984). The laboratory interacts with gender and other dimensions of social experience in ways that potentially may be understood, but most often are not.

The laboratory is almost too easy a target for critique on gender studies. Surveys, observations, or even interviews, relatively more "radical" methods in standard psychology, can also distort gender if applied without attention to power asymmetries, context, and meaning. While they may claim dispassionate investigation by isolating and/or creating an individual woman, psychological observations, surveys, and interviews typically gather data from a woman alone, as if she were in her natural habitat. With power unexamined, context and background whited-out, women's meanings translated *for* her, and universal laws sought, such decontextualized psychology obfuscates the woman (Fine, 1986; Sherif, 1987). We offer two negative examples of gender-neutral research to illustrate the need for feminist *interruption* of traditional methods.

In an essay published a few years ago, I wrote about Altamese—a woman whom I met in a hospital emergency room. She had just been raped and it was my job to counsel her (Fine, 1984a). The piece chronicles our evening together, mostly my silly class- and race-biased assumptions about how one copes with the violence, the randomness, and the insanity of rape inside a community in which neither police nor courts are trusted, in which "to tell" is to "send a boy to a white man's jail" and make one's self, mother, and children only more vulnerable to further violence. I wrote the piece because in the course of that evening it grew more and more apparent to me that as a feminist, as a psychologist, and as a rape crisis counselor all that I thought I knew about "coping" was tainted by a white and privileged set of social understandings, and all that Altamese (that is what I renamed her) understood as "coping" would have been perverted into "helplessness" if not "masochism" by a standardized psychological survey, observation, or interview.

She was unwilling to prosecute, see a therapist, or confide in a family member. She thought I was naive to imagine any of these strategies to be useful. "Who would believe me?" was her response to my idea about prosecution; "Only feels worse when you get home" was the answer to therapy; and "If I tell my mother, she or my brothers will go out and kill the guys . . . makin' it worse" was the reason not to confide in kin. I came to understand the need to unearth power, contexts, and local meanings, if we were to understand how and why women act as they/we do. A simple survey, observation, or interview conducted as if neutral with respect to power or gender would have distorted her experience, her decisions, and her commitment to resist the ways of coping that I deemed "normal."

Another negative example describes feminist research which unearthed women's meanings—but which could as easily (again) have obfuscated power, context, and meaning. Demie Kurz, sociologist at the Philadelphia Health Management Corporation and University of Pennsylvania, gathers divorced women's oral biographies of their lives with former husbands, focusing particularly on child support payments and experiences with domestic violence. Kurz relies on multiple methods, including standardized survey instruments and in-depth interviews. Among these, she invites women to complete Strauss' Conflict Tactic Scale. Respondents circle the number of acts of violence they and their spouse enacted over the past year, and then Kurz invites the women to explain their ratings. One woman completed the Strauss Conflict Tactics Scale by circling almost identical numbers and frequencies of violent acts for herself and her spouse. Another proudly circled more for self than spouse. Trying to present a neutral face, Kurz asked, "So, you and he, you were violent together? You hit him and he hit you?" Both women—independently—laughed and said some version of, "What would you do if he hit you, sit there and smile?"

A third interviewee explained to Kurz that her former husband cleaned out their home one Sunday afternoon. "So he came when you weren't home and took everything?" "No, he used his car—he's too cheap to rent movers—and made 10 trips, back and forth. And I stood there and watched." Typical passive woman, right? Wrong. "You didn't do anything?" asked Kurz. "Are you kidding, he was so violent with me I was terrified, and glad only to get him out of the house."

Without the feminist sensibilities to probe for power, context, meanings, and braided subjectivities, these women's lives and psychologies would go unrecorded or substantially misrepresented through traditional research methods (see Lather, 1986). Women can appear victimized, not coping, even "co-violent," helpless, or passive if researchers fail to probe for power asymmetries, to unearth the constraints and opportunities of context, and to interrogate local meanings (see Kurz, 1988). In such circumstances, the presumption of gender neutrality—within a laboratory, survey, interview, observation, and archival analysis—will undermine all that can be understood about gender and power. By masking asymmetries such research may discover "differences" and then ascribe them to biology or social roles, all the while obscuring power.

Reframing the Notion of Transformation: Toward Politics/Despite Psychology

The discipline of psychology has appropriated and depoliticized feminism in two ways: through the search for gender differences and through the presumption of gender neutrality. The argument for *neutrality* suggests that no feminist effort need be asserted to unpack power, context, or meaning; and the search for gender *differences* flattens the asymmetries that organize gender relations while promoting heterosexuality as the exclusive frame for viewing social relations.

If feminist transformations of psychology per se have been disappointing in the mainstream and even within the pages of our own journal *PWQ*, there nevertheless exists an explosion of feminist critique, epistemologies, theories, methods, and politics emerging from the corners of the academy and beyond, with psychologists co-creating, disrupting, advocating, listening, writing, screaming, and whispering (see Deaux, 1984, for review). While we make no attempt to be comprehensive, we merely note *In a Different Voice* (Gilligan, 1982), *Women's Ways of Knowing* (Belenky et al., 1986), *Lesbian Psychologies* (Boston Lesbian Psychologies Collective, 1987), *The Psychology of Women: Ongoing Debates* (Walsh, 1987), *The Black Woman* (Rodgers-Rose, 1980), a recent volume of *PWQ* devoted to the study of Hispanic women (Amaro & Russo, 1987), a current bibliography of psychological work on women of color (Mays, undated), *Tomorrow's Tomorrow* (Ladner, 1972), *Women with Disabilities: Essays on Psychology, Culture and Politics* (Fine & Asch, 1988), and *Representations: Social Constructions of Gender* (Unger, in press), which collectively enrich, finesse, critique, and create feminist psychologies. In each of these volumes the tensions of our work are explored, the relationships between researcher and researched unpacked. Subjects get to be subjects, complexity and diversity are sought and welcomed, notions of objectivity are reformulated if not finally buried, and constructions of gender stretch broadly to encompass social and economic arrangments, ideologies, personal relationships, and inner selves. In the next section we explore feminist psychologists' attempts to interrupt that which we have inherited from the fathers of psychology, and reproduced in our own work. We look to the example of feminist therapy to help us imagine how we might evolve a truly political feminist project.

A PROJECT OF POLITICAL FEMINIST PSYCHOLOGY

The question of a political feminist psychology automatically raises the question of audience. For whom are we writing/researching? A few position themselves toward "regular" women. Some write for/with activists and practitioners and an even smaller group write for lawyers and potential jurors, as in the case of expert witnesses working for the defense of battered women who kill (Blackman, 1989) or adolescent women who seek confidential abortions (see Melton & Russo, 1987). However, our analyses in the form of the penetration, ovulation, and transformation indices suggest that, for the most part, we are addressing psychologists, even between the relatively safe covers of *PWQ*. This may be due to concerns over tenure, professional acceptability, legitimacy, or the limits of our training. The consequences, however, are extreme.

While feminist psychology exists as a *potentially* expansive field of intellectual and political inquiry, it remains bound by a discipline designed to flatten, depoliticize, and individualize. These unacknowledged contradictions fill that which is called feminist psychology. They pervert our scholarship, as they erode the politics of our work. Perhaps more than in other disciplines, feminists inside psychology, however, have choices. While broadening our audience beyond the discipline may be costly to those who remain in the academy, it is also compelling to imagine psychology deployed in ways that demystify ideology, that disrupt the seeming neutrality of relationships and structures, and that open ideological and material choices for all women. But a glance at the complexities confronted by feminist psychologists who do posit audiences outside the mainstream of psychology will help prevent romanticization of an idealized political feminist psychology. Whether we collaborate with activists, as in the work of Rhoda Linton and Michele Whitham on the Women's Peace Movement; with legal advocates for battered women who kill, as in the work of Julie Blackman, Lenore Walker, and Angela Browne; or with public educators (see Fine, 1986; Lather, 1986; McIntosh, 1983), the contradictions inside these relationships are by no means resolved.

If seeking social change rather than universal laws is our goal, we are still vulnerable to the possibilities of *gender essentialism* and *racial/ethnic/class erasure*. How can *woman* be represented as a social and political category if not by camouflaging all the complexities and contradictions among us? We are still vulnerable to *ignoring social context* and *contingencies*—for how else can we generate courtroom strategies and public policies that can "generalize" across situations? And we are still vulnerable to *hegemony*, this time representing as "true" that which we believe, instead of that which men proclaim. It is sometimes hard to remember that *our* hegemony is little better than *theirs*.

In working with activists, we do not resolve these questions of power, context, and meaning simply by revealing the multiplicity of women's voices, the complexities of their contexts, and the contingencies of social arrangements. Nor can they be resolved by relying on the varied meanings women inscribe on their own lives or by representing individual psychologies within frames of inequitable power. By doing so we merely relocate the contradictions and the discussions among "ourselves," but we still inherit dilemmas.

To illustrate: In rural Tennessee, Dr. Jacqui Wade, Director of Afro-American studies at Penn and I (MF) were hired to evaluate a series of battered women's shelters. It took little genius to notice the whiteness of staff and residents. It required little insight to hear that the women's needs were not always compatible with their children's needs (as in the desire to see paternal grandparents). Our work was conceived as collaborative with the shelters. Yet we ultimately generated what we considered to be important critical commentary—about race and racism, and about children—which was not entirely shared by our collaborators. On these topics we departed sharply from the women of the shelters. While they were the *subjects* of the research, the ones *for whom* the research was conducted, within the report which we wrote and narrated, they may have felt like objects. We discussed, negotiated, and traded insights. Yet there were moments of splitting and moments of critique. This is all to say that feminist psychologists writing within the academy do not have a monopoly on contradictions. Involvement in activist research does not relieve feminist psychologists of the hypocrisies with which we live daily. If we are compelled to social action, policy, legal advocacy, and/or practice, then we find ourselves back at the central dilemmas—framed in much more interesting and significant areas than in the academy—but the central dilemmas of feminist psychology nevertheless.

We turn to imagining a project of political, feminist psychology, advanced through novel *ways of learning*, knitted to the conditions, complexities, asymmetries, pleasures, and dangers of women's lives. To excite feminist imaginations toward interruptive questions of epistemology, methodology, methods, and politics (Harding, 1987), we offer a project that weaves four such ways of learning. Interrogating that which women do *traditionally*—sustain relationships and maintain social secrets—and that which women do *subversively*—generate feminist politics and imagine possibilities, we invite a project of psychology which empowers as it exposes, which offers critique as it reveals not only what is not, but what could be. These four ways of learning are selective, not comprehensive. They challenge the authoritative position of the researcher; unsettle claims about objectivity, bias and truth; and confuse intentionally the accepted segregation of social theory, method, and politics. All these posit political social change as the task of feminist psychology, and all these generate far more questions than answers.

To Unpack the Traditional Work of Women

I. Interrogating the Stuff of Relationships

If you really want to know either of us, do not put us in a laboratory, or hand us a survey, or even interview us separately alone in our homes. Watch me (MF) with women friends, my son, his father, my niece, or my mother and you will see what feels most authentic to me. These very moments, which construct who I am when I am most me, remain remote from psychological studies of individuals or even groups. In the Psychology of

Women class which I teach, students interview a woman "who is different from you in terms of race/ethnicity, social class, sexual orientation or disability and write about her, yourself, and what transpired between," or they "write a three generation analysis of some issue that affected your grandmother, mother, and self." The resulting essays are rich, filled with the stuff of relationships, the ways in which women blend together, and the ways in which women split off, positioned through and in opposition to other women:

What did ever happen to you and I? We were the best. I always knew I could count on you. . . you were better than a sister. I was happy for and with you when you got married. I knew it was right for you. But I resented his intrusion into us. Our friendship had to be worked into his schedule. Somehow it didn't seem as bad when you were just dating him. You were always around. . . . But when you got married it was almost like I had to make dates with you. . . and they always had to be at times that were convenient for him. . . almost like I could have whatever was left of you after he had taken his fill. I didn't like that. . . and then along came baby one. . . you were into things that I had no interest in and they seemed to swallow you whole. I guess it was easier to just find other things. . . and other people than to try and compete. And I guess I envied you in some ways. I was working myself into exhaustion when you were on maternity leave picking out wallpaper for the nursery. You had someone to take care of you. . . I only had myself to take care of me and that scared me a lot. . . . You scared me. . . I didn't know who you were anymore, but I'm not sure who I am all the time either now. . . .

This is a small piece of Pam. In an attempt to capture the essence of this stranger who used to be my best friend. Pam was not what I expected. My rose colored vision of a happy woman in complete control of her life didn't match the woman who opened the apartment door. Was the vision I had created of Pam for the past 18 years naive? Probably but at the same time perhaps it served a purpose in giving me an "ideal vision" when I felt things in my own life were less than ideal. It's interesting that Pam also has an ideal vision of my blissfully married life in suburbia, cat, dog and children in tow that served as a reference point for measuring her life. How sad that we were both measuring our lives by an imaginary ideal of the other's life. Our time together [they got together on Valentine's Day] showed us both that our unhappiness had just taken different forms. Pam focuses on what's missing from her life—the companionship, affection and sex she would have were she not living alone. I focused on the burdensome aspects of the same companionship, affection and sex that Pam craves. Two sides of the same coin. . . .

I find myself growing tired of being patient and waiting for a "distant day." I feel a sense of urgency to no longer simply let my life lead me instead of leading my life. I must do something with this strong sense of connectedness I feel for this woman whose life is so different from mine. This woman who could be me. This woman who I could be. [This paper was situated inside a discussion of compulsory heterosexuality (Rich, 1980)].

                                                                                    Jill Tillman

As an adult my interviewee remains active in social change. Fighting strong against laws which place a disproportionate amount of minorities behind bars, yet offers probation and light sentences to white men who commit the same crimes.

This challenge of the system strikes me as brave particularly since her family of origin distilled in her a fear of authority figures. I have never questioned the system in this way. I have advocated through personal experience the importance of changing some of these laws. However I have never stood up against them. I black and she white.

Recounting a piece of my childhood I asked my interviewee whether the police had held such a strong arm in her community as they had done in mine. She said not. She could not imagine the cops chasing men down the streets and shooting at them ill-respective of others in the range of gunfire. She could not imagine radical, militant groups like the Black Panthers living a half a block away and watching fearfully as the police raided their home and dragged them all out one by one. She could not imagine seeing teenage men crippled for life from gang wars, drug wars and the like. And yet she fights for causes which have not touched her life, but instead the lives of others, mostly black men and black women, hispanic men and hispanic women.

I am black and she is Jewish. I cannot escape my skin color and the texture of my hair can only be changed temporarily. She can waltz in and out of invisibility, utilizing her white skinned privileged for protection or gain. I do not have this option. I am not shielded from racism as she can sometimes be from anti-semitism. Gomez recounts, "1980, my lover, white and Jewish, did not understand my outrage when she told me her friend, a white woman, had decided to cut off the nappy hair of her black, adopted daughter, rather than learn to deal with it. My lover understood oppression and discrimination but as a white skinned woman with the approved hair texture she'd never thought about the years of insidious assault black women face daily."

We emerge with our differences: Jewish, black, middle-class, working class, straight, lesbian, motherless and mother. Yet there are also common differences which have brought us closer together in reaching towards the same goals and fighting against the same obstacles: abolishment of racism and anti-semitism, equal opportunity in jobs, housing and education. We have experienced the wrath of dysfunctional families and emerge as strong and capable women, perhaps not so different after all.

Allener Rogers

We have no easy way to analyze these essays, and yet inside them we find both the "stuff" of relationships, and the "stuff" of women's identities. The *subject* is constructed as she constructs herself, in reflection, relation, and in resistance to the *other* (see Fisher and Galler, 1988). Psychological analyses of individuals, alone or in isolation, render invisible these relational aspects of self (Hooks, 1981; Mead, 1934, Bhaba, 1983). To begin research inside women's relationships and to work through these data are to seek *women* in a fundamentally radical and nonindividualistic way.

II. On Social Secrets: Desilencing the Social Underground

We know from feminist investigations that women are nestled not only inside relationships but precisely inside the most contradictory moments of social arrangements. Indeed, it is often women's work to be stuffed inside such spots and to testify that *no contradiction* exists (Smith, 1987). *No seams* wrinkle. *Nothing* shatters our coherent social existences. Wives are not supposed to give away the secret of male dependence although they have plenty of evidence; secretaries are not supposed to tell about male incompetence or the incoherence they make presentable; lesbian women are not supposed to "flaunt" their sexualities (Nestle, 1983); mistresses are not supposed to tell about the contradictions inside heterosexuality, monogamy, and the promises of marriage; women with disabilities are not supposed to expose social obsessions with attractiveness and illusions of life-long independence and health; prostitutes are not supposed to tell about the contradictions of intimacy and sexuality; daughters are not to speak of incest; and maids or domestics are not supposed to talk about the contradictions of the world of paid work and family life under advanced capitalism.

Women of all colors and classes are nestled inside these contradictory spots in which the pressures and structures of the economy rub against the pressures and structures of racism, sexism, and heterosexism. Women are sworn to both invisibility and secrecy (see Delacoste and Alexander, 1988). Whether we turn to Judith Rollins' (1985) or Shellee Colens' (1986) stories of the relationships between domestics and the women who employ them, or the *Village Voice* article on the relationships between black child care workers and the white children they tend to (Dobie, 1988), we hear the screams and the silences that fill the contradictory spots. Whether we turn to Susan Schechter's (1983) account of black and Latina women residing in battered women's shelters under the rules and notions of "appropriate behavior" generated typically by white and affluent feminist women, or we turn to my own work on rape survivors asked to cope in ways that privileged women and psychologists might (Fine, 1984a), we see the contradictions that women are forced to swallow. Whether we ask disabled women about the value of feminism as currently practiced (Blackwell-Stratton, Breslin, Mayerson, and Bailey, 1988), or ask lesbian women who have just come out to their now distant (straight) best friends, whether or not they believe that heterosexual women are really more relational and connected than are men (Golden, 1987), we understand that women collect the data on social contradictions between but also within the genders.

We share Jean Baker Miller's insight that women are responsible not only for the maintenance of these relations and the repair of fractures but also for keeping silent about the extent to which men depend on women at home, at work, and on the street (see also Jane Flax, 1987, for a more psychoanalytic account). Across social contexts, women's unpaid work includes collecting, retaining, and never revealing social secrets about men's and women's lives; about oppressive social and economic arrangements and the ideologies that make it "go down easier." This second way of learning—desilencing—calls for a moratorium on secret keeping. It tells—through letters, diaries, and groups, in contexts of relative safety and risks.

Because women need to tell and because women—and girls—need to know.

To unearth the secrets is also to tap the costs of the silencing. Given that women are the repositories of social secrets and made to feel responsible for social problems, the hegemonic system works perfectly. Women traditionally have not needed to be coerced into secrecy. To speak has been to betray self. So many have preserved systems for which they have been held accountable; systems that betray, as they sustain them.

If they told, secrets of privilege, sexuality, danger, terror, violence, oppression, dependence, and fears would be exposed/transformed. We invite feminist scholars of psychology to engage in precisely these tasks; to unearth the psychologies of women and men by identifying and invading those moments of social silencing and secrecy. Sitting at the margins, forced to the margins, or appropriated once at the margins, women collect social controversy and are sworn—typically through the "privilege" of heterosexuality—to secrecy. The "data" would expose a system that survives on the backs of women—disproportionately low income women of color.

ON SUBVERSION: WOMEN'S OTHER WORK

III. On Politics: Untying the Knots of Political Contradictions

If we move the project of feminist psychology from what women have *traditionally* done to the arena of *subversion*, our investigation detours from what has been to what could be. The unearthing of secrets—now "inside" feminist politics and practice—is a significant task. When battered women's shelters are disproportionately white in staff and residents, and defend this position because "black communities seem to take care of themselves better;" when feminist health collectives take on an AIDS testing program but refuse populations of IV drug-using women because "we're not ready to take this on"—then researchers can be helpful in unfreezing moments of political decisionmaking. We can learn the histories of such decisions and the care with which they are made and help unpack the dilemmas made in the name of politics and practice. (What may *appear* to feminist researchers to be an abdication of feminist principles needs to be explored through conversation with participants and decisionmakers.)

This way of learning unfreezes and unties political contradictions. It involves inviting staff, residents/clients, advocates, and professionals from within and outside the organization to come together for group sessions to unravel the contradictions, dilemmas, and choices: to unpack the politics, consequences, and costs. Freezing these moments to unfreeze the conversations enables this mode of feminist research (Gordon, 1988). Researchers may pose questions that practitioners/activists seek to avoid and may engage probes that threaten the impression of institutional coherence.

Questions and ethical dilemmas will emerge, of course, about who owns the data, whose voice/analysis/critique should be privileged, what happens to organizational health once disrupted, and who gets to publish what. This project is potentially both problematic and liberatory. Collaborative study and writing, in common and separate voices, can enable a multiplicity of positions to be stated, critiqued, unraveled, and repacked (Lewis and Simon, 1986). Theory, practice, politics, and methods fuse inside this moment of feminist scholarship.

IV. On Possibilities: Studies of What Is Not

Theresa de Laurentis (1987) argues that the subject of feminism involves "the movement back and forth between the representation of gender (in its male-centered frame of reference) and what that representation leaves out or, more pointedly, makes unrepresentable. It is the movement between the (represented) discursive space of the positions made available by hegemonic discourses and the space-off. . . those other spaces, both discursive and social, that exist since feminist practices have (re)constructed them, in the margins. . . of hegemonic discourses, and in the interstices of institutions, in counter practices and new forms of community" (p. 26).

In order to understand gender as a relational concept and one with elastic boundaries, we need to investigate not only what is represented and experienced as gender, but also what is not represented, what is not known, and what is not imaginable about gender and about women. We need to disrupt prevailing notions of what is inevitable and "natural" (see Tiefer, 1987), as we invent images of what could be.

To *illustrate what is not measured*: In the battered women's shelter research, the Conrad Hilton Foundation asked Michelle Fine and Jacqui Wade to itemize a cost–benefit analysis of providing services per women/child head. We agreed but insisted that we would also calculate the cost of *not* providing services per woman/child. We asked each respondent—mothers and children—to help us think about what would have happened to them had *no* service been available. They itemized easily: broken bones, missed days at school, foster care, employee absenteeism, welfare, moving children and/or mother to another state, fires, destroyed furniture, perhaps murder.

To *illustrate what is not illustrated*: Feminist psychologists typically study a slice of the individual woman, as she pops up in her multiple roles—student, mother, friend, sexual object/subject, worker, daughter, and/or all of these. Less often studied are women inside collectives, women in their relationships (Simon, 1988), the transformation of women over time (Baruch, Biener, & Barnett, 1987), women in collaboration with women (Brodkey, 1988), and women inside categories and communities we cannot yet imagine.

To *illustrate what is not grieved*: When injustice persists with no evidence of unhappiness, rebellion, or official grievance, we need to study the reasons why. An effective system of social injustice requires no coercive agents—only the strength of hegemony and/or punishment for dissent (Gramsci, 1973). The most comprehensive system of injustice is one in which victims are victimized, nonvictims benefit, and "consensus" prevails that victims either "enjoy it" or at least they "don't mind." As Faye Crosby and her colleagues demonstrate (see Chapter 4 in this volume), the absence of grievance cannot be read as an indication of consent.

Feminists need to interrogate the absence of grievances, appeals, and rebellions by problematizing those factors that contribute to the social construction of quiescence (Gaventa, 1980; Kaminstein, 1988). For example, at the University of Pennsylvania, as elsewhere, conservative faculty and administration have taken the position that the very few incidents of formally filed sexual and racial harassment grievances signify the absence of harassment. Faculty, staff, and students in the feminist and Afro-American communities have argued, in contrast, that the *absence* of grievance substantiates the very depth of and terror imposed by harassment. Feminist research must get behind "evidence" that suggests all is well. We must demonstrate that which misrepresents justice, consensus, and "brotherhood" while silencing women. Feminist psychology can reframe what is, as it activates images of what could be.

This proposed project engages critique, enables transformation, and invites the unearthing of possibility in feminist research. Although it may seem impossible, we propose that there is already precedent for the making of feminist critique, the transformation of tradition, and the creation of novel possibilites. This precedent exists in the practice of feminist psychotherapy.

A MOMENT ON FEMINIST PSYCHOTHERAPY

Constructed out of the same contradictions and tensions as those found in academic and activist feminist psychology, feminist therapists have reformulated a variety of psychotherapies, ranging from behavioral to family systems to psychodynamic modalities. The tensions that confront academic and activist researchers—acknowledgement of biases, the uses and misuses of power, and the importance of gender in developmental and situational issues—also challenge feminist therapists (Lerman, 1986). Feminist therapies differ from other therapeutic approaches in so far as the "samples" and "topics" have changed dramatically. Physical and sexual abuse, harassment, depression, the body, relationships, assertiveness, and development are addressed in their social contexts, instead of boxed as pathology or explained as individual in origin. However, far more fundamental, radical principles of practice (Gilbert, 1980) unite feminist therapists. The personal is considered political; the therapist–client relationship is viewed as optimally egalitarian; social transformation—through individual and group change—is recognized as the desired outcome.

Feminist therapists critique white heterosexual male assumptions that have organized traditional therapies by stepping outside them and interrogating questions of power, personal meaning, and social context. They reconstruct these models to work within feminist assumptions, and out of the contradictions and tensions inherent within these principles they create novel ways of doing therapy and of doing work together (see Broverman et al., 1972; Chesler, 1972; Greenspan, 1983; Lerman, 1986).

But inside the transformation of practice, like the transformation of academic psychology, paradox lingers. Consider, for example, feminist reworkings of psychoanalytic theory, which have rejected the Oedipal stage as the crux of female personality development and have concentrated instead on the earlier mother–daughter relationships (Chodorow, 1978; Dinnerstein, 1976). Although gender development now shifts from a focus on what women lack (an Oedipal penis) to what women possess (a pre-Oedipal "good enough" mother), the feminist object-relations school still essentializes mothering and ignores the importance of context, diversity, history, race/ethnicity, and class. Human behavior (both male and female) is typically reduced to gender-specific terminology. In one particular case, a psychodynamic family systems model (Comprehensive Family Therapy) appropriates the language of the "mothering one" to describe *either* parent who displays nurturant behaviors. By including fathers in early childrearing, Kirschner and Kirschner (1986) aim to avoid sexist and gender-specific roles for parents, but the language they deploy inherently associates nurturance with the female.

Transforming therapeutic practice, like transforming therapeutic theory, confronts many of these same dilemmas. Two primary principles of feminist therapy—that the personal is political and that the therapeutic relationship should be egalitarian—embody inherent contradictions and tensions. A few years ago one of us (Susan Gordon) interviewed three therapists about their identifications as feminists and their practice of feminist modes of therapy. The two who did not identify strongly as feminists could not even consider the therapeutic value of educating a client to social inequities or guiding her toward social change. The third, who strongly identified herself as a feminist, nevertheless hesitated to address social inequities within her counseling sessions with her clients, lest she impose her own values on them. Feminists tread a fine line between helping clients distinguish individual pathology from societal oppression and imposing a political consciousness on them.

Issues of political awareness then are tied to both the client's consciousness and to the power dynamics of the therapeutic relationship. The nature of therapy—feminist and not—is inherently unequal. Power lies on the side of the one who does not self-disclose—the therapist. Regardless of whether the therapist views herself and is viewed by her client as an omnipotent healer or as an educated helper, the client sits in a subservient position. She needs the assistance that the therapist can provide. An impossible situation in which to imagine equality? Perhaps, but acknowledgment of the *principle* of egalitarian relationship opens the feminist therapeutic conversation to explore the dynamics of power in therapy. Fee setting, appointment breaking, touching, dual relationships with clients, and other ethical issues can then be negotiated and studied inside power.

Finally, feminist therapy is even more than critique and therapeutic transformation. It also enables the powerful creation of novel ways of organizing *practice*. Egalitarian settings in which therapists collaborate may perhaps represent the most significant instance of transformation. Seven years ago the Feminist Therapy Institute first met in Vail, Colorado. Lynne Rosewater described this meeting as "electrifying and powerful" (personal communication, March 21, 1988). Fifty therapists who had been practicing for at least five years, all advanced practitioners and well versed in feminism, set as their goal the sharing of innovations and of problems inside the practice of feminist therapies. Instead of following the traditional conference arrangement of few presenters and many listeners, the Institute called on each of the 50 participants to present and listen to each other. Egalitarianism moved through the basic fabric of the Institute. All members, even the founders, complete a lengthy application process. The annual conference is open to the first 60 members who apply—this year some members of the steering committee waited too long and were not accepted. FTI takes as its task proactive work for social change. Instrumental in the political movement to stop the sexist gains in DSM III, they are developing a code of feminist ethics in therapy and examining cultural diversity and anti-racism by interrogating their own racism and by assuring the representation of women of color at the next conference—for whom slots are reserved. In FTI, as in other such settings, therapists experiment with working in nonhierarchical and collaborative ways. Able to explore questions that otherwise would not have surfaced, they offer a vision of transformation and creation for feminist research psychologists.

Feminist Psychology: An Inherent Contradiction?

Feminists inside research psychology suffer from extreme ambivalence. Trained and immersed in a highly positivist tradition, a discipline suffering from what Evelyn Fox Keller calls "physics envy" and yet rich with data about women (and men) which expose the superficiality of notions of objectivity, truth, stages, and even gender, it is not surprising that we are ambivalent.

To answer the most simple question, have we transformed psychology? We would have to say, barely. When Michelle was up for tenure, a colleague, in an effort to be supportive, explained: "It's a pleasure to have someone doing feminine psychology around here."

Have we decentered the white, male, heterosexual, affluent, non-disabled standard? Probably not. Do we care? I'm not so sure. Within psychology we have achieved a small space for the intellectual and political nurturance of each other, our students, activists, practitioners, and policy-makers. Our work—in quite explicitly feminist and in quite deformed ways—pops up in the public media (see Chapter 6 in this volume). We are on television defending battered women who kill (Blackman, 1986; Walker, 1984); in print denouncing sexual harassment (B. Gutek, personal communication); in courtrooms defending the rights of young women to attend the finest all-male public high school in the city of Philadelphia (Fine, 1983; Unger, 1983); and arguing that anti-abortion clinic protestors constitute a violation of the free speech of women seeking confidential abortions (M. LaFrance, personal communication). Feminist works are cited by some mainstream journals—at substantial rates given the paucity of explicitly feminist journals—and feminist scholars are being published inside the mainstream, particularly when we abide by the rules of traditional psychology.

But our impact on the discipline has ultimately been limited. Unlike sociology and anthropology departments, which seem to at least *know* that they need "a gender person," psychologists in psychology departments do not scramble to fill "the gender spot." In part, feminist psychologists have selected audiences elsewhere. But we have also been too sweet, asked nice questions, used "their" methods uncritically, and *not* been hysterical. We have typically failed to address systematically the notions of power; the dialectics of social inequity and individual psychologies; the braiding of gender, class, and race/ethnicity with age, disability, and sexual orientation. We have yet to develop a language for articulating that which is negotiated "in-between" structures of oppression and individual/group psychologies (Bourdieu, 1977). We have found no way inside the discipline to discuss "resistance" without it appearing childlike or overemotional. And we have been as shy about introducing politics explicitly into our work as we have been about exposing the inherently conservative politics that organize the field of psychology (Apfelbaum, 1979; Buss, 1979; Furby, 1979; Wexler, 1983).

Feminists can fit into psychology all too easily. We can do it by pretending that psychology is an apolitical discipline; by representing ourselves uncritically as "objective" researchers; by misrepresenting gender, within frames of sex roles, sex differences, or gender-neutral analyses without discussing power, social context, and meanings; and by constructing the rich and contradictory consciousness of girls and women into narrow factors and scales. But by so doing, we reproduce and legitimate the individualism, conservatism, and dangers of psychology. We collude in the sexist and racist stances built into gender and race research which claims to be "power neutral" but is actually power justifying. Then we—like the women we study—sit inside moments of social contradiction and we keep our mouths shut. We may build a humble critique from within the field which will undoubtedly be tamed and appropriated. Perhaps all psychologists will eventually include girls and women in their studies. Psychology, however, will then even more resiliently mask the power asymmetries that define gender, race/ethnicity, sexuality, disability, and class relations.

Feminist psychologists can enrich feminism inside psychology. But more important in the 1980s we can transform politics through feminist psychology. Psychology can be reconstituted as the stuff that fills women's (and men's) minds, bodies, and relationships; that feels so personal, rings so political, and has yet to be articulated between the two. Feminist psychologists must enter that space—to interrogate how women (and men) position and are positioned in ways that relay, inscribe, experience, and critique the social as a personal moment. And then we must learn how those personal moments can be strung together like beads into collective and disruptive feminist movements of politics and scholarship.

REFERENCES

Amaro, H., & Russo, N. (1987). Hispanic women and mental health. *Psychology of Women Quarterly, 11,* 393–407.
Apfelbaum, E. (1979). Relations of domination and movements for liberation: An analysis of power between groups. In W. Austin and S. Worchel (Eds.), *The social psychology of intergroup relations.* Monterey, CA: Brooks/Cole.
Baruch, G.K., Biener, L., & Barnett, R.C. (1987). Women and gender in research on work and family stress. *American Psychologist, 42,* 130–136.
Belenky, M.F., Clinchy, B.M., Goldberger, N.R., & Tarule, J.M. (1986). *Women's ways of knowing: The development of self, voice and mind.* New York: Basic Books.
Bem, S. (1974). The measurement of psychological androgyny. *Journal of Clinical and Consulting Psychology, 42,* 155–162.
Bernstein, M.D., & Russo, N.F. (1974). The history of psychology revisited: Or, up with our foremothers. *American Psychologist, 29,* 130–134.
Bhaba, H. (1983). *The other question—the stereotype and colonial discourse. Screen, 24,* 18–36.
Blackman, J. (1986). Potential uses for expert testimony: Ideas toward the representation of battered women who kill. *Women's Rights Law Reporter, 9,* 227–238.
Blackwell-Stratton, M., Breslin, M.L., Mayerson, A.B., & Bailey, S. (1988). Smashing icons: Disabled women and the disability rights and women's movements. In M. Fine and A. Asch (Eds.), *Women with disabilities: Essays in psychology, culture, and politics* (pp. 306–332). Philadelphia: Temple University Press.
Boston Lesbian Psychologies Collective (Eds.) (1987). *Lesbian psychologies.* Urbana: University of Illinois Press.

Bourdieu, P. (1977). Cultural reproduction and social reproduction. In A.H. Halsey and J. Kauabel (Eds.), *Power and ideology in education* (pp. 487–551). New York: Oxford University Press.

Brodkey, L. (1988). *Academic writing as social practice*. Philadelphia: Temple Univeristy Press.

Broverman, I., Vogel, S., Broverman, D., Clarkson, F., & Rosenkrantz, P. (1972). Sex-role stereotypes: A current appraisal. *Journal of Social Issues, 28*(2), 59–78.

Brown, L.S. (1987). Lesbians, weight, and eating: New analyses and perspectives. In Boston Lesbian Psychologies Collective (Eds.), *Lesbian psychologies* (pp. 294–309). Urbana: University of Illinois Press.

Browne, A. (1987). *When battered women kill*. New York: Macmillan/Free Press.

Buss, A. (Ed.) (1979). *Psychology in social context*. New York: Irvington.

Caplan, P.J., & Hall-McCorquodale, I. (1985). Mother-blaming in major clinical journals. *American Journal of Orthopsychiatry, 55*, 345–353.

Chesler, P. (1972). *Women and madness*. New York: Doubleday.

Chodorow, N.J. (1978). *The reproduction of mothering: Psychoanalysis and the sociology of gender*. Berkeley: University of California Press.

Cole, J.B. (Ed.) (1986). *All American women: Lines that divide, ties that bind*. New York: Free Press.

Colen, S. (1986). "With respect and feelings:" Voices of West Indian child care and domestic workers in New York City. In J.B. Cole (Ed.), *All American women: Lines that divide, ties that bind* (pp. 46–70). New York: Free Press.

Collins, P. (Spring 1988). *Black feminist thought*. Paper presented at the Penn Mid-Atlantic Women's Studies Seminar. University of Pennsylvania, Philadelphia.

Crawford, M., & Marecek, J. (1988). *Psychology reconstructs the female: 1971–1988*. Presented at Nags Head Conference on Sex and Gender, Nags Head, North Carolina.

De Laurentis, T. (1987). *The technologies of gender: Essays on theory, film, and fiction*. Bloomington: Indiana University Press.

Deaux, K. (1984). From individual differences to social categories. *American Psychologist, 39*, 105–116.

Deaux, K., & Major, B. (1987). Putting gender into context: An interactive model of gender-related behavior. *Psychological Review, 94*, 369–389.

Delacoste, F., & Alexander, P. (Eds.) (1988). *Sex work: Writings by women in the sex industry*. Pittsburgh: Cleis Press.

Dill, B.T. (1987). The dialectics of black womanhood. In S. Harding (Ed.), *Feminism and methodology: Social science issues* (pp. 97–108). Bloomington: Indiana University Press.

Dinnerstein, D. (1976). *The mermaid and the minotaur: Sexual arrangements and human malaise*. New York: Harper & Row.

Dobie, K. (1988). "Black women, white kids." *Village Voice*. Jan. 12, pp. 20–27.

Eichenbaum, L., & Orbach, S. (1983). *Understanding women: A psychoanalytic approach*. New York: Basic Books.

Espin, O.M. (1987). Issues of identity in the psychology of Latina lesbians. In Boston Lesbian Psychologies Collective (Eds.), *Lesbian psychologies* (pp. 35–55). Urbana: University of Illinois Press.

Fine, M. (1983). Expert testimony delivered in *Newberg* v. *Board of Public Education*, Philadelphia.

Fine, M. (1984a). Coping with rape: Critical perspectives on consciousness. *Imagination, Cognition and Personality: The Scientific Study of Consciousness*, *3*, 249–267.

Fine, M. (1984b). Perspectives on inequality: Voices from urban schools. In L. Bickman (Ed.), *Applied social psychology annual IV* (pp. 217–246). Beverly Hills: Sage.

Fine, M. (1985). Reflections on a feminist psychology of women: Paradoxes and Prospects. *Psychology of Women Quarterly*, *9*, 167–183.

Fine, M. (1986). Contextualizing the study of social injustice. In M. Saks and L. Saxe (Eds.), *Advances in applied social psychology. (III)*. Hillsdale, NJ: Erlbaum.

Fine, M., & Asch, A. (1988). *Women with disabilities: Essays in psychology, culture, and politics*. Philadelphia: Temple University Press.

Fisher, B., & Galler, M.J. (1988). Friendship and fairness: How disability affects friendship between women. In M. Fine and A. Asch (Eds.), *Women with disabilities: Essays in psychology, culture, and politics* (pp. 172–194). Philadelphia: Temple University Press.

Flax, J. (1987). Postmodernism and gender relations in feminist theory. *Signs: Journal of Women in Culture and Society*, *12*, 621–643.

Foucault, M. (1972). Intellectuals and power. *TELOS*, *16*, 103–109.

Furby, L. (1979). Individualistic bias in studies of locus of control. In A. Buss (Ed.), *Psychology in social context* (pp. 169–190). New York: Irvington.

Gaertner, S.L., & Dovidio, J.F. (1981). Racism among the well-intentioned. In E. Clausen and J. Bermingham (Eds.), *Pluralism, racism, and public policy: The search for equality* (pp. 208–220). New York: G.K. Hall.

Gaventa, J. (1980). *Power and powerlessness: Quiescence and rebellion in an Appalachian valley*. Urbana: University of Illinois Press.

Gilbert, L.A. (1980). Feminist therapy. In A.M. Brodsky and R.T. Hare-Mustin (Eds.), *Women and psychotherapy: An assessment of research and practice* (pp. 245–265). New York: Guilford Press.

Gilligan, C. (1982). *In a different voice: Psychological theory and women's development*. Cambridge, MA: Harvard University Press.

Golden, C. (1987). Diversity and variability in women's sexual identities. In Boston Lesbian Psychologies Collective (Eds.), *Lesbian psychologies* (pp. 18–34). Urbana: University of Illinois Press.

Gordon, S. (1988). *Evolution of a research proposal: The personal becomes methodological*. Unpublished manuscript. University of Pennsylvania, Graduate School of Education, Philadelphia.

Grady, K.E. (1981). Sex bias in research design. *Psychology of Women Quarterly*, *5*, 628–636.

Gramsci, A. (1973). *Letters from prison*. New York: Harper & Row.

Greenspan, M. (1983). *A new approach to women & therapy*. New York: McGraw-Hill.

Harding, S. (1986). *The science question in feminism*. Ithaca, NY: Cornell University Press.

Harding, S. (Ed.) (1987). *Feminism and methodology: Social science issues*. Bloomington: Indiana University Press.

Hare-Mustin, R.T., & Marecek, J. (August 1987). *The meaning of difference: Gender theory, postmodernism, and psychology*. Paper partially presented at the meeting of the American Psychological Association, New York.

Hartsock, N.C.M. (1987). The feminist standpoint: Developing the ground for a specifically feminist historical materialism. In S. Harding (Ed.), *Feminism and methodology: Social science issues* (pp. 157–180). Bloomington: Indiana University Press.

Henley, N.M. (1985). Psychology and gender. *Signs: Journal of Women in Culture and Society, 11*, 101–109.

Hooks, B. (1981). *Ain't I a woman: Black women and feminism.* Boston: South End Press.

Huddy, B., & Goodchilds, J. (1985). *Older women in action: The influence of personal interests on collective action.* Paper presented at the annual meeting of the American Psychological Association, Los Angeles.

Joseph, G.L., & Lewis, J. (1981). *Common differences: Conflicts in black and white feminist perspectives.* New York: Anchor Press.

Kaminstein, D. (1988). The rhetoric of science and toxic waste dumps: A study of community quiescence. Unpublished manuscript. University of Pennsylvania, Graduate School of Education, Philadelphia.

Keller, E.F. (1982). Feminism and science. *Signs: Journal of Women in Culture and Society, 7*, 589–602.

Kirschner, D.A., & Kirschner, S. (1986). *Comprehensive family therapy: An integration of systemic and psychodynamic treatment models.* New York: Brunner/Mazel.

Kurz, D. (1988). Presentation to research seminar in social methods at the University of Pennsylvania, Graduate School of Education, Philadelphia. Unpublished raw data.

Ladner, J.A. (1972). *Tomorrow's tomorrow: The black woman.* Garden City, NY: Doubleday.

Lather, P. (1986). Research as praxis. *Harvard Educational Review, 56*, 257–277.

Lerman, H. (1986). *A mote in Freud's eye: From psychoanalysis to the psychology of women.* New York: Springer-Verlag.

Lewis, M., and Simon, R. (1986). A discourse not intended for her: Learning and teaching within patriarchy. *Harvard Educational Review, 56*, 459–472.

Linton, R., & Whitham, M. (1982). With mourning, rage, empowerment and defiance: The 1981 women's Pentagon action. *Socialist Review, 12*(3–4), 11–36.

Lott, B. (1985). The potential enrichment of social/personality psychology through feminist research and vice versa. *American Psychologist, 40*, 155–164.

Lykes, M.B. (in press). Dialogue with Guatemalan Indian Women: Critical perspectives on constructing collaborative research. In Rhoda Unger (Ed.), *Representations: Social construction of gender* (pp. 167–185). Farmingdale, NY: Baywood Publications.

Lykes, M.B. (1986). *The will to resist: Preservation of self and culture in Guatemala.* Presented at the Latin American Studies Association Meetings, Boston, October.

Lykes, M.B., & Stewart, A.J. (1986). Evaluating the feminist challenge to research in personality and social psychology: 1963–1983. *Psychology of Women Quarterly, 10*, 393–412.

Mayo, C. (1982). Training for positive marginality. *Applied Social Psychology Annual, 3*, 57–73.

McHugh, M.C., Koeske, R.D., & Frieze, I.H. (1986). Issues to consider in conducting nonsexist psychological research: A guide for researchers. *American Psychologist, 41*, 879–890.

McIntosh, P. (1983). *Interactive phases of curricular re-vision: A feminist perspective*. Monograph. Wellesley College.

Mead, G.H. (1934). *Mind, self and society*. Chicago: University of Chicago Press.

Melton, G.B., & Russo, N.F. (1987). Adolescent abortion: Psychological perspectives on public policy. *American Psychologist, 42*, 69–72.

Miller, J.B. (1976). *Toward a new psychology of women*. Boston: Beacon Press.

Miner, V., & Longino, H.E. (1987) *Competition: A feminist taboo?* New York: Feminist Press.

Nestle, J. (1983). My mother liked to fuck. In A. Snitow, C. Stansell, and S. Thompson (Eds.), *Powers of desire: The politics of sexuality* (pp. 468–470). New York: Monthly Review Press.

Parlee, M. (1979). Psychology and women. *Signs: Journal of Women in Culture and Society, 5*, 121–133.

Parlee, M. (1981). Appropriate control groups in feminist research. *Psychology of Women Quarterly, 5*, 637–644.

Poovey, M. (1988). Feminism and deconstruction. *Feminist Studies, 14*, 51–65.

Rich, A. (1980). Compulsory heterosexuality and lesbian existence. *Signs: Journal of Women in Culture and Society, 5*, 631–660.

Rodgers-Rose, L. (Ed.) (1980). *The black woman*. Beverly Hills: Sage.

Rollins, J. (1985). *Between women: Domestics and their employers*. Philadelphia: Temple University Press.

Rosewater, L.B., & Walker, L.E.A. (Eds.) (1985). *Handbook of feminist therapy: Women's issues in psychotherapy*. New York: Springer-Verlag.

Rubin, G. (1984). Thinking sex: Notes for a radical theory of the politics of sexuality. In C.S. Vance (Ed.), *Pleasure and danger: Exploring female sexuality* (pp. 267–319). Boston: Routledge & Kegan Paul.

Rubin, L.B. (1976). *Worlds of pain: Life in the working-class family*. New York: Basic Books.

Schechter, S. (1983). *Women and male violence*. Boston: South End Press.

Scott, J.W. (December 1985). *Is gender a useful category of historical analysis?* Paper presented at the meeting of the American Historical Association, New York.

Sears, D.O. (1986). College sophomores in the laboratory: Influences of a narrow data base on social psychology's view of human nature. *Journal of Personality and Social Psychology, 51*, 515–530.

Sherif, C.W. (1987). Bias in psychology. In S. Harding (Ed.), *Feminism and methodology: Social science issues* (pp. 37–56). Bloomington: Indiana University Press.

Shields, S. (1975). Functionalism, Darwinism and the psychology of women. *American Psychologist, 30*, 739–754.

Simon, B.L. (1988). Never-married old women and disability: A majority experience. In M. Fine and A. Asch (Eds.), *Women with disabilities: Essays in psychology, culture, and politics* (pp. 215–225). Philadelphia: Temple University Press.

Smith, D.E. (1987). Women's perspective as a radical critique of sociology. In S. Harding (Ed.), *Feminism and methodology: Social science issues* (pp. 84–96).

Bloomington: Indiana University Press.

Smith, A., & Stewart, A.J. (1983). Approaches to studying racism and sexism in black women's lives. *Journal of Social Issues*, *39*, 1–15.

Stacey, J., & Thorne, B. (August 1984). *The missing feminist revolution in sociology*. Paper presented at the annual meeting of the American Sociological Association, San Antonio, TX.

Tiefer, L. (1987). Social constructionism and the study of human sexuality. In P. Shaver and C. Hendrick (Eds.), *Sex and gender* (pp. 70–94). Beverly Hills: Sage.

Unger, R.K. (1983). Expert testimony delivered at *Newberg* v. *Board of Public Education*, Philadelphia.

Unger, R.K. (August 1987). *The social construction of gender: Contradictions and conundrums*. Paper presented at the meeting of the American Psychological Association, New York.

Vanderslice, V.J. (in press). Separating leadership from leaders: An assessment of the effect of leader and follower roles in organizations. *Human Relations*.

Walker, L.E. (1984). *The battered woman syndrome*. New York: Springer-Verlag.

Wallston, B.S. (1981). What are the questions in psychology of women? A feminist approach to research. *Psychology of Women Quarterly*, *5*, 597–617.

Walsh, M.R. (Ed.) (1987). *The psychology of women: Ongoing debates*. New Haven, CT: Yale University Press.

Weitz, R. (1984). What price independence? Social reactions to lesbians, spinsters, widows, and nuns. In J. Freeman (Ed.), *Women: A feminist perspective*, 3rd ed. Palo Alto, CA: Mayfield.

West, C., and Zimmerman, D.H. (1987). Doing gender. *Gender and Society*, *1*, 125–151.

Wexler, P. (1983). *Critical social psychology*. Boston: Routledge & Kegan Paul.

Wittig, M.A. (1985). Metatheoretical dilemmas in the psychology of gender. *American Psychologist*, *40*, 800–811.

8
Illness and Imagery: Feminist Cognition, Socialization, and Gender Identity

Nancy Datan

In 1980, the feminist poet Audre Lorde wrote in *The Cancer Journals*: "May these words serve as encouragement for other women to speak and to act out of our experiences with cancer and with other threats of death, for silence has never brought us anything of worth" (1980a, p. 10). With her encouragement, today I will explore a web of taboos and silences that surround breast cancer, a disease that affects so many of us that we can all expect a friend, if not ourselves, to experience it. Breast cancer currently affects one of every eleven women and is expected to affect one out of ten in the near future. Of those, some will inevitably be feminists. I am one of them.

It is a central tenet of feminism that women's invisible, private wounds often reflect social and political injustices. It is a commitment central to feminism to share burdens. And it is an axiom of feminism that the personal is political. It is in that spirit that I ask you to come with me in imagination where I hope nobody will ever go in fact, to a hospital bed on the morning after a mastectomy, where I found new expression for a recent theme of the *The Journal of Social Issues*, "Social Issues and Personal Life: The Search for Connections" (Clayton & Crosby, 1986).

Studies of women with breast cancer typically focus on women's responses to the disease. This chapter is a naturalistic ethnography which explores a stimulus designed to shape women's responses: the Reach to Recovery material presented to women after surgery. Crisis demands coping: Reach to Recovery is an effort to shape coping responses.

In its own words, "Reach to Recovery is one woman reaching out to share and support another in time of need. . . . Reach to Recovery works through carefully selected and trained volunteers who have fully adjusted to their surgery. . . . The volunteer visitor brings a kit containing a temporary breast form, manuals of information and appropriate literature for husbands, children, other loved ones, and friends. The visitor can provide information on types of permanent prostheses and lists of where they are available locally. . . . Reach to Recovery can provide information to women interested in breast reconstruction" (American Cancer Society,

1982b). Thus the first message of Reach to Recovery is that one's body has been mutilated and that steps must be taken to remedy its deficiency.

My Reach to Recovery volunteer brought a kit with exercise equipment, cosmetic disguise, and a collection of reading material, all for me to keep; and three samples of breast prostheses for me to examine. The exercise equipment consisted of a small rubber ball attached to a length of elastic cord and a length of nylon rope knotted at each end with two wooden tongue depressors to be inserted into the knots. The cosmetic disguise was a small pink nylon-covered, dacron-filled pillow, which proved more useful and safer for throwing exercises than the rubber ball intended for that purpose, which rebounded on its elastic cord painfully into my chest when I threw it.

Substitute breasts of various sorts outweighed everything else in the Reach to Recovery visitor's kit; a corresponding weight was found in the reading material. A crude quantitative analysis of the Reach to Recovery reading material offers a preview of the emphasis on the prosthetic.

One-page pamphlets or form letters:

- What is Reach to Recovery?
- After Mastectomy: The Woman on Her Own
- "An Ounce of Prevention:" Suggestions for Hand & Arm Care
- How to examine your breasts
- A letter to husbands
- A letter to daughters
- A letter to sons

And, at greater length:

- Exercises after Mastectomy: Patient Guide (8 pages)
- Helpful Hints and How To's (8 pages)
- After Mastectomy: A Patient Guide (10 pages)
- Prostheses List 1984–1986 (14 pages)
- Breast Reconstruction Following Mastectomy (20 pages)

Buried in this material is the fact that a mastectomy may bring disability and even occasionally death as a consequence of damage to lymphatic circulation, which may produce permanent arm swelling. Of a total of 67 pages of information, only one page addresses this issue. Surgery limits arm motion: exercises that promote recovery and help prevent arm swelling take up an additional eight pages. Thus only about 10% of this material is actually addressed to health considerations. What then is the nature of the "recovery" to which one is supposed to reach?

The principal focus of this material, the exclusive focus of three of the five multipage pamphlets, of 42 of a total of 67 pages of information, is on strategies for temporary or permanent substitutes for the missing breast. Thus on quantitative grounds alone, the woman who has just had a mastectomy is overwhelmed by the message that her body is now defective and that her first priority will be to seek an artificial, cosmetic remedy. Her kit provides her with an emergency solution—the small pink pillow that can be pinned into her clothing even before her bandages are removed. It is illusory comfort, like the promise of ice cream after a tonsillectomy to a child who wakes up to discover a throat too sore to swallow. But throats do heal, so the illusion and the consequent disillusion are short-lived. Reach to Recovery offers a woman a lifetime of disguise. What this kit does not provide is room to accept the loss of a breast, the wound, and the scar that healing will bring.

I came to surgery with a very different view of mastectomy, which I owe to Audre Lorde, whom I first discovered in April 1980, when *Savvy* carried her article "After Breast Cancer: I am a Warrior, not a Victim." She described her rejection of the physical pretense in the cosmetic emphasis of Reach to Recovery in words that transcended the experience she had just had and I never anticipated:

Implying to a woman that, with the skillful application of a lambswool puff or an implantation of silicone gel, she can be the same as before surgery prevents her from dealing with herself as real, physically and emotionally. . . . We are expected to mourn the loss of a breast in secret, as if it were a guilty crime . . . [but] When Moshe Dayan stands before Parliament with an eye patch over his empty eye socket . . . he is viewed as a warrior with an honorable wound. . . . Well, we are warriors also. I have been to war, and so has every woman with breast cancer, the female scourge of our time. . . . "Nobody will know the difference," said the Reach to Recovery volunteer, with her lambswool puff. But it is that very difference which I wish to affirm, because I have lived it, and survived it and grown stronger through it. I wish to share that strength with other women. (1980b, pp. 68–69)

In 1980 it seemed so simple. Even in 1986 it did not seem so complex: Audre Lorde had spoken first and assured me a voice for my autonomy and my grief. As she did, I mourned my breast. It was the first breast to develop erotic feelings, the first breast to fill with milk, the first breast my firstborn child suckled, and the last breast my last child suckled. That breast carried a special aura into middle age: one summer afternoon our small red dog shepherded me into a hike with a leap and nip exquisitely and precisely placed at the very tip of my nipple. I also remembered the last time that breast was part of my body in lovemaking, just a handful of hours before surgery. As Audre Lorde had done, I intended to grieve, and to go on, with gratitude to her for going before me and making it easier.

I had rejoiced in Audre Lorde's rejection of a prosthesis and shared her horror at the reprimand her surgeon's nurse issued:

"We really like you to wear [a prosthesis] when you come in. Otherwise it's bad for the morale of the office."
I could scarcely believe my ears [wrote Lorde]. Every woman there had either had a mastectomy, or might have a mastectomy. Every woman there could have used

the reassurance that having one breast did not mean life was over, nor did it mean she was condemned to using a placebo in order to feel good about herself and the way she looked . . . . I refuse to have my scars hidden or trivialized behind a puff of lambswool or silicone gel (1980b, p. 69).

If the need for defiance was regrettable, it was not incomprehensible: ground rules for public appearance occupy fashion pages in the daily newspaper. To flout them is to defy culture, and Lorde was clearly, intentionally doing precisely that. I looked forward to joining her in revolution. But it had not occurred to me until I found myself in a hospital bed with a lapful of Reach to Recovery material that it would be war 24 hours a day. A mastectomy, it seems, ushers in a lifetime of round-the-clock disguise: so I discovered after I found that I underestimated the power of a nonconscious ideology. Breast cancer is not a cosmetic disease, but it is embedded in a larger social and political context in which the cosmetic industry is itself a social and political phenomenon. Thus, if one rejects the a priori assumption that a missing breast demands an all-out coverup, one finds oneself at war with the very material that is meant to promote healing. This discussion follows the course of a naturalistic ethnography which I undertook involuntarily in my hospital bed, reading the Reach to Recovery material with the vulnerability that comes after surgery and the educated cynicism that comes from years of feminist analysis.

In 1964, driving down Jaffa Road in Jerusalem, pregnant with my second child, my breasts swelling and my brassiere confining, I reached under my shirt in the middle of traffic, unhooked it, removed it, and never expected to think about brassieres again. But on December 3, 1986, as a conscientious patient intending to learn all I could about mastectomy and the healing process following surgery, I read every word of the Reach to Recovery material, and the first lesson I learned was that I was expected to resume wearing a brassiere as part of my recovery: "Reach to Recovery suggests and encourages each woman to wear the bra in which she is most comfortable. When your doctor says you are ready, you should be fitted with the breast substitute—prosthesis—suited to you," instructs the cover page of the *Prostheses List, 1984–1986* (American Cancer Society, 1984).

That imperative is twofold if one has not worn a brassiere for 22 years: not only should you be fitted with a substitute breast—Audre Lorde had prepared me for that —but you should wear a brassiere. And nothing prepared me for that. If, for whatever reason—political principle or personal comfort—one has discarded a brassiere, both freedom and comfort come to an end with breast cancer: research has shown that discomfort in wearing a prosthesis is a commonly reported physical complaint following mastectomy (Meyerowitz, Chaiken, & Clark, 1988). Yet this instruction—no mention of the discomfort—is the message a woman gets on the first morning after surgery.

The invasion of the brassiere was just the beginning. The booklet *Helpful*

Hints and How To's assured me that leisure and sleep bras "provide a solution for the woman who feels she needs to wear a breast form in bed. Women who do not want to wear a bra and form to bed, but still want contour on the side of the surgery might want to make a form similar to the temporary form in the Reach to Recovery kit and attach it inside the bodice of their sleepwear garment. Nylon netting can be gathered in a round shape and with some experimentation can also be attached inside a loose garment to simulate the contour of the natural unsupported breast" (American Cancer Society, 1982a, pp. 1–2).

It is not enough to deceive the public; not even enough to deceive one's mate—I assumed that "the woman who feels she needs to wear a breast form in bed" does not sleep alone. *Helpful Hints and How To's* encourages the woman who has had a mastectomy to deceive herself. A reader of Audre Lorde's *The Cancer Journals* (1980a) might assume that "making your own form" refers to the construction of a dressmaker's form adapted to one's altered body. But no: "form" takes on new meaning after breast cancer and is used as a presumably innocuous substitute for "substitute breast." The reader is warned that such a "form," if not weighted properly, will cause that side of the brassiere to ride up on the body (p. 5). The Reach to Recovery solution: "use the pocket of the temporary Reach to Recovery form as a pattern and fill it with birdseed, rice, barley, small plastic beads. . . drapery weights, fishing sinkers, gunshot or BB's" (p. 1).

My first reaction to this suggestion was the cognitive equivalent of wound shock. Surely this represented a merger of Frederick's of Hollywood, Ace Hardware, and the American Cancer Society. Yes, one possible first response to this suggestion is to assume that it is a bad joke and to fight off the assault on one's intelligence with better jokes.

But when the initial shock wears off, the imagination does not have to work very hard to call up the confining sensation of a brassiere, the discomfort compounded by one side riding up over wounded or scarred flesh, and the remedy proposed by Reach to Recovery and published with the seal of the American Cancer Society: a pouch of birdseed or gunshot, lying against the body where there was once the first touch of a boy's hand or a baby's mouth—or even a small dog's teeth. In 1980, I agreed immediately with Audre Lorde when she declared: "For not even the most skillful prosthesis in the world could undo that reality, or feel the way my breast had felt, and either I would love my body one-breasted now, or remain forever alien to myself" (1980a, p. 44). It seemed to me then, and still does, that hers was the most elemental of protests: do not add insult to injury. I had no way of guessing how outrageous these insults could be.

The pièce de resistance, most extensive and handsomest of the material put into my hands the day after surgery, is a 20-page pamphlet, nearly one-third of the total number of pages in my kit, on breast reconstruction, urging that the most effective treatment for breast surgery is more surgery. I thought I was prepared for this as well: breast reconstruction had been mentioned by every doctor I had seen from the time I was first told that I had cancer. Since no surgeon could restore the flesh that had swollen first with desire and then with milk, it seemed pointless to me until I inquired about the procedure itself. A mastectomy, I was told, is comparatively simple surgery—45 minutes or so. A reconstruction is more complex—it may involve several operations, the removal of muscle from the back to be inserted into the chest wall, and the subsequent insertion of a silicone implant. When I asked my oncologist why any woman would subject herself to that, he explained that it would avoid the inconvenience of a prosthesis that might slip out of place. Surely if one rejected the first premise, that would be that.

But I was wrong again. The war on cancer patients is being fought with as much or more determination as the war on cancer. The booklet on breast reconstruction goes beyond the helpful hints and how-to's which keep one's bra from riding up and "allow" one to wear one's favorite clothes. It redefines one's sexual identity at the very moment that identity is most vulnerable. This booklet is written in question and answer format. It should be required reading as part of training in questionnaire construction and restricted to graduate students. Instead, it is distributed to women on the morning after surgery.

Question: "Should every woman have a breast reconstruction after mastectomy?" Answer: "Every woman should know that breast reconstruction is possible and make her own decision. Some women seem to be able to adapt psychologically to the post-mastectomy physiological change. Others who opt for breast reconstruction are usually the strongly motivated patients who are willing to undergo an additional operation" (pp. 5–6). As someone with a high need for achievement, I read this material with the best of intentions, hoping to make the most of my experience. I graduated from college with honors, had managed other life transitions with some distinction, and meant to do the same with cancer. I had always considered myself to be strongly motivated. And so, as students of cognitive dissonance will understand, I turned to the title page to find out who the responsible reference group was, so that I could dissociate myself from it and retain my claim to strong motivation.

Like everything else about the cosmetic approach to breast cancer, that seemed easy enough at first. Unlike every other item in my kit, this was not the work of Reach to Recovery, but of the American Society to Plastic and Reconstructive Surgeons, Incorporated. Like the birdseed breast, it seemed at first to be a bad joke. But if one is trying to make sense of a new experience, one seizes upon whatever is offered; in an understimulating hospital room, one reads whatever is available; and, although knowledge of the distorting effects of questions and answers skewed in the direction of presumed social desirability, like any other knowledge, provides some power, on the first day after surgery one is simply not powerful enough to dismiss casually such statements as the following:

If you are like most women, your breasts have great psychological significance to you and you will feel more feminine and more secure socially and sexually with a reconstructed breast following mastectomy for cancer. (p. 6)

In other words, your sisterhood or your scar: if your breast has mattered to you, and mine certainly had, you are told that you will want the benefit of "surgical advances [which] have provided plastic and reconstructive surgeons with techniques to create the appearance of breasts" (p. 4). If not, Aristotelian logic leads the reader to believe, you are not like most women. And if so, you have cancer, you are groggy from surgery, and you are all alone.

Here I distinguish between the 20,000 women who undergo breast reconstruction every year, according to this booklet, and the authors of the booklet. Two Reach to Recovery volunteers came to my bedside, the first, like me a runner, as part of her scheduled round and the second, like me a cross-country skier, at my surgeon's request. The first had run a 10K and the second had skied the Korteloppet after surgery; that bonded us. Both had had "implants," as they termed them; that divided us. Which took priority, our commonalities or our differences?

Virginia O'Leary offers a model for the reconciliation of our differences in her Division 35 presidential remarks, "Musings on the Promise (and Pain) of Feminism" (1987). She notes: "The very intensity of involvement that makes women's connections with women so rewarding has the potential to evoke pain as well. . . . Trashing someone usually involves impugning her (feminist) motives." Since I have identified myself with feminist Audre Lorde and have agreed that the cosmetic response to breast cancer leads to self-alienation, does it follow that I am forced to deny the feminism implicit in my visitors' athletic efforts, or for that matter in their volunteer participation in a program of women helping women? Indeed not. If a hospital room is no place for a crash course in Total Womanhood, neither is it the place for retroactive consciousness raising. Breast cancer is a trauma; if a woman feels she is entitled to four silicone breasts after a mastectomy, I applaud her originality, and, as O'Leary does, I urge tolerance of the diversity of interpersonal styles, in sickness as well as in health. It is precisely the question of tolerance for diversity which was the issue in my hospital room.

In the spirit of tolerance for diversity, I considered breast reconstruction. In the words of its advocates, the American Society of Plastic and Reconstructive Surgeons, Incorporated, a breast reconstruction

will not only provide greater physical self-confidence, but will also enable you to wear a wide range of clothing. After reconstruction, you need not worry about "slipping" or displacement of the prosthesis which may occur with external devices. (p. 7)

However, it is acknowledged that even modern surgery will not bring you everything:

The reconstructed breast will look reasonably normal when covered with an undergarment but will show scarring and subtle imperfections when you are nude (p. 9). . . . Breast reconstruction cannot restore normal sensation to a breast after mastectomy (p. 14). . . . Most women say it may take a while to get used to the reconstructed breast . . . there may be some tenderness and discomfort when you [sleep on your stomach] . . . when people hug you they may not be able to distinguish any difference in the feel of the breasts. In some cases, however, the contraction of your body tissues around the implant may cause the reconstructed breast to feel firmer than your other breast. (p. 15)

Furthermore,

Complications can occur. . . . If an infection or heavy bleeding occurs around a breast implant, it sometimes has to be removed but it can usually be replaced after a period of several months. If the implant shifts to an undesirable location or feels hard due to the contraction of the tissue, an additional surgical procedure may be required to release it. (p. 9)

Finally,

A small number of recurrences [of cancer] occur on the chest wall itself and breast reconstruction might delay but would not prevent detection of these. (p. 14)

Thus, in the words of a pamphlet intended to promote the process, breast reconstruction makes it easy to wear clothes, but not to go naked. The public self is affirmed, but it is at the expense of discomfort to the private self, who wants to hug or to sleep on her stomach. The surgery carries a risk of complications and further surgery and might delay detection of a recurrence of the cancer—and this procedure, it is claimed, provides "greater physical self-confidence" (p. 7).

My quarrel is not with the women who choose this procedure but with the surgeons who assert that physical self-confidence will be enhanced by this painful, potentially dangerous invasion of the body. It is one option. Another option is to live, as Audre Lorde inspired me to do, without any thought of disguise: this enables one to hug, to find erotic nerves reawakening even before the mastectomy incision is fully healed, and to sleep on one's stomach, all components of my physical self-confidence.

Now the time has come to get out of the hospital bed and to resume my identity as a feminist social scientist. What if this experience is not merely an illness, but a naturalistic experiment designed by Rhoda Unger as a test of my epistemology? In that case it is not my body which is in need of reconstruction—it is reality.

I begin by disputing a 1983 volume of *The Journal of Social Issues* (Janoff-Bulman & Frieze, 1983) which takes as its theme "Reactions to Victimization," among whom are numbered cancer victims. I read those words without a pause in 1983, not even the briefest of pauses to consider that Audre Lorde's 1980 article, which I remembered nearly verbatim, had been entitled, "After Breast Cancer: I am a Warrior, not a Victim." However, the word "victim" becomes far more salient when it refers to oneself. And, after a while, it becomes offensive. One is "stricken," "afflicted," maybe even "victimized" by cancer at first. But months later? Years? Have I earned tenure as a victim?

The term victim suggests passive acceptance, when responding adequately to cancer demands continuous active coping. Consider the distinction Bruno Bettelheim makes of the Holocaust: its victims are those who were buried; those who go on are survivors. Circumstances victimize; the individual coping response is part of the struggle for survival. Bettelheim states:

[Holocaust] survivors are not alone in that they must learn to integrate an experience which, when not integrated, is either completely overwhelming, or forces one to deny in self-defense what it means to one personally in the present. . . . Engaging in denial and repression in order to save oneself the difficult task of integrating an experience into one's personality is of course by no means restricted to [Holocaust] survivors. . . . Survivors have every right to choose their very own way of trying to cope. The experience of being a concentration camp prisoner is so abominable, the trauma so horrendous, that one must respect every survivor's privilege to try to master it as best they know and can. . . . But to have come face to face with such mass murder, to have come so close to being one of its victims, is a relatively unique, psychologically and morally most difficult, experience. It follows that the survivor's new integration will be more difficult—and, one may hope, also more meaningful—than that of [those] spared subjection to an extreme experience. (1979, pp. 24, 33, 34)

Denial or integration, the polarities of response to the Holocaust described by Bettelheim, parallel those found in Reach to Recovery and in Audre Lorde's response: oblivion or awareness. Oblivion is a form of death of the self. Yet awareness in an oblivious world is agony, as Wisconsin naturalist Aldo Leopold observed:

One of the penalties of an ecological education is that one lives alone in a world of wounds. Much of the damage inflicted on land is quite invisible to laypersons. Ecologists must either harden their shell and make believe that the consequences of science are none of their business, or be the doctor who sees the marks of death in a community that believes itself well and does not want to be told otherwise. (1953, p. 165)

Substitute feminism for ecology and we see a spectrum of social ills which feminism has rendered visible. The woman who has been raped or might be, the mother seeking child care, or the woman seeking an abortion, all face issues that once were defined as personal and private and now are seen as public and political. Breast cancer too can be seen as more than a singular affliction, as feminists consider rape to be not an isolated personal trauma but an expression of a larger social context in which male sexuality, the patriarchal family, and aggression against women are blended. Similarly, breast cancer is not a solitary ordeal but an illness of the community, to which the community responds with an expression of communal values, which may certainly include repudiation, denial, and isolation.

These communal values are highlighted by issues in gender identity specific to particular illnesses (Meyerowitz et al., 1988). As journalist Martha Weinman Lear observes:

> To be American, male, in one's fifties, a compulsive worker—as who of them is not—worried about cholesterol and unpaid bills, working under stress and watching old friends succumb, one by one, to that crisis of the heart . . . I do not suppose women can fully understand that fear. Not that particular one. We agonize instead over cancer; we take as a personal threat the lump in every friend's breast. (1980, p. 11)

Many researchers (Meyerowitz et al., 1988; Rosen and Bibring, 1968) have noted that heart attacks strike at masculine values: aggression, achievement, striving, and sexuality come to have new meanings. Rosen and Bibring (1968) suggest that heart attacks in young men accelerate issues of aging and dependency, since the immediate treatment demands enforced passivity. Breast cancer strikes at the core of femininity: as Rossi observes, "in contemporary Western societies the breast has become an erotic symbol," rather than a functional component of reproduction (1986, p. 120).

Recovery from a heart attack is measured by renewed participation in activities: for example, some survivors of heart attacks go on to run marathons. No such physical triumphs are celebrated by recovery from breast cancer, which is measured by the restoration of appearance. To put it another way, the implied identities regained by men and women recovering from these gender-specific illnesses are that of the midlife jock and the would-be perpetual cheerleader. Last year I ran my first marathon, at the age of 45. As Audre Lorde wrote after her Reach to Recovery volunteer had visited her: "I ached to talk to women about the experience I had just been through, and about what might be to come, and how were they doing it and how had they done it. But I needed to talk with women who shared at least some of my major concerns and beliefs and visions, who shared at least some of my language" (1980a, p. 42). I have never been a cheerleader, and I could not see trying out for the part with falsies. I want to run another marathon, and nothing at all in Reach to Recovery tells me about my prospects as a distance runner.

I propose that Reach to Recovery is, however inadvertently, an example of what sociologist Irving Rosow (1974) terms the socialization to old age, which he views as socialization to a normless, devalued status. As a heart attack accelerates passivity and dependency and other issues of aging for men, breast cancer accelerates the progress of women toward the double standard of aging (Bell, 1970; Sontag, 1972): not merely devalued, but devalued and dependent sooner, and desexualized as part of the devaluation. The image of women presented in Reach to Recovery material underscores the status of victim and trivializes the victimization. One is victimized not by a disease but by its cosmetic consequences: the threat of a desexualized body. The effectiveness of this process rests on the circumstances of socialization, which is facilitated by the ambiguity and anxiety that are abundant on surgical wards. The message, which does not stand up well under critical scrutiny, depends on the power of a nonconscious ideology.

Years ago, I was introduced to the power of a nonconscious ideology when I conducted a small experimental study of mothers' responses to an infant presented in pink or in blue clothing, designed as a modest test of the nature–nurture question (Will, Self, & Datan, 1976). On the one hand, proponents of the "nurture" perspective argue that differences in sex-role socialization reflect the imposition of gender roles which may or may not be appropriate for any given individual; thus mothers inflict social norms on their children before the children are able to express independent preferences. On the other hand, proponents of the "nature" perspective argue that these differences are the outcome of presocial, innate dispositional differences in female and male infants who present different cues to mothers; thus, by socializing sons and daughters differently, mothers are responding effectively and indeed with sensitivity to biologically based differences in individuals.

We tested this question by presenting a single five-month-old baby, whose dispositional cues would not vary across settings, dressed as a boy and as a girl, to mothers who were asked to interact "naturally" with the baby and were provided with a doll, a fish, and a train. If cultural norms shaped the mother's behavior, we anticipated differences in the treatment of the same baby depending on whether it was wearing pink clothing and identified as "Beth" or wearing blue clothing and identified as "Adam." If, on the other hand, the baby's needs determined the mother's response, we would expect no variation in the treatment of the baby.

It will not surprise this audience that mothers handed "Beth" the doll, held her close, touched her, comforted her if she expressed distress, and told us during debriefing that they "knew" she was a girl because she looked so feminine and soft, while "Adam" was given a train, less often cuddled or comforted if he expressed distress, and "looked strong" or "masculine." Mothers further asserted during debriefing that they did not believe in treating sons and daughters differently and did not treat their own sons and daughters differently in any way. Yet these mothers' behavior offers a glimpse at their children's future, which is less egalitarian than the mothers' declared attitudes: girls who will outperform boys on tests of verbal ability, boys who will show deficits in social skills as early as high school; women who will choose affiliation over achievement and pay for their choice with impoverished old age, men who will choose achievement over affiliation and pay for their choice by dying sooner.

To conclude: It has been a task of feminist psychology to expose, explore, and ultimately reject the inequities that begin in the nursery and accumulate over the life course. This chapter has explored some inequities that are part of the social response to breast cancer. It can be seen as a special case of a recent theme of *The Journal of Social Issues*: "Social Issues and Personal Life: The Search for Connections." As I learned, women with breast cancer soon discover that they are in the middle of a minefield of taboos. Feminist epistemology proves invaluable as a mine detector and has been a tool for me in guiding this effort to transform victims into survivors. If socialization is viewed as the transmission of values from one generation to the next, it may be argued that feminists are failures in socialization, and this chapter can be seen as yet one more instance of a repudiation of culture, its nonconscious ideology, and its oppressions.

Cancer is a powerful stimulus word which, thanks to a growing number of survivors, has recently begun to shed first one taboo status, that of unspeakability, and then another, that of death sentence. Breast cancer partakes of a third taboo status: it represents an assault on a symbol of sexuality (Rossi, 1986). In a review of studies of psychological research on women's responses to breast cancer, Meyerowitz et al. (1988) note: "Unfortunately, at times there has also been a tendency for authors to draw conclusions that may be founded more in stereotypes of women and their needs than in sound data." A typical statement of this stereotyped concern is expressed by Derogatis, who asserts as a hypothesis that "the fundamental female role is seriously threatened by breast cancer" (quoted by Meyerowitz et al., 1988). But as Meyerowitz, Taylor, and others have shown, it is by no means clear that cancer itself poses such a universal threat (see Meyerowitz et al., 1988; Taylor, Lichtman, & Wood, 1984; Taylor, Wood, and Lichtman, 1983).

Yet the very material intended to promote recovery assumes that breast cancer is a threat to sexual identity and imposes this assumption on women just as they are most in need of reassurance. Cancer may go into remission, but breasts do not grow back; to accept the message of Reach to Recovery is to accept mutilation as a core feature of one's postsurgical identity, and thus to accept the status of victim. And for victims the most appropriate response is grief. Survivors, by contrast, command our respect—and speaking for myself, I have done my grieving and am ready for some applause.

REFERENCES

American Cancer Society (1982a). *Reach to Recovery: Helpful hints and how to's*. (Available from the American Cancer Society, 777 Third Avenue, New York, NY 10017.)

American Cancer Society (1982b). *Reach to Recovery: What is reach to recovery?* (Available from the American Cancer Society, 777 Third Avenue, New York, NY 10017.)

American Cancer Society (November 1984). *Prostheses list: 1984–1986*. (Available from the American Cancer Society, 777 Third Avenue, New York, NY 10017.)

American Society of Plastic and Reconstructive Surgeons, Incorporated (January 1982). *Breast reconstruction following mastectomy*. (Available from American Society of Plastic and Reconstructive Surgeons, Incorporated, Patient Referral Service, 233 North Michigan Avenue, Suite 1900, Chicago, IL, 60601.)

Bell, J.P. (November–December 1970). The double standard. *Trans-Action*, pp. 23–27.

Bettelheim, B. (1979). *Surviving and other essays*. New York: Knopf.

Clayton, S.D., & Crosby, F. (Eds.) (1986). Social issues and personal life: The search for connections. *Journal of Social Issues*, *42* (2), 1–221.

Janoff-Bulman, R., & Frieze, I.H. (Eds.) (1983). Reactions to victimization. *Journal of Social Issues*, *39*(2), 1–227.

Lear, M.W. (1980). *Heartsounds*. New York: Simon & Schuster.

Leopold, A. (1953). *Round river*. New York: Oxford University Press.

Lorde, A. (1980a). *The cancer journals*, 2nd ed. San Francisco: Spinsters Ink.

Lorde, A. (April 1980b). After breast cancer: I am a warrior, not a victim. *Savvy*, pp. 68–69.

Meyerowitz, B.E., Chaiken, S., & Clark, L.K. (1988). Sex roles and culture: Social and personal reactions to breast cancer. In M. Fine & A. Asch (Eds.), *Women with disabilities: Essays in psychology, culture, and politics* (pp. 72–89). Philadelphia: Temple University Press.

O'Leary, V. (Winter 1987). Musings on the promise (and pain) of feminism. *Psychology of Women*, pp. 1, 3.

Rosen, J.L., & Bibring, G.L. (1968). Psychological reactions of hospitalized male patients to a heart attack: Age and social-class differences. In B.L. Neugarten (Ed.), *Middle age and aging*. Chicago: University of Chicago Press.

Rosow, I. (1974). *Socialization to old age*. Berkeley: University of California Press.

Rossi, A.S. (1986). Sex and gender in the aging society. In A. Pifer & L. Bronte (Eds.), *Our aging society* (pp. 111–139). New York: Norton.

Sontag, S. (1972, October). The double standard of aging. *Saturday Review*, pp. 29–38.

Taylor, S.E., Lichtman, R.R., & Wood, J.V. (1984). Attributions, beliefs about control, and adjustment to breast cancer. *Journal of Personality and Social Psychology*, *46*, 489–502.

Taylor, S.E., Wood, J.V., & Lichtman, R.R. (1983). It could be worse: Selective evaluation as a response to victimization. *Journal of Social Issues*, *39*, 19–40.

Will, J.A., Self, P., & Datan, N. (1976). Maternal behavior and perceived sex of infant. *American Journal of Orthopsychiatry*, *46*, 135–139.

Editors' Note. Dean Rodeheaver's response to Nancy's paper, written from his perspective as her spouse, was presented at the 1987 conference. A copy may be obtained by writing: Dean Rodeheaver, Human Development, College of Human Biology, Univeristy of Wisconsin at Green Bay, Green Bay, WI 54311–7001.

Index